PSYCHOANALYSIS AND RELIGIOUS EXPERIENCE

Psychoanalysis and Religious Experience

W. W. MEISSNER, S.J., M.D.

YALE UNIVERSITY PRESS
NEW HAVEN AND LONDON

Published with assistance from
the Louis Stern Memorial Fund.

Designed by Sally Harris
and set in Times Roman type.
Printed in the United States of America by
Edwards Brothers, Inc., Ann Arbor, Michigan.

Library of Congress Cataloging in Publication Data

Meissner, W. W. (William W.), 1931–
  Psychoanalysis and religious experience.

  Bibliography: p.
  Includes index.
  1. Psychoanalysis and religion. 2. Freud, Sigmund,
1856–1939. 3. Experience (Religion)—Psychological
aspects. I. Title.
BF175.M453 1984   200′.1′9   83–51296
ISBN 0–300–03049–5
    0–300–03751–1 (pbk.)

The paper in this book meets the guidelines
for permanence and durability of the
Committee on Production Guidelines for
Book Longevity of the Council on Library Resources.

10 9 8 7 6 5 4 3 2

CONTENTS

PREFACE

The history of the dialogue between psychoanalysis and religion is fraught with mutual antagonism. On the one side, psychoanalysis has followed a path, with rare exceptions, of seeing religious experience in essentially reductive or, even more prejudicially, psychopathological terms. The analytic emphasis has tended to fall on the unconscious and irrational aspects of religious behavior. Undoubtedly, Freud's own biases were a major influence in this development. On the other side, religious and theological reflection has tended to ignore considerations of human drives and needs, focusing primarily, almost exclusively, on man's supernatural potential, on the life of the spirit as abstracted from the vicissitudes of man's carnal immersion, and on the economy of salvation.

These various currents and influences are still very much alive in the ongoing dialogue between psychoanalytic and religious thinking. Today the opposition between these two currents has taken on a new coloration, as it expresses itself in new and varied modalities and flourishes in quite a different intellectual climate and context, but the same issues remain and set the terms of the continuing discussion. In light of these considerations, it seems essential to a basic understanding of this dialogue that the Freudian argument be reassessed and recast.

It seems clear that Freud's religious views, perhaps more than any other aspect of his work and his psychology, reflect underlying and unresolved ambivalences and conflicts stemming from the earliest psychic strata. Behind the Freudian argument about religion stands Freud the man, and behind Freud the man, with his prejudices, beliefs, and convictions, lurks the shadow of Freud the child. A basic psychoanalytic insight says that the nature and content of any thinker's or creative artist's work reflect essential aspects of the dynamic configurations and conflicts embedded in the individual's personality structure. Freud is no exception, and his religious thinking unveils these inner conflicts and unresolved ambivalences more tellingly than any other aspect of his work. A review and synthesis of Freud's inner psychic conflicts and the basic interplay of forces, defenses, fantasies, ideals, ambitions, and beliefs that played themselves out in his inner life form the essential backdrop for the ensuing discussion (chapter 2).

At the same time, we are not in any sense dealing with a reductive approach. If we were to persuade ourselves that Freud's own unresolved psychological conflicts, giving rise to and influencing the course of his argument about religion, substantiated the conclusion that the validity of that argument rests on its psychological underpinnings, we would be making an egregious error—an error of which psychoanalytic thought has too often been guilty. On the contrary, the Freudian argument on religion must be addressed on its own ground and in its own terms. The argument stands or falls—or, perhaps, limps—quite independently of the psychological determinants that might have given rise to it and influenced the manner in which it was shaped.

With this in mind, I have taken up a detailed discussion of the argument of *The Future of an Illusion* (Freud 1927). The objective of that discussion (chapter 3) is not so much refutation—although there are a number of critical points at which the Freudian argument can be effectively challenged. Rather, my concern is to refocus and recast the Freudian argument in the interests of preserving and extending the ensuing dialectic. One of Freud's unique gifts was that even when he was mistaken about a particular concept or proposition he was able to approach it in a way that provided important psychological insight. Consequently, in my approach to the understanding of the Freudian argument about religion, I have been wary of adopting the adversarial logic that all too often ends by throwing the baby out with the bathwater.

As I have noted, and as will become apparent, there were powerful historical and conceptual reasons why Freud took his position regarding religious thinking. But we need not allow these historical accidents to distract us from the fundamental insights Freud brought to his understanding of religious phenomena. Perhaps the most far-reaching and profound of those insights is Freud's understanding that man's religious experience —and indeed his spiritual experience—takes place in the context and on the basis of the psychological realities of his human existence. Despite his iconoclasm and rejection of religious beliefs, Freud by virtue of his genius brought us to the interface of man's religious life with his psychological life, in a more poignant and telling way than ever before in human history. If the dialectic between religion and psychoanalysis is to have any meaning at all, we cannot afford to retreat from that vital and sensitive frontier.

Freud's thinking about religious subjects became considerably more nuanced and ambivalent as it progressed and displayed itself over the years. There is no better means available to grasp the complex facets of Freud's thinking about religion than his lifelong friendship and interchange with his colleague Oskar Pfister. Pfister was a Lutheran pastor who remained active in the practice of his ministry for nearly forty years. Through most of that time he was a devoted follower of Freud and an enthusiastic devotee of psychoanalysis.

Pfister was one of the first to bring the resources of psychoanalytic thinking and techniques to the service of pastoral needs and objectives. Consequently, he stands forth as one of the progenitors of the pastoral counseling movement. I have tried to reconstruct the major elements of the lifelong correspondence between Pfister and Freud and their climactic debate on the occasion of Freud's publication of *The Future of an Illusion* (chapter 4). Following the progression of the debate offers us an opportunity for a much more nuanced appreciation of Freud's religious outlook. But far more significantly, the lifelong debate between these two great antagonists enunciates many of the basic arguments that have characterized the discussion in the ensuing half century.

Freud's remarkable *Moses and Monotheism* (1934–38) fills out this conceptual reworking of the Freudian argument. When he wrote this book, Freud was very old; indeed, he was near death. His life had been made a torment of pain by a remorseless cancer that gnawed away at his face and palate. In this context, the writing of the Moses book was for Freud one last, valiant effort to set straight within his own mind the deeper conflicts and ambivalences that had plagued him all his life. His relationship to the figure of Moses and the basic psychological issues it reflected are distilled in this last flamboyant gesture of defiance (chapter 5).

One of the interesting aspects of the Moses book is that in it Freud reflects, in somewhat idiosyncratic fashion, some of the best convictions and understanding of the biblical scholarship of his day, building his argument out of bits and pieces of the prevailing views regarding the Moses narrative, the Exodus events, and the development of the concept of monotheism.

The argument of the Moses book, however, never found wide acceptance among scholars in biblical archeology, biblical criticism, or even anthropology. Subsequent years have subjected the whole area of biblical studies and criticism to a radical revision that makes it clear that the fundamental points of view on which Freud based his synthetic reconstruction were themselves faulty and misleading. From this perspective, we can take another look at the possible psychoanalytic implications of a revised and updated evaluation of the events surrounding the Exodus of the Chosen People from Egypt and their entrance into the Promised Land. Our understanding of the origins of monotheistic ideas has similarly undergone, and continues to undergo, radical revision at the hands of biblical scholars and archeologists. The pattern of events and cultural influences is neither so simple nor so direct as in the accounts that captured Freud's imagination in his writing of the Moses book.

While a critical reevaluation of the underlying argument of the Moses book seems to be important and useful, it is perhaps more important to pay attention to the line of continuity that runs from the earliest levels of Freud's psychological experience and to the very last battle of the intrepid conquistador of illusion. Fascinatingly, the same issues and ambivalences that appeared in the early infantile strata of Freud's psychic life once again emerge in the conflictual efforts of the eighty-year-old Moses who has never been allowed to reach his Promised Land and who stands on the threshold of death.

Starting from this revised assessment of the Freudian argument and its implications for the psychoanalytic understanding of religious phenomena, I have undertaken a more explicit consideration of the ways in which psychoanalysis can begin to interpret religious phenomena. As indicated above, an important dimension of this reconsideration is the attempt to preserve Freud's fundamental insights even as we put aside what seem to be the misguided or incorrect aspects of his thinking. One of these insights, evident not only in his thinking about religion but in the general develop-ment of the psychoanalytic perspective, is the effort to understand the organization and functioning of the human personality in specifically developmental terms.

It has been a staple of the psychoanalytic orientation since Freud's day that the structures in terms of which personality organization and function-ing can be analyzed have a genetic history. They come about through a progression of stages of development that reflect in some fundamental fashion the continual interplay of intrinsic maturational forces in the organism with the environment—both physical and social or personal. For reasons that are poorly understood but seem to be related to his own unresolved conflicts and inner prejudices, Freud somehow failed to bring this fundamental insight to bear on his thinking about religious phe-nomena. Instead, he was able to understand and articulate only a limited range of religious manifestations that reflect only a narrow spectrum of developmental influences. His model of religious development therefore was limited almost exclusively to a kind of infantile and neurotic base, largely focusing on the developmental levels that give rise to obsessional and ritualistic practices.

Nonetheless, the fundamental developmental perspective and the genetic metapsychological assumption apply across a broad range of reli-gious manifestations and dispositions. Consequently, my effort in address-ing this issue is not merely to articulate the developmental aspects of religious experience but also to integrate various aspects of the develop-mental progression, which is substantially epigenetic in character. In so doing I hope to provide the basis for a possible typology of religious experience that relates certain key developmental parameters in a more synthetic fashion. Thus, in chapter 6 I have attempted to integrate the developmental lines having to do with narcissism, object relationships, and faith into a coherent schema. The hidden assumption of this approach is that the shape of the faith experience as it evolves developmentally is contingent on and reflects, as well as conditions, the developmental vicissitudes of both narcissism and object relations. While a more or less satisfactory account of personality organization and the integration of faith can be achieved within this perspective in terms of both narcissism and object relations, obviously the process is much more complex and opens itself to more broadly conceived cognitive, affective, and dynamic considerations.

In a further effort to focus the conceptual terms in which psychoanalysis can approach religious phenomena, I have attempted to bring to bear the genial insight of Donald Winnicott, especially his theory about the transitional realm of experience (chapter 7). I can claim no originality in the development of these concepts; indeed, the notion of transitional objects and transitional phenomena has been extant for decades. But it seems to me that this fundamental formulation has not been brought to bear on our understanding of religious phenomena with the degree of elaboration or emphasis it deserves. Winnicott was more or less satisfied with a passing reference to cultural and religious applications of the notion of transitional phenomena. After all, his concern was with their role in the developmental process itself, particularly in the infantile development of object relationships. But the concept provides a kind of breakthrough that allows us to move in new and, I think, stimulating directions. Freud's thinking seems in retrospect to have been trapped in a kind of Cartesian dichotomy, between the world of objective (scientific) phenomena and concepts, on the one hand, and the world of subjective (wish-fulfilling) concepts and phenomena, on the other. If he had to make a choice, it was clear that he would choose scientific objectivity over wishful illusion.

But the notion of an area of transitional phenomena that remains open to input from the realms of both the subjective and the objective, without being reduced to either one or the other, provides a middle ground in which fruitful explorations of the psychic reality and validity of man's religious experience can be carried out without being forced into polarized or prejudicial positions.

I should emphasize that in these chapters we are not dealing with relatively hardened positions that have found their way with confidence into the main line of psychoanalytic thinking about religious concerns. Rather, they are tentative hypotheses that are tantamount to stumbling first steps in the direction of a more deeply searching and profoundly understanding psychoanalytic approach to religious phenomena. These hypotheses must be tested through further exploration and scrutiny and through a continuing effort to explore their application to various problems within the religious perspective. Putting behind us the limitations and misconceptions of the Freudian approach to religious phenomena only opens the path to a more challenging, more difficult, but, I hope, more accurate and meaningful understanding of man's relationship to his God and to himself.

A basic tenet of this volume is that the psychoanalytic perspective on religious thinking has moved well beyond the positions taken by Freud, which are both limited and scientifically and culturally embedded. The foundations for the continuing dialogue between scientific psychoanalysis, on the one hand, and theologically based religious conceptualization, on the other, have become considerably more nuanced and sophisticated. In advancing conceptualizations for what I conceive to be the direction of the dialogue in the future, I have attempted to articulate areas of both congruence and divergence that seem to me to obtain in the current intellectual climate.

I have attempted to reformulate the issues in terms of the fundamental images of man that prevail in the psychoanalytic and religious perspectives (chapter 8). These images of man do not stand in radical opposition but, rather, enter into a process of continuing dialectical transformation that has allowed the basic understanding of human nature to evolve gradually on both sides. The psychoanalytic view of human nature has come a long way since Freud's early and simplistic version, which saw man as a creature dominated and determined almost exclusively by his instinctual life. Concepts relating to the organization and functioning of ego and superego have led to a more nuanced and generalizable account of human psychic activity. More currently, supraordinate concepts of the self and its relationship to higher levels of psychic activity have become part of psychoanalytic lore.

Similarly, the view of human nature in religious and theological circles has gradually retreated from the hard line which idealistically (and again simplistically) regarded man almost purely in terms of his higher functions —that is, his distinguishing capacities for operations of intellect and will, as well as for a spiritual life. Largely under the growing impact of psychoanalytic and other psychological input, religious thinkers have increasingly come to terms with and taken into account the basically biological, we might even say instinctual and motivational, aspects of man's existence.

Within this evolving intellectual climate, growing areas of congruence between the respective approaches have been delineated. By the same token, the remaining areas of as yet irreducible divergence have become more clearly understood. Basing the argument on the fundamental images of man and their gradual evolution, I have attempted to articulate these areas of congruence and divergence in the interface between psychoanalysis and religion (chapter 9).

One such area of convergence has been in psychoanalytic and religious attitudes toward freedom. Working self-consciously with a theological anthropology that takes into greater account the basic biological and dynamic nature of man's existence, theological thinking about freedom has become much more attuned to the exigencies of man's physical and material existence. Consequently, the contemporary account of freedom is no longer one that is cast in excessively abstract, idealized, or spiritualized terms. The implications of these developments for the dialectic of psychoanalysis and religion are detailed in chapter 10.

Looking at the difficult path that lies ahead, I must warn the reader that my argument will often lead into strange byways that may seem alien or disconcerting. This is perhaps unavoidable in an interdisciplinary work, which seeks to bridge conceptual chasms—and in the process demands considerable stretching. The problem partly stems from trying to address different audiences—reaching out to religious thinkers and theologians on one side, and to psychoanalytic thinkers on the other. It also derives from the need to dip into a variety of fields of expertise that bear on particular questions. In such instances, I have sought assistance in the work of scholars who are more at home in such esoteric byways, but without, I hope, losing the basic thread of the argument. To the extent that the enterprise falls short of its objectives, I beg the reader's indulgence.

Part 1

INTRODUCTION

1. TOWARD A PSYCHOLOGY OF
   RELIGIOUS EXPERIENCE

PSYCHOANALYSIS VERSUS RELIGION

Traditionally there has been a powerful opposition posed between psychoanalysis and religious thinking. The reasons for this are multiple, not only
having to do with Freud's own iconoclastic and atheistic posture but also
reflecting the basic nature of psychoanalytic concepts as they emerged
historically. The concepts of psychoanalysis emphasized a reductive view
of man—that is, a view of man that focused primarily on the instinctual
roots of behavior. The psychoanalytic account, at least in its beginnings,
emphasized the sexual-libidinal aspects of human behavior. Consequently,
psychoanalytic explanations for a wide range of human behaviors were cast
in terms of a reductive frame of reference that related such phenomena to
the causal aspects of the libido theory.

But the form of psychoanalytic explanation cannot bear the full weight
of responsibility for this state of affairs. Psychoanalysis arose in a cultural
context in which powerful forces were at work that were basically antithetical to a religious orientation. When Freud entered the picture, scientific
rationalism and naturalism had reached their high watermark. The scientific world in which he took his place was the world of Newtonian physics,
of determinate and determinable causes and effects, all of which could be
accurately and definitively measured and quantified. The universal laws
that had only recently been discovered were thought to govern all natural
processes, physical and psychological, animate and inanimate.

The laws of thermodynamics provided the context for Freud's scientific
thinking. These laws governed all natural processes, including the direction and exchange of energy, the thresholds of stimulation and response,
and the principles of inertia and constancy—processes that served as a
basis for Freud's attempts to construct a model of the mind, as well as
for broader scientific explanations of cause and effect. It was a world of

An earlier version of this chapter appeared in *Communio* 4 (1977): 36–59.

universal scientific determinism. The scientific mind of Freud's day thought it had found the universal key to understanding all natural phenomena. Nothing existed but particles and forces—all else was illusion.

Freud himself served as an eloquent disciple of this scientific attitude and its tradition; his *Project for a Scientific Psychology* (1950b) reflects the strength and extent of his assimilation of it. Although this attempt to physiologize his psychology was doomed to failure, given the tools with which he had to work, it continued to exercise a powerful influence on the direction of his thinking and psychoanalytic theorizing. Needless to say, such a naturalized and secularized view of nature was antithetical to any view that allowed for forces outside the range of these explanatory concepts. Consequently, anything that smacked of the spiritual or the "supernatural" was anathema.

Such an attitude left little room for religious ideas. Religious thinkers could not help viewing not only psychoanalysis in its earliest forms but also the whole scientific mentality of the day as threatening and as inevitably working to undermine and overthrow religion. Freud thus walked in the footsteps of Charles Darwin, who had preceded him by roughly half a century. Darwin's view of man and his origin was an affront to the religious thinkers of his day. And if the intensity and bitterness of the debate over Darwin's ideas was cast at a higher pitch than the argument over Freud, it was undoubtedly only because Darwin was a goodly step ahead of Freud. The argument was essentially between Science with a capital S and Religion with a capital R. It took another century before the fundamental ideas had been sufficiently worked through to allow for an amplified understanding that there were no inherent contradictions between the religious and the scientific views and that the respective conceptual systems could coexist with mutual respect and even reinforcement.

This enlightened view has by no means achieved universal acceptance. The teaching of evolutionary theory, for example, is still challenged in parts of the United States, usually by fundamentalist religious groups.

Over the years, repeated attempts to address, rethink, and reshape this adversarial dialectic have achieved considerable success. Thoughtful religious men have carefully weighed Freudian arguments and have gradually come to see that there is no necessary connection between Freud's scientific thinking and his religious persuasions. Here and there, intrepid souls might even be found who could embrace psychoanalysis as a conceptual framework and as a therapeutic technique without finding themselves compelled to surrender their religious orientations and convictions. Freud's student Oskar Pfister, a Lutheran pastor, was one, and as we shall see Freud himself begrudgingly conceded that psychoanalysis might have a place in thinking about and dealing with souls, even those in spiritual distress.

But, despite such pioneering efforts, the opposition between psychoanalysis and religious thought persists in the minds of less informed individuals, whose thinking has not advanced beyond the adversarial opposition of the 1920s. The number of religiously minded persons who are terrified by the thought of exploring their unconscious lives, whether in the context of psychoanalysis or even psychotherapy, is by no means insignificant. Despite many years of effort by pastoral counselors of all religious faiths, an attitude persists among the clergy that is antithetical to any psychiatric, psychological, or psychoanalytic intervention. The stalking-horse of Freud's secular and antireligious pronouncements and the myth of libidinal license still haunt the view of many.

The maxim has it that "people who live in glass houses shouldn't throw stones." If the psychoanalytic house is not made of glass, nonetheless it has a number of transparent panes. Psychoanalysts are not comfortable with religion. They tend to regard religious thinking and conviction as suspect, even to hold them in contempt at times. There is a latent persuasion, not often expressed or even articulated with the inner voice, that religious ideas are inherently neurotic, self-deceptive, and illusive. These are the residues within the psychoanalytic tradition of Freud's own idiosyncratic attitudes. Psychoanalysis lives on the inheritance of his fundamental insights; even though the science has moved well beyond the limited perspective he provided, his basic positions remain a powerful force in the thinking of many psychoanalysts. The prejudices are rarely expressed and remain more or less implicit, but at times they can be heard with striking impact.

I do not wish to give a false impression of psychoanalysts and their thinking about religion, so I must hasten to add a qualifying note. The psychoanalytic community is strikingly—I would even say amazingly—open-minded. By and large, practicing clinical psychoanalysts keep open and often surprisingly accepting minds regarding religious thoughts, feelings, beliefs, fantasies, and convictions. They are respectful of their patients' religious beliefs and values, more out of a sense of psychoanalytic ethics than because of any regard for religious ideas as such. The good analyst knows his place, knows that it is not his role to shape, modify, or mold the patient's beliefs or values; rather, it is his function in the psychoanalytic situation to help the patient to explore the roots, causes, meanings, and implications of whatever beliefs, values, convictions or attitudes he holds.

Where infantile residues, areas of conflict, and neurotic organizations can be identified, the potentiality exists for further exploration, understanding, working-through, and resolution. If an individual's religious orientation rests on neurotic foundations, the analytic supposition is that they will be eroded and the patient will either retreat from his religious views or replace them with a new constellation of religious orientations, whose basis is more adaptive and less reflective of underlying psychopathology. If the patient's religious orientations have a relatively healthy, adaptive, realistic, and psychologically mature basis, they will only find reinforcement and amplification through psychoanalytic inquiry. The situation is not much different from that of the patient who is troubled by an unsatisfactory marital relationship. If the relationship is based on neurotic components, the analytic effort, insofar as it serves to expose these components and to resolve the underlying issues, will lead to the dissolution of the marriage. Where elements of solid and meaningful relationship, love, and mutual respect can be identified, the expunging of neurotic contaminants can only strengthen that relationship.

When we turn to the enterprise of establishing the basis for a meaningful psychoanalytic account of religious experience, we are faced with some difficult questions that require preliminary discussion, concerning the broader context within which a psychoanalytic study of religion would take place. These questions have to do with the nature of a scientific psychology of religion, the role of such a psychology in relation to religious experience, and the potentialities and limitations of such an enterprise. A subject as complex and rich as the psychology of religious experience requires that we remind ourselves of the inherent limitations arising from the nature of the science and its methodology.

The first important point is that the psychology of religious experience is before all else a science of human behavior and experience; insofar as religious experience can be focused and understood through the methodology of such a science, it must be seen as specifically human experience. The implications of this limitation are considerable. There is no area of human endeavor or existential involvement more profound, more far-reaching, more full of implication and significance than religious experience. But through the eyes of psychology, such experience remains essentially human in its dimensions.

The guiding supposition is that a psychology of religious experience can grapple with this profound realm of human experience only in terms of the impact of this experience on man's psychic capabilities. Whatever else one may say about religious experience, it is inherently a human experience and can be approached and understood from that perspective. Thus, a psychology of religious experience does not concern itself with the suprahuman—the supernatural or divine aspects that may be intermingled with the human elements in given religious context or manifestation. The psychology of religious experience in fact must pass over the suprahuman precisely because it has no resources even to attempt to understand that loftier dimension.

This does not imply that a psychology of religious experience must be inherently reductive or must deny the supernatural dimension. Rather, it can remain openly and authentically empathic to the supernatural dimension while it goes about its business on the natural level. The psychologist studies religious experience or behavior as a psychologist, and the methodology and means of conceptualization at his command belong to the science of psychology. Thus, the psychological approach puts aside the supernatural character of religious phenomena and restricts itself more or less to their natural manifestations.

Consequently, we may say that the psychology of religious experience does not pay attention to the formally supernatural or specifically religious qualities of the phenomena it observes, describes, and tries to understand. It does not depend on the verification or acceptance of a revelation, for example. It in no way requires a faithful acceptance of or commitment to a set of religious beliefs or categories in order to do its work. While we can readily admit that the account that a given psychologist renders of religious experiences may be more or less sympathetic, depending on his own religious convictions, nonetheless it remains true that those convictions do not and should not serve as the basis of his psychological understanding.

While an insistence on psychological and methodological purity has its place, science, it turns out, is not always scientific. A case can and should be made for the usefulness of empathic observation or even participation in the psychological approach to religious phenomena. Freud's limitation was that he was not a believer, and that he held fixed and prejudicial ideas about the role of religion in human life, so that he could not be an objective or perceptive observer of it. There is much in his life history that gave rise to this posture, but here it is sufficient to note that such influences do play a significant role.* We might argue, then, that the psychologist who sets out to study religious experience must possess an empathic openness to and a respect for the meaning and relevance of the phenomena he studies. His own religious experience may supply important data, but it also runs the risk of creating a tension between his respective roles of scientifically objective and critical observer on the one hand and emotionally and cognitively involved participant on the other. Interestingly enough, this was precisely Freud's dilemma in his attempts to analyze and understand his own dreams (Freud 1900).

The psychological approach assumes that in every religious experience there is a specifiable and analyzable human dimension. Even the phenomena of the most exalted mystical states do not take place in vacuo but find their expression and their realization within the human psyche; further, they are substantially an expression of dynamic mental forces and functions. Consequently, the psychology of religious experience would reject any form of spiritualism that attempted to categorize religious experience in transcendent spiritual terms beyond the reach of inherently human

*An extended reflection on the influence of Freud's own psychology on his religious attitudes and doctrines can be found below, in chapter 2.

experience. An effective psychology of man's religious experience would see it as integrated with the other realms of human experience and as reflecting many of the drives, impulses, and affective and cognitive resources that characterize these other realms.

The psychology of religious experience, then, must take its place in the ranks of other human sciences that address the understanding of man's religious experience. Much depends on what one chooses to examine. Religious behaviors and experience, even of individuals, range from the more or less superficial patterns of behavior involved in religious rituals and in extrinsic forms of religious activity to the profoundly moving and uplifting experiences of the loftiest mystical states. They may also include dimensions of group behaviors. If the natural scientist chooses to study patterns of behavior in groups, we are more likely to call him a sociologist than a psychologist; if he focuses his attention on individual behaviors and experience, we tend to regard his approach as psychological. But even within these denominations, what one chooses to examine, and the methods by which it is examined, vary widely.

From this point of view, the psychologist would insist that behavior is behavior even when it occurs within a context that we generally accept as religious in connotation and implication. But there is a wide variety of theoretical contexts within which the analysis of religious experience can be articulated and through which the attempt to understand religious behavior and experience can be undertaken. One can study religious behaviors of almost any kind—church attendance, birth-control practices, frequency of confession, religious rites, and so on—or survey attitudes and beliefs by means of interviews and questionnaires.

Beyond this, however, lies the vast range of private, intrapsychic religious experience, not merely the inner set of lived beliefs by which a believer guides his life, but more particularly the quality of inner experience, affective and cognitive, that characterizes the believer's approach to his realized and lived experience of a relationship with his creator. Once we have taken the focus of our concern away from the superficial and behavioral aspects of religious experience, which can be evaluated by extrinsic and peripheral techniques, we are left with a subject that is extremely complex, ephemeral, difficult to elicit and to study, and yet of the most profound significance to man's existential reality. We must employ a method of study that is adequate to the sensitivity, depth, and elusiveness of the subject.

WHAT CAN ONE EXPECT OF A PSYCHOLOGY OF RELIGIOUS EXPERIENCE?

If we accept these potentialities and limitations in our putative psychology of religious experience, we are led to a further question of particular relevance to the emerging dialogue between theological and behavioral sciences. Simply put, the question is, What can one expect of a psychology of religious experience? In other words, what kinds of questions can a psychology of religious experience answer? What kinds of understanding can it bring to the theological enterprise?

The answer is obviously not simple or very straightforward. It depends in part on the methodology of our science and on the kinds of behavior we choose to study. If we adopt a behavioral approach and decide to study certain patterns of action characteristically found in people who profess religious adherence, our psychological understanding will have a correspondingly limited scope. Even here, however, there is a great deal to be studied and learned. Many otherwise unusual states or patterns of behavior that are of considerable inherent interest to the psychologist occur more frequently within religious contexts. These include forms of ecstatic behavior, mystical trances, glossolalia, pentecostal experiences, and a host of other phenomena. If, however, we are convinced that man's religious experience is primarily and centrally a phenomenon of his inner psychic life, then mere behavioral observation will have only limited use in approaching its core, and we must appeal to alternate methodologies.

Guided by the dual theologically derived suppositions that *gratia perficit naturam* and that the core of human religious experience under grace has to do with specifiable aspects of man's subjective experience, unconscious as well as conscious (Meissner 1964, 1966a), we can take a further step. The theory of human functioning and of the organization of the human psyche that lends itself most powerfully and convincingly to the exploration of man's subjective experience is that of psychoanalysis. Consequently, our approach to the questions we have posed will be taken from the psychoanalytic perspective and will focus primarily on the subjective aspect of human experience, conscious and unconscious, as it plays itself out in the realm of religious participation.

What, then, might one expect? This question is related to an equally important question, namely, What is religious experience? A primary task of a psychology of religious experience is description. We do not have an adequate description of the varieties of religious experience. Very little has been done to extend or amplify William James's seminal but rudimentary work at the turn of the century ([1902] 1961). Following his lead, we are able to sketch out the general terrain and find reasonable agreement on the broad categories of religious experience, but a detailed and penetrating descriptive analysis remains to be done. This task must essentially fall to a descriptive introspective psychology.

A first step in addressing the question of what constitutes religious experience is to determine what religious experience is *not*. One reason why the psychology of religious experience remains an area of chronic fascination to the psychologist is precisely that it overlaps, and to a significant degree is intertwined with, mental processes that, from a clinical perspective, can be described as pathological. This point brings us to an extremely complex area, since it is not always easy to draw a line between what is pathological and what is not. Often the behavior itself or the state of mind involved serves adaptive functions within a specific social or cultural context; what we might describe in clinical terms as disordered behavior or disordered mental states nonetheless is acceptable in such a context and in fact is often abetted by forces within that context, in order that the disordered behavior may be put at the service of cultural objectives. This problem is particularly pertinent to the outer reaches of religious experience, where various mystical states, for example, may seem to the clinical observer to be full of pathological elements.

The problem, incidentally, is identifiable not only at those far reaches of religious experience but also in the ordinary range of religious thoughts and feelings. Religious observance and the adherence to credal systems can become a vehicle for pathological tendencies and needs in individual believers. More often than not, such adherences are a matter of common acceptance and fall well within the limits of unremarkable socially and culturally adaptive behaviors, but at times they may express underlying prejudicial attitudes and in extraordinary circumstances may escalate to the level of paranoid distortions. One need only think of religious wars and persecutions to be convinced of this point.

Despite these complexities, the question of what religious experience is not remains a valid one, on which the psychological observer can often cast considerable light. Thus one frequently enough encounters pseudomystical or conversion experiences that may be the external expression of underlying pathological processes. To take a gross example, mystical experiences may be hallucinatory and may manifest a paranoid delusional system. Or a sudden, dramatic, and seemingly inexplicable conversion may be a form of resolving impending psychotic chaos. I am not raising the important question of the value of such phenomena, but wish only to indicate that they cannot be taken at face value, and that the trained psychological observer is best equipped to discriminate between authentic religious phenomena and pathological distortions.

Besides the consideration of psychopathology, there are more subtle issues surrounding the relation between the supernatural and the natural in human experience. Within a theological context that allows for divine influence on human experience through the action of grace, the question of how the supernatural and the natural are integrated and with what effect becomes one of central importance.

Whatever else we can say about religious experience, we can postulate that the form of divine intervention does not violate the nature and functioning of man's capacities—*gratia perficit naturam*—and that the form of the experience is determined significantly by the nature of the psychic organization and functioning of the person affected. The analysis of this experience is not merely a process of teasing out the effects of grace from those of nature; rather it is an attempt to understand the way in which man's natural capacities and propensities become the vehicle for divine action. While grace must act through nature, in so doing it must shape and adapt itself to nature—not in a general or absolute sense, but concretely and particularly to the characteristics and capacities of the given recipient of grace. The task of describing, studying, and understanding the various components of man's nature and functioning, particularly in individual personalities, is the work of psychology.

While the science of psychology generally undertakes to describe man's psychological functioning, psychoanalysis and the psychological approaches derived from or influenced by it have contributed most significantly to the study of individual personalities. It is in this area of psychological endeavor that it seems to me the richest fruit is to be sought for an evolving psychology of religious experience. The understanding of any personality requires an exploration of that individual's capacities, inclinations, attitudes, and beliefs, and includes an understanding of the affective and dynamic concerns that form the fabric of his motivational life.

Each human personality is the product of a personal history and a course of development. The residues of that history and development are embedded variously in each personality, with varying outcomes. The analytic understanding of these components directs its attention to the way in which the residues of previous developmental experiences become incorporated into the personality structure and affect the way in which the individual adapts to his environment. Such issues are of primary importance to the understanding of religious experience. It was Freud who originally pointed out that the believer's attitude toward God may contain resonances and residues of earlier attitudes toward parental figures. This critical insight has provided a firm basis for an analytic psychology of religious experience. One of the challenges for an analytic psychology of religious experience, then, is to explore the ways in which early development phenomena interact with other forces to produce various religious experiences.

The Relevance of a Psychoanalytic Psychology of Religious Experience for Theology

The question of the relevance of religious experience to the enterprise of theology has arisen explicitly only in contemporary contexts. Previously in the history of theology, concern with religious experience was left pretty much in the realm of connotation or implication. Although the traditional methodology of theological reflection was the somewhat bookish *lectio meditativa,* the lectio was not carried out in isolation from the lived subjectivity of the lector. But the role of that subjectivity in the genesis of theological reflection was left muted and unfocused. Contemporary theological reflection, however, is considerably more self-conscious and inclined to include reflection on one's subjective experience among the creative roots of theology (Bozzo 1970). My point is that theological reflection has never been actually divorced from religious experience and in fact has constantly been derived from and powerfully influenced by it.

If we accept this point of view, the psychoanalytic psychology of religious experience becomes a basic science to which theological reflection must turn in order to explore one source of its own vitality. Theological reflection is not sustained in terms of its object alone; that is, it does not carry out its complex function simply in a frame of reference articulated by scripture and tradition. Rather, it gains its impetus and impact by reflecting on the roots of the religious impulse embedded in the ongoing current of psychic experience; thus it has its origin in the interior grasp of a lived and experienced faith that is nourished and enriched by grace. Moreover—to turn the process around—theological reflection does not serve as an end in itself, but has a further objective: to enrich the experienced life of faith by giving it form, shape, and substance.

This way of looking at things opens the way to mutual interaction, translation, and communication. We are trying to define an area of interdisciplinary collaboration between the psychoanalyst who is concerned with religious experience and the theologian who is concerned with deepening the resources of theological reflection on that experience. The theologian must base his reflection to some extent on an underlying theological anthropology. That anthropology has often been implicit in the theological enterprise. More often than not its elements have been drawn from philosophical sources. A ready example is the Thomistic synthesis, in which an elaborated rational psychology provides the image of man and his nature with which the theological enterprise works and on which it bases its understanding of the theological dimensions of the existence of that human nature. This is not the place to go into the inadequacies of that psychological view and its correlative anthropology; suffice it to say that it has been bypassed by contemporary modes of thinking and has proven entirely too static and abstract to reflect the more dynamic and specific emphases reflected in contemporary psychological accounts.

In any case, the point I would like to make is that the theological enterprise cannot do without a sound and informed theological anthropology as one of its basic underpinnings. It would serve the theologian well, therefore, to enrich his reflection with the resources of a more sophisticated and developed psychological science. Here the theologian is in a position analogous to that of the contemporary historian. The historian's methodology does not allow him to deal simply in terms of verifiable external facts and data. Rather, his account must embrace important elements of the psychology and motivation of the historical figures he deals with. It is difficult or impossible, in rendering a historical account, to recapture the specifics of motivations that were often hidden or even unconscious. Consequently the historian must infer such motivations from the data at his command. But this aspect of his historical reconstruction rests upon an implicit psychology. It is this difficulty that has given rise to the interdisciplinary effort known as psychohistory. Psychohistory attempts to replace supposedly commonsense but often erroneous approaches to psychological interpretation with a sounder, more sophisticated and scientifically verifiable account of psychological parameters.

Even if one regards the objective as praiseworthy, it is evident that the enterprise is fraught with difficulty. From the psychologist's point of view, it is hampered by the inadequacy of data, which often leads the psychohistorian beyond the appropriate range of his methodology. Despite the limitations, many psychohistorians hasten to point out that the result is far preferable to that of the previous uninformed approach and should therefore be pursued. Many historians, however, are uncomfortable with a methodology that is quite foreign to their own and frequently conflicts with it.

The picture I am painting is analogous to what I see as the area of overlap between a psychology of religious experience and theological reflection on that experience. While theological reflection cannot take place without a presumptive underlying anthropology, it is equally true that the psychological attempt to understand religious experience will remain naive and misguided unless it is informed to a significant degree by theology. Unfortunately this interdisciplinary effort has remained hesitant and inchoative. The sustained and systematic reflection this important area requires has not yet risen to the level of a felt need for either psychologists or theologians.

Part of the problem is that the whole area has an unfortunate history of mistakes, misunderstandings, misconstructions, and even plain paranoid distortions on both sides—in the psychological naiveté of theological accounts when they touch upon aspects of religious experience, and in the theological naiveté, or even simple ignorance, of psychological attempts to penetrate and understand religious experience. Ignorance and prejudices aside, the two disciplines desperately need each other but seem unable or unwilling to collaborate in their mutually implicating and potentially enriching enterprises.

Some Perspectives on the Psychology of Religious Experience

I would like to turn to more substantive issues within the psychology of religion itself that may, I hope, advance the dialogue to some degree. Too often the discussion of religious experience remains trapped in more or less classic categories, to the considerable disadvantage of any attempt to illuminate it. The psychological resources that could be brought to bear on it have been considerably enriched in recent years, but little attempt has been made to exploit them for this purpose. This is particularly true in the framework of psychoanalytic thinking, which has often maintained a stereotypic adherence to a Freudian perspective. However, other perspectives have emerged to enrich and expand the original Freudian perceptions which consequently promise a considerably more penetrating and nuanced account of religious experience.

These issues will be developed later in greater depth. A preliminary discussion at this juncture has a twofold merit. It will provide the reader with a concrete appreciation of the kinds of psychoanalytic perspectives I have been describing—perhaps clarifying my argument. It may also provide the reader with a focus and a sense of direction as he pursues the path ahead.

One of the important perspectives to emerge within psychoanalysis is the developmental perspective. It was of course Freud who gave the original developmental impetus to analytic thinking and applied the developmental analogue to the understanding of religion. His premise was that religious experience, in common with all areas of human experience, is influenced by and expresses the residues of earlier development. This basic premise remains valid and extremely important as a guiding principle for the exploration of religious experience. Freud's limitation was that he saw religion *only* in terms of a pathological model—as a vehicle for the expression and maintenance of infantile needs and dependencies (Ricoeur 1970). He argued that religion was essentially an expanded form of obsessional neurosis, serving the neurotic infantile needs of many in the larger cultural context, rather than the intrapsychic neurotic conflicts of one. In religion we were all children, related in our trusting infantile dependence on a powerful god who replaced the oedipal parents. Thus religious dependence and faithful acceptance of belief systems were for Freud a regressive expression of human needs that he hoped could be overcome through the more realistic and mature efforts of science. Freud's own scientific account therefore became restricted by his prejudicial view of religion and his theological ignorance.

If we suspend for the moment Freud's judgments on the matter, it seems reasonable to maintain the basic developmental premise. We can characterize levels of religious experience as reflecting various phases of development from very primitive infantile stages to the most mature, integrated, and adaptive levels of psychic functioning. Limited by his predilections and frame of reference, Freud was able to envision only a segment of the broader developmental spectrum. He focused his account primarily on the infantile elements, which he considered characteristic of religious experience, and in fact limited most of his account even more narrowly to the obsessional and ambivalence-ridden developmental conflicts of the anal period.

We now understand that developmental vicissitudes are considerably more complex, and that their expression in religious phenomena may derive either from even more primitive strata of developmental experience or from more advanced and more highly integrated and differentiated levels. Frequently religious experience may express residues from a number of developmental strata, but usually they are integrated in an overlying modality of personality functioning that predominantly reflects the attainments of one developmental phase (Meissner 1978b).

The developmental perspective is readily supported in these terms by the experience of anyone who deals in a pastoral relationship with religiously inclined individuals. The most primitive levels of infantile fusion and narcissistic omnipotence can be found in the religious delusions of psychotics. A caricature of religion, which Freud himself employed as an analogy to obsessional states, is not infrequently found among religious people in whom blind adherence to ritual and scrupulous conscientiousness, as well as conscience, dominate religious life. In fact, we can safely say that the great mass of believers lend credence to Freud's formulations.

More mature and integrated forms of religious experience are modestly distributed among the people of God. Those who reach the highest level of religious experience and achieve the maximum expression of religious ideals are very rare indeed. The argument here rests not on statistics, but rather on an understanding of the quality of religious experience. The psychologist is frequently limited in his attempts to understand religious experience by the fact that those with whom he deals have integrated their religious lives in only a limited and often immature fashion. Unfortunately, to study the religious experience of those more advanced and saintly souls who have gained a high level of religious maturity, we must rely on secondhand historical accounts that leave many questions unanswered and unapproachable. One of the recurrent gaps between the account of the psychology of religious experience and the theological account has to do with this distributive factor: the psychologist generally deals with some limited degree of religious attainment or some relatively impaired form of religious experience, while the theologian directs his attention to a more or less idealized, rarely attained level of religious maturity. Nonetheless, the developmental perspective provides a framework within which a more comprehensive understanding of religious phenomena can be attempted.

An important dimension is added to this perspective through the object relations approach. The developmental progression is intertwined with the individual's history of object relations. Each step in the developmental schema is characterized by a different quality of object relations, moving from symbiotic dependence in the early phases to an increasing capacity for independence and for establishing more differentiated and mature object love. The object relations point of view was more or less implicit in Freud's formulations, but has been articulated as an approach within psychoanalysis only in recent years.

An important line of thinking and investigation has been opened up by the work of D. W. Winnicott (1971), particularly in his notion of transitional phenomena. Winnicott starts with the idea of the "transitional object" in the developmental experience of infants. In the earliest days of life infants are generally capable of a variety of autoerotic stimulation and of pleasurable attachment to the mothering figure, focusing particularly on the gratification derived from sucking on the breast. Within a few months, however, one may see the infant transfer his attachment, often fiercely, to the first "not-me" possession—a doll, a toy, or a blanket, for example. The child may suck it or cling to it; he cannot be without it. In Winnicott's view, the transitional object represents the infant's first attempt to relate to the world outside of the mother. Moreover, it is a replacement for the mother and indicates the child's emergent capacity to separate from the mother and to make substitutions for her as he grows into an individual in his own right.

The analysis of the transitional object leads to a consideration of transitional phenomena in general. These can be categorized as having neither totally subjective nor totally objective status. Rather, they share in elements of both realms, so that the child's original transitional object, for example, has in addition to its objective reality a transitional quality that depends on what the child contributes from his subjective inner world. The interaction of the subjective and the objective creates a psychologically intermediate area of illusion within which the child can play out the drama of separation and attachment.

Winnicott's point is that all children pass through stages of transitional relatedness to objects and gradually refine such transitional experiences, becoming increasingly capable of responding to objects in the environment in terms of their objective reality rather than their transitional illusoriness. But the need for a capacity for illusion, however modified or diminished by the growth of objectivity and realistic adaptation, is never completely eliminated. In fact, in a healthy resolution to crises of development, there emerges a residual capacity for illusion that is among the most significant dimensions of man's existence. Within this area of illusion Winnicott locates man's capacity for culture, creativity, and, of particular relevance to this study, religion and religious experience. He writes:

> I am here staking a claim for an intermediate state between a baby's inability and his growing ability to recognize and accept reality. I am therefore studying the substance of *illusion*, that which is allowed to the infant, and which in adult life is inherent in art and religion, and yet becomes the hallmark of madness when an adult puts too powerful a claim on the credulity of others, forcing them to acknowledge a sharing of illusion that is not their own. We can share a respect for *illusory experience*, and if we wish we may collect together and form a

group on the basis of the similarity of our illusory experiences. This is a natural root of grouping among human beings. (Winnicott 1971, 3)

Consequently, when we address ourselves to religious experience in these terms, we are not talking about a phenomenon in terms of its objective reality, nor are we focusing on a derivative of total subjectivity. The former is essentially beyond the realm of mere human experience, and the latter falls in the realm more of delusion than of illusion. Psychotic delusion is wholly made up of the subject's disordered imagination and his fragmented relationship to reality. Illusion, on the other hand, retains not only its ties to reality but also the capacity to transform reality into something permeated with inner significance. Man cannot do without illusion, since it gives meaning and sustenance to his experience of himself.

The concept of transitional phenomena and its role in structuring the area of illusion opens the way to a more profound exploration of the psychology of religious experience. On the one hand, it allows us to explore the dimensions of that experience without being driven into a reductive posture that truncates, minimizes, or abolishes the specifically theological or divine influence embedded in it; at the same time, it allows a fuller scope to the exploration of psychological factors in that experience. Moreover, the transitional object schema focuses the issues around specific developmental components, particularly those derived from the child's pattern of relationships with significant objects. It creates the potential not only for an analysis of the pathological and infantile determinants of some forms of developmentally impoverished religious experience but also for an enriching investigation of mature, integrated, and developmentally advanced modalities of faith and religious commitment.

The analysis can be carried a step further. Transitional phenomena are composed, as psychological constructions, from elements of subjective experience. The image of a divine being, a godhead, that every man shapes for himself within this area of illusion, is comprised of objective elements that may derive from a variety of sources but are generally regulated and sustained by a communal belief system within a given credal society. Within an organized religious system, the church authoritatively teaches and proposes a specific set of concepts that provides the dogmatic context for the idea of God. That image, formed and held internally as a significant psychological possession, is combined with elements derived projectively from the inner world of the experiencing believer. Thus it is personalized and carries idiosyncratic elements corresponding to those inherent in the believer's sense of self—the distinctive qualities and characteristics that distinguish him from other men. Consequently, in psychological terms, each man creates his own image of God, even though that individualized image is in contact with a shared set of communal beliefs that delineates a concept of God to which the group of believers adheres.

This consideration introduces us to the complex world of psychic mechanisms by which these processes arise. The projective elements that are embedded in the illusory experience and in the formation of transitional components are derived from the organization of the inner world of the experiencing and believing subject. The processes by which the inner world arises are termed "internalizations" in the parlance of analytic thinking. The basic notion is that the inner world takes shape through the child's evolving developmental experience, whose course is shaped by the internalization of the child's relationships to specific objects. Thus the child's evolving psyche is formed under the influence of his object relationships and comes to bear their imprint, no longer as a force extrinsic to his experience, but as an internal possession through which his own internally constituted and subjectively grasped sense of self comes into existence.

It is from these internalized elements that the projective components of transitional illusion arise. They reflect dynamic elements of the believing subject's inner world; at the same time, they cannot be sustained merely by the motivational forces that drive them from the subjective side. Rather, they require stabilization and integration in terms of the larger, objective frame of reference. These subjective derivatives and projections, as part of the complex of transitional illusory constructions, are embedded in and reinforced by larger cognitive schemata, which take the form of credal systems, dogmatic formulations, doctrinal assertions, and a wide range of cognitive organizations and integrations that carry doctrinal or dogmatic impact.

The whole network of projections, transitional formulations, and sustaining cognitive and credal systems serves the important psychological purpose of sustaining the integrity and cohesion of the believer's sense of self; ultimately the power of belief is inextricably linked with the forces that sustain a consistent and coherent sense of personal identity. I have attempted to describe these complex mechanisms elsewhere (Meissner 1978a). It is clear that the religious sphere is not the only realm of human experience within which these forces are at work, but within it they operate with particular poignancy, significance, and intensity.

The study of the psychology of religious experience is undergoing considerable flux, even within the perspective of psychoanalysis. The historical development of this perspective has often been rehearsed, but I have tried to emphasize current and emerging trends that promise a more profound capacity to understand the human dimensions of even the loftiest and most developed forms of religious experience.

I have, however, been suggesting the direction of *future* trends in this field. The work by and large remains to be done, particularly on the level of concrete and specific clinical investigation. Here again, as in so many areas, the fields are ripe for the harvest, but the laborers are few. Not only is there great challenge in this for those who have the interest and capacity to investigate these matters, but there is a pressing urgency for efforts in the psychology of religion to be informed by astute and informed theological opinion.

Psychoanalysis has advanced well beyond the limited perspective that Freud's understanding of psychic functioning allowed him. Psychoanalytic theory today is considerably more nuanced and sophisticated and allows us to approach the understanding of religious phenomena without necessarily being reductive or being forced to deal with religious experience in the limited terms of psychopathology.

Nonetheless, the divergences in points of view, the differentiation of respective philosophical perspectives and orientations, and even the tensions and disagreements over the uses of terminology need to be articulated and understood in order for the dialogue between psychoanalysis and theology to advance in any useful way. In this respect, then, it becomes essential to explore and compare the implicit nature of psychoanalytic understanding and the characteristic dimensions of religious understanding. It is only when these different emphases and their implications, particularly the nature of the understanding appropriate to each field, are adequately grasped that their capacity to complement each other in the central task of understanding human existence becomes apparent.

Part 2

FREUD AND RELIGION

2. FREUD'S RELIGION

Any attempt to approach the psychoanalytic study of religion cannot ignore the contributions of Sigmund Freud. Psychoanalysis is his creation, and to an overwhelming degree the psychoanalysis of religion is the product of his thinking. In its short historical course, psychoanalysis has nonetheless come to appreciate that one cannot divorce the works of man from man himself; the products of human creativity in any realm—art, poetry, music, architecture—reflect some of the basic motivations and conflicts of human psychology. Much of the continuing effort of applied psychoanalysis is focused specifically on the exploration of the dynamic forces and conflicts that lie behind human creativity in all its forms and expressions.

One of the paradoxes of Freud's life is that although he was a self-professed agnostic, religion remained one of his predominant preoccupations. References to religion can be found among his earliest writings and letters, and his first paper dealing specifically with religion was published in 1907. Three of his major works—*Totem and Taboo* (1912–13), *The Future of an Illusion* (1927), and *Moses and Monotheism* (1939)—are devoted to aspects of the psychoanalytic understanding of religious phenomena. Why was it that a "godless Jew," as Freud referred to himself, would so preoccupy himself with God and the things of God?

Needless to say, to find an answer is not an easy or simple task since it involves examination of overlapping and intermingling aspects of Freud's life experience and of the manner in which religious matters touched upon that experience. At the same time, we need to search below the surface of things to the inner realm of conflict and personal meanings that religious influences held in Freud's mind. Fortunately, we have the advantage of previous guides who have mapped out, at least in part, aspects of this complex problem.

We will have to take into consideration Freud's exposure to religion in childhood, his familial influences with their inherent conflicts and ambivalences, his fascination with superstition and the occult, and the somewhat mystical tendencies that were a marked part of his personality. In addition, important questions arise in terms of Freud's religious affiliation, particularly his connection with the Jewish religion and his sense of identity as a Jew. Then there are the complex implications of Freud's lifelong preoccupation with death. All these elements, intertwined and interwoven, provide a potentially valuable insight into Freud's religious convictions and form the backdrop and perhaps even the source of his view of religious experience.

EARLY RELIGIOUS EXPERIENCE

From his earliest days Freud was exposed to a variety of religious experiences. His parents were both believers, although not very orthodox in the practice of their faith. Jones (1957) notes that Freud's parents were rather freethinking, and that after the move to Vienna the family dispensed with Jewish dietary observances and most of the customary rituals, with the exception of the Seder on the eve of Passover. Their practice in the preceding years in Moravia is not known. Jakob, Freud's father, was a thoughtful and reflective man who was fond of reading the Torah. But it seems that his interest in the problems of life was governed more by a philosophical than by a religious concern. On the whole, therefore, the family was undoubtedly Jewish, but basically nonreligious. Nonetheless, they followed some of the usual religious practices, and there is evidence that Freud received lessons in Hebrew from one Professor Hammerschlag from the ages of seven to thirteen even though, curiously, he later denied any knowledge of the language.

Jones (1957) also notes that Freud was conversant with the Bible and could quote readily from either testament. At an early age, young Sigmund was attracted by Ludwig Philippson's remarkable edition of the Bible, which his family possessed. In this edition, the text is accompanied by numerous illustrations and woodcuts and is complemented by a learned commentary that includes numerous discussions of early history and comparative religion.

Some years later, when Freud turned thirty-five, his father, then seventy-five, sent him the same Bible as a birthday gift, with the following inscription in Hebrew:

> My dear Son,
>   It was in the seventh year of your age that the spirit of God began to move you to learning. I would say that the spirit of God speaketh to you: "Read in My book; there will be opened to Thee sources of knowledge and of the intellect." It is the Book of Books; it is the well that wise men have digged and from which lawgivers have drawn the waters of their knowledge.

Thou has seen in this Book the vision of the Almighty, thou hast heard willingly, thou hast done and hast tried to fly high upon the wings of the Holy Spirit. Since then I have preserved the same Bible. Now, on your thirty-fifth birthday, I have brought it out from its retirement and I send it to you as a token of love from your old father. (Jones 1953, 19)

The letter certainly confirms Freud's own observation in his *Autobiographical Study* (1925a) that he had been deeply engrossed in the Bible almost as soon as he was able to read anything, and that this had an enduring effect on him. It is curious that his father here addressed him in Hebrew, a language that the adult Freud claimed not to know. Was there in this use of Hebrew an implicit appeal, or an implicit rebuke, against Freud's drifting from his religious heritage?

Bergmann (1976) notes that this letter makes it apparent that Jakob Freud was neither a devout nor a nationalistic Jew but rather a member of the Haskala, a movement that saw Judaism as the epitome of rational and philosophic enlightenment. He observes:

No orthodox Jew would speak lightly about the Spirit of God, speaking to a seven-year-old. Nor would any religious Jew see the Bible as belonging to mankind as a whole. Biblical flowery language [*melizot* in Hebrew] also marks Jacob Freud as a member of the Haskala. It was this aspect of the Jewish tradition that Freud learned from his father, and he could, therefore, equate the freedom to use the intellect with his Jewish heritage. (p. 4)

An additional fact of Freud's early life that is given varying weight by different authors is that from birth to the age of two-and-a-half he had a Catholic nanny who frequently took him to church services. When little Sigmund got home, he would imitate the preaching he had heard, to the great amusement of the family. But this nanny also taught him about hellfire and damnation and about salvation for the good and obedient. Zilboorg (1958) discusses the impact of these teachings on the child's impressionable mind and presumably on his adult attitudes. He suggests that the discovery of this woman's thievery and her consequent dismissal must have caused the young child considerable disillusionment and might have contributed to his jaundiced view of religion in general and of Catholicism in particular. Jones (1957) on the contrary discounts the idea that this series of events had any lasting influence.

Freud was undoubtedly fond of the nanny, to whom he referred at times as "that prehistoric old woman" (Jones 1953, 6). Even more important, however, are the circumstances under which she fell into disfavor. Jones reports that her dismissal took place soon after the birth of Freud's sister, when his mother was still in bed with the new baby. Freud learned years later that the nanny had been caught stealing and sent to jail. At the time, however, when he asked in bewilderment what had happened to her, his older half-brother Philip, who seems to have been involved in the discovery and accusation, merely said: "*Sie ist eingekastelt*" ("she is locked up"). The child took the reply literally to mean that the nanny had been locked in a chest rather than that she had been put in prison.

Jones relates this misunderstanding to Freud's analysis some forty years later of a memory from his childhood (Freud 1901). He recalled standing before a chest and tearfully demanding something from Philip, who was holding the chest open; then his mother entered the room, notably thin— that is, not pregnant. Freud thought at first that the memory must refer to some episode of his half-brother's teasing, but his analysis of it brought to light quite a different picture. He had missed his mother, who had apparently gone out, and so had anxiously turned to this half-brother who had figuratively put his nanny in a chest, begging him to release his mother from that same chest. When his brother opened the chest to reassure him that his mother was not within, he began to cry. Undoubtedly the loss of the nanny was a significant event for Freud, coinciding as it did with the loss of his mother during her confinement and with the appearance of an interloper and rival in his childish claims for exclusive maternal attention.

FREUD'S SUPERSTITION

For the hardheaded agnostic and objective scientist that Freud professed to be, he was an uncommonly superstitious man. This fact has not escaped observation. Jones (1955) comments on Freud's tendency to "unrestrained imagination," and Jung (1963) mentions the mystical side of himself that Freud seemed to have to deny—an aspect that Jung himself would hardly have overlooked. As Wittels puts it,

> In Freud's mentality the mystical gift of the seer is continually at war with the need for mechanical description. . . . He is afraid of his own supreme talents, and throughout all of his life as an investigator he has been imposing a curb on himself. (Wittels 1931, 79–80)

Freud's preoccupation with superstition was lifelong. Jones recounts the earliest known example of it. During their betrothal, Freud told Martha that as a boy he had chosen the number seventeen in a lottery that was supposed to reveal one's character. The word that came out was "constancy"; he pointed out that it was on the seventeenth day of the month that they became engaged. Schur (1972) notes that the number seventeen resembles the Hebrew spelling of "good." Freud and Martha continued to celebrate this good day for many years.

At times Freud came close to acknowledging such elements in himself. Commenting on his numerical associations, he says:

In analyses of this kind which I conduct on myself, I find two things particularly striking: firstly, the positively somnambulistic certainty with which I set off for my unknown goal and plunge into an arithmetical train of thought which arrives all at once at the desired number, and the speed with which the entire subsequent work is completed; and secondly, the fact that the numbers are so freely at the disposal of my unconscious thinking, whereas I am a bad reckoner and have the greatest difficulties in consciously noting dates, house numbers, and such things. Moreover, in these unconscious thought-operations with numbers, I find that I have a tendency to superstition, whose origin for long remained unknown to me. (Freud 1901, 249–50)

In the 1901 and 1904 editions the paragraph continues: "I generally come upon speculations about the duration of my own life and the lives of those dear to me; and the fact that my friend in B[erlin] has made the periods of human life the subject of his calculations, which are based on biological units, must have acted as a determinant of this unconscious juggling." The passage is omitted from the 1907 edition on. The reference is undoubtedly to Wilhelm Fliess, Freud's confidant and correspondent in Berlin.

Certainly a variety of elements contributed to this lifelong preoccupation. Not only were such superstitions common in the Jewish cultural community in which Freud was reared but, as Schur (1972) comments, "It can be assumed that a family [such as Freud's] stemming from Tysmenica would be well-acquainted with this type of knowledge, because Tysmenica was the seat of one of the several dynasties of Hasidic rabbis" (p. 26). Jones (1953) also notes that the Philippson Bible to which Freud was devoted in childhood is filled with numerological symbolism and commentary.

Perhaps the primary example of the Pythagorean tendency in Freud's personality was his well-known *Todesangst,* or fear of death. One of the earliest references to this anxiety is in a letter to Fliess in 1894:

What is less obvious, perhaps, is my state of health in other respects. For several days after the deprivation [of tobacco] I felt moderately well, and started to write down my present position on the neurosis question for you. Then came a sudden cardiac oppression, greater than I had before giving up smoking. I had violent arrhythmia, with constant tension, pressure, and burning in the region of the heart, burning pains down the left arm, some dyspnoea—suspiciously moderate, as if organic—all occurring in two or three attacks extending continuously throughout part of the day, and accompanied by a depression of spirits which expressed itself in visions of death and departure in place of the normal frenzy of activity. (Freud 1954, 83)

Freud had convinced himself that he was suffering from a mild carditis and that his life was thereby foreshortened.

Wallace (1978) has suggested that this upsurge of Todesangst was related to Freud's underlying conflicts with his father. It occurred in the wake of the deaths of two important father figures in Freud's career: Meinert, who had been his preceptor in psychiatry, and Brücke, whose influence on Freud may have outweighed that of all others and who had advised Freud to abandon his interest in research. This was also the period when Freud was undoubtedly plagued with considerable guilt over his role in the cocaine addiction of his friend Fleischl, which had subsequently resulted in Fleischl's death. In addition, Freud's relationship with Breuer was deteriorating, and his father's health was on the decline. At the same time, his friendship with Fliess was becoming both more intense and more ambivalent. Later in the year, just before his father died, Freud suffered a recurrence of the Todesangst.

Shortly after the death, Freud set upon the course of self-analysis that was ultimately to lead to one of his most important achievements, the uniquely self-revelatory *Interpretation of Dreams* (1900). Schur (1972) has examined in great detail the relationship between some of the dream material provided in *The Interpretation of Dreams* and the underlying themes of ambivalence and conflict in Freud's relationship to Fliess as well as to his father. Schur suggests that Freud's lack of awareness of these conflicts, which in turn were rooted in early infantile conflicts, and his failure to work them through in their adult, transference-like forms were responsible for the persistent recurrence of Freud's obsessive preoccupation with the date of his own death. The theme running through the dreams in question is that of "the guilt of the survivor" (p. 154).

In the so-called *non vixit* dream, which occurred in 1898, Freud tries to explain to Fliess, who has come to visit him, that another person with them is not alive (*"non vivit"*), but says by mistake *"non vixit"* ("he did not live"). Freud turns a piercing look on the ghost, who melts away. The deceased figure of Freud's mentor Fleischl also appears in the dream, and Freud realizes that he too is only an apparition. The thought then occurs to Freud that people of that sort exist only as long as one wishes and could be gotten rid of if someone else wished to do away with them.

Fleischl had been an associate of Brücke, in whose laboratory Freud had worked. He was a brilliant investigator, whom Freud had undoubtedly envied. But Fleischl had injured his hand, and the resulting infection necessitated amputation of several fingers. The site subsequently developed neuromas causing severe pain, which Fleischl tried to alleviate with morphine. Freud tried to help cure the resulting addiction by giving him cocaine, whose anesthetic properties he had been investigating. Fleischl soon developed a cocaine addiction that proved to be even more disastrous, leading to physical and mental deterioration and to his death in 1891. These events were rendered all the more painful to Freud because he had introduced Fleischl to cocaine in the first place; his guilt feelings surfaced in the *non vixit* dream.

The other ghost in the dream, the figure whom Freud annihilates by his piercing gaze, is Joseph Paneth. Paneth had taken Freud's place as an assistant in Brücke's institute and had also lent Freud considerable amounts of money. He had had ambitions for Fleischl's position, but died before him. In recounting his associations Freud comments:

> Not unnaturally, a few years earlier, I myself had nourished a still livelier wish to fill a vacancy. Whenever there is rank and promotion, the way lies open for wishes that call for suppression. Shakespeare's Prince Hal could not, even at his father's sick-bed, resist the temptation of trying on the crown. But, as was to be expected, the dream punished my friend, and not me, for this callous wish. (p. 484)

Another stimulus to the dream was an operation that Fliess had just undergone and Freud's fears for his friend's life. Also, a few days prior to the dream Fliess had celebrated his fortieth birthday. Freud's preoccupation with the date of his death was originally focused on the numbers forty-one and forty-two, and later even more intensely on the number fifty-one. In 1899, the numbers that preoccupied him were sixty-one and sixty-two, and finally in 1936 the dominant number was eighty-one-and-a-half. Fliess himself had developed a system of critical dates in periodic cycles that he believed determined birth, illness, and death. The fortieth birthday represented the onset of one of these critical periods, and Schur (1972) suggests that this fact supports the assumption that Freud's preoccupation with such dates developed out of a partial identification with Fliess.

The night after his father's funeral, almost two years to the day before the *non vixit* dream, Freud had had a dream in which the motive he discerned was the feeling of self-reproach that death generally creates among the survivors. In 1899, when Freud was analyzing the *non vixit* dream, he was unaware of the significance of anniversaries, particularly of deaths. His associations to the dream moved from rivalries and conflicts with his colleagues to those of his early childhood. He thought of his nephew John, the son of his half-brother Philip. Until Freud's third year, he and John, who actually was a year older than Freud, had been inseparable. When Freud was three, John had moved with his family to England, but had reappeared, like the dream figures, when the family returned to Vienna in 1870. Freud was then fourteen. He recalled that at the time, he and his nephew would enact the parts of Caesar and Brutus. He comments:

> My emotional life has always insisted that I should have an intimate friend and a hated enemy. I have always been able to provide myself afresh with both, and it has not infrequently happened that the ideal

situation of childhood has been so completely reproduced that friend
and enemy have come together in a single individual—though not, of
course, both at once or with constant oscillations, as may have been
the case in my early childhood. (Freud 1900, 483)

By a circuitous series of associations, Freud arrived at a connection
between Julius Caesar and his nephew John. Schur (1972) points to a series
of connections that Freud in fact omitted from his interpretation of the
dream. In the same letter to Fliess in which he recounts his recovery of
memories concerning John, Freud writes:

that I greeted my brother (who was a year my junior and died after a
few months) with ill-wishes and genuine childish jealousy, and that his
death left the germ of self-reproaches in me. I have also long known
the companion in my evil deeds between the ages of one and two. It
was my nephew, a year older than myself, who is now living in
Manchester and who visited us in Vienna when I was fourteen. . . .
This nephew and this young brother have determined what is neurotic, but also what is intense, in all my friendships. (Freud
1950a, 262)

Freud did not mention the association to his brother Julius in his interpretation of the dream, even though its manifest content included Fliess's visit
to Vienna in July. Fliess was born in 1858, the year in which Julius died.
Consequently, Fliess was the substitute figure for Freud's dead younger
brother.

Of Paneth, who had sought Fleischl's position and whom Freud annihilates in the dream, Freud says, "As he was ambitious, I slew him," just as
Brutus had slain Caesar. Freud translates the dream thoughts as follows:

"It's quite true that no one is irreplaceable. How many people I've
followed to the grave already! But I'm still alive. I've survived them
all; I'm left in possession of the field." A thought of this kind,
occurring to me at a moment at which I was afraid I might not find my
friend Fl[eischl] alive if I made the journey to him, could only be
construed as meaning that I was delighted because I had once more
survived someone, because it was *he* and not I who had died, because
I was left in possession of the field as I had been in the phantasied
scene from my childhood. (Freud 1900, 485)

The references to Brutus and Caesar, as it turns out, come not from
Shakespeare but from Schiller's *Die Räuber*. This tragedy centers around
the vicious sibling rivalry between a deformed and ugly younger brother
and an older brother who is a born leader of superior abilities. The scene to
which Freud refers takes place after the battle of Philippi. Caesar's ghost
appears to Brutus, and in the dialogue that follows calls Brutus his son,

saying he has become the greatest Roman of all by plunging his sword into his father's chest. Brutus replies, "Where Brutus lives, Caesar must die."

As Schur (1972) comments, both the relationship of Prince Hal to his royal father and that of Brutus to Caesar were prime examples of oedipal conflict, which Freud avoided, disguising them as more mature conflicts of rivalry and ambition. This may be explained by the fact that the *non vixit* dream was for Freud a form of anniversary reaction to his father's death as well as an elaboration of the survival-guilt dream that he had reported to Fliess two years before. The *non vixit* dream reflects the growing sense of conflict and ambivalence in Freud's relationship with Fliess (Schur 1966). In the dream this had become a matter of survival and of Freud's need to do away with Fliess. He needed to maintain the approval and admiration of Fliess, his alter ego, yet he knew that Fliess's theories were scientifically valueless. Like Freud's father, Fliess too would soon have to be left by the wayside; he would have to be killed off.

Among the death ages that preoccupied Freud was fifty-one. The first mention of it is in a letter to Fliess on 22 June 1894, in connection with the death of Freud's friend Kundt, a physicist (Schur 1972). Freud mistakenly identified Kundt's age at death as fifty-one; in fact he was fifty-four. The matter surfaced again in a dream in which Freud receives a hospital bill for someone who had been in his house in 1851. Freud was amused at this since he was not alive in 1851, and at the time of the dream his father was already dead. In the dream, to clear up the matter, Freud goes into the next room where his father is lying and tells him about it. His father replies that once in 1851 he got drunk and had to be detained. Freud associated the number fifty-one with an age of particular danger for men and commented to Fliess that he had had colleagues who had dropped dead at that age, apparently thinking of Kundt. This association related in turn to Freud's fear that the age of fifty-one would be the limit of his own life.

By this time, Fliess had arrived at his theory of periodicity, in which the male period of twenty-three and the female period of twenty-eight were used to determine critical periods of life, illness, and death. Fliess predicted that the total of the two periods, fifty-one, would be the limit of Freud's life, or would at least be a critical period for him. Although Freud consciously and explicitly put no credence in Fliess's theories, they nonetheless continued to exercise an unconscious hold on him. Many of his dreams from the period are filled with complex calculations, most of them also having some connection with questions of birth and death.

The theme of death plays a considerable role in many of Freud's dreams. His father's death in particular is a frequent and recurrent theme in Freud's dreams and associations. He comments:

It is true that dreams of dead people whom the dreamer has loved raise difficult problems in dream-interpretation and that these cannot always be satisfactorily solved. The reason for this is to be found in the particularly strongly marked emotional ambivalence which dominates the dreamer's relation to the dead person. (Freud 1900, 431)

In his dream of the castle by the sea, Freud appears as a volunteer naval officer. It is wartime, and there is fear of attack from enemy ships. The governor of the castle has to leave and gives Freud instructions what to do in the event of attack. As he is about to leave, however, he falls down dead. Suddenly, ships appear; Freud's brother cries out that they are warships, but it turns out that they are only merchant vessels. Then, suddenly, a small ship that is cut off in the middle in a rather comic fashion appears, with curious cup- or box-shaped objects on its deck. At this point everyone calls out, "That's the breakfast ship!" (Freud 1900, 463).

The dream occurred during Fliess's illness and after his recently published work containing his discoveries of biological cycles had been declared the work of an insane man. Freud had written to him more or less ignoring Fliess's troubles and telling him about his own enjoyable trip during the recent Easter holiday. In addition, Freud was just then on the verge of reaching a new understanding of the functioning of the human mind. As Schur (1972) notes, Freud had to pay for this by identifying himself with the dead governor. Once again, the motif of the guilt of the survivor surfaces. The basic theme of the dream is guilt over happiness and success that the dreamer feels have been gained at the expense of a beloved friend. Freud saw that the governor was a substitute for himself and that the dream thoughts dealt with his concerns about the future of his family after his own premature death. These dream thoughts were associated with happy recollections of his travels in the Adriatic. Warships are changed into harmless vessels, even into a breakfast ship. But the containers on its deck reminded Freud of Etruscan black pottery, which he took as a direct reference to death:

It was precisely behind this memory of the most cheerful *joie de vivre* that the dream concealed the gloomiest thoughts of an unknown and uncanny future. (Freud 1900, 466)

At a later date, Freud's preoccupation focused on the numbers sixty-one and sixty-two as his death ages. He admits this in a letter to Jung and recounts how on a trip to Greece with his brother Alexander these numbers kept cropping up in an uncanny fashion. He traced this preoccupation to the year 1899, in which he completed writing *The Interpretation of Dreams*. In the same year, Freud received a new telephone number, 14362. Freud was then forty-three and took the terminal digits of his telephone number, sixty-two, as predicting the end of his life. He comments: "The superstitious notion that I would die between the ages of sixty-one and sixty-two proves to coincide with the conviction that with

The Interpretation of Dreams I had completed my life work, that there was nothing more for me to do and that I might just as well lie down and die. . . . Moreover, the hidden influence of W. Fliess was at work; the superstition erupted in the year of his attack on me. You will see in this another confirmation of the specifically Jewish nature of my mysticism" (McGuire 1974, 219–20).

Freud was not unaware of the roots of his own superstition. In the 1904 edition of *The Psychopathology of Everyday Life* (1901) he comments:

Rage, anger, and consequently a murderous impulse is the source of superstition in obsessional neurotics: a sadistic component, which is attached to love and is therefore erected against the loved person and repressed precisely because of this link and because of its intensity. —My own superstition has its roots in suppressed ambition (immortality) and in my case takes the place of that anxiety about death which springs from the normal uncertainty of life. (p. 260)

And again in the edition of 1907:

Anyone who has had the opportunity of studying the hidden mental impulses of human beings by means of psycho-analysis can also say something new about the quality of the unconscious motives that find expression in superstition. It can be recognized most clearly in neurotics suffering from obsessional thinking or obsessional states— people who are often of high intelligence—that superstition derives from suppressed, hostile and cruel impulses. Superstition is in large part the expectation of trouble; and the person who has harbored frequent evil wishes against others, but has been brought up to be good and therefore repressed such wishes into the unconscious, will be especially ready to expect punishment for his unconscious wickedness in the form of trouble threatening him from without. (p. 260)

As early as 1897, Freud had formulated his notion of oedipal conflict and rivalry with the father, even to the point of murderous wishes. His self-analysis, in addition, had uncovered his own murderous wishes against his younger brother Julius and an intense rivalry with his sister. Julius had died in 1858, only to be succeeded within months by a sister. Blum (1977) notes the significance of these events in Freud's developmental progression; they occurred in the rapprochement stage of separation-individuation, with its associated vulnerability to object loss and ambivalence. Freud applied his insights about these events to his 1907 analysis of religious practices as obsessional acts. Soon after, he began treatment of a case of obsessional neurosis, the famous Rat Man (1909b). Freud interprets the patient's obsessional preoccupation with his father's death as an unconscious wish. He then connects this to Brutus's relationship to Caesar: "As Caesar loved me, I weep for him; as he was fortunate, I rejoice at it; as he was valiant, I honor him; but, as he was ambitious, I slew him." Had Freud at this point forgotten the *non vixit* dream and the fact that he had at one time played Brutus to his Julius?

Some years later, Freud (1936) described his experience on the Acropolis during the trip to Athens with his brother. At that time Freud experienced what he called a disturbance of memory, which was actually a transient state of derealization, of disbelief in the reality of what lay before his eyes. He had even to ask his brother if it were really true that they were on the Acropolis. Freud was able to relate this to a sense of guilt attached to his satisfaction at having achieved something his father had been unable to achieve. He writes: "It was something to do with a child's criticism of his father, with the undervaluation which took the place of the overvaluation of earlier childhood. It seems as though the essence of success was to have got further than one's own father, and as though to excel one's father was still something forbidden. . . . The very theme of Athens and the Acropolis in itself contained evidence of the son's superiority. . . . Thus, what interfered with our enjoyment of the journey to Athens was a feeling of filial piety" (pp. 247–48).

Shengold (1966) has discussed the connections between this experience on the Acropolis and Freud's Roman neurosis. The longing to see Rome represented a childhood wish connected "with my schoolboy hero-worship of the Semitic Hannibal" (Freud 1954). The conquest of this longed-for city, the *Roma virum genetrix,* reflects the fulfillment of an incestuous childhood wish, the realization of an oedipal triumph. Like Hannibal, Freud descended from the Alps into Italy. And when he stood on the crest of the Acropolis, his wish both to surpass his father and to possess his mother came into symptomatic conjunction. To stand on the height, on the crest of the hill, came to represent possession of the mons veneris, the taking of the father's place and the fulfillment of incestuous desires.

But Freud did not mention that the 1904 experience on the Acropolis followed Fliess's accusation, only a week before Freud's trip, that Freud had stolen Fliess's ideas on bisexuality. The theme of undervaluation taking the place of previous overvaluation applied to Freud's deteriorating relation with Fliess no less than with his father (Schur 1969). Fliess had explained his ideas on bisexuality to Freud in 1897, but Freud, forgetting this, had presented these same notions to his friend three years later as his own. In the face of Fliess's accusations, Freud had been quite upset and had confessed the possibility that he had been motivated by a wish to rob Fliess of his originality, reflecting Freud's envy and hostility. Freud described the episode in his own words:

One day in the summer of 1901 [actually 1900] I remarked to a friend [Wilhelm Fliess] with whom I used at that time to have a lively exchange of scientific ideas: "These problems of the neuroses are only to be solved if we base ourselves wholly and completely on the assumption of the original bisexuality of the individual." To which he replied: "That's what I told you two-and-a-half years ago at Br. (Breslau) when we went for that evening walk. But you wouldn't hear of it then." It is painful to be requested in this way to surrender one's originality. I could not recall any such conversation or this announcement of my friend's. One of us must have been mistaken and on the "cui prodest?" principle it must have been myself. Indeed, in the course of the next week I remembered the whole incident, which was just as my friend had tried to recall to me; I even recollected the answer I had given him at the time: "I've not accepted that yet; I'm not inclined to go into the question." But since then I have grown more tolerant when, in reading medical literature, I come across one of the few ideas with which my name can be associated, and find that my name has not been mentioned. (Freud 1901, 143–44)

Freud was apparently unable to work through his guilt and his doubts about his originality. The Acropolis event was symptomatic of Freud's infantile wish for power, his guilt over the oedipal conquest of the father, the residues of sibling rivalry and survivor guilt, and his need for punishment. It represented a form of identity crisis (Harrison 1966) that reflected basic aspects of Freud's neurotic conflicts. Freud later wrote an open letter about his experience on the Acropolis to Romain Rolland, the French author and mystic, on the occasion of Rolland's seventieth birthday. Freud himself was eighty at the time and caught in the grip of a remorseless cancer (Freud 1936). Once again he was preoccupied with his own identity, threatened this time by pain, increasing helplessness, and approaching death. The identity crisis on the Acropolis resurfaced and challenged Freud to reassert his power and creativity by reasserting the power of the repressed (Stamm 1969). The episode was, in addition, a working-through and an attempt at mastery of basic lifelong conflicts that come into focus in relation to Rolland, the proponent of religion and mysticism. We can infer that it was part of Freud's lifelong struggle to overcome his powerful tendencies to superstition and mysticism.

In the years of the First World War Freud's Todesangst seemed to grow more intense. He was, in fact, approaching the ominous ages of sixty-one and sixty-two. Jones (1955) comments on Freud's continuing superstition about these ages. Schur (1972) recounts that Freud was bothered by the further thought that both his father and eldest brother had died at age eighty-one-and-a-half and by the prospect of passing even that advanced age. At the time, he was close to finishing his metaphysical papers, and this triumph, together with the thought of surpassing his father in longevity, added to his burden of unconscious guilt.

The preoccupation with his death during these years was intensified by his fear for the life of his son Martin, who was fighting at the front. This fear was both an expression of Freud's oedipal aggression and a punishment, since in his superstition the year 1918 would bring death to both of them. Freud knew "that the fear of death, which dominates us oftener than we know . . . is usually the outcome of a sense of guilt" (Freud 1915a, 297). His hostility was related to oedipal ambivalence and to intense sibling rivalry.

By the time the war ended, Freud had passed the critical age of sixty-two, and his mind seemed to turn to telepathy and the occult. *Beyond the Pleasure Principle* appeared in 1920. Two tragic events weighed heavily on Freud's mind at the time and undoubtedly had a great deal to do with his attempt to come to terms with death and with his ultimate formulation of the "death instinct." The first was the death of his young friend Anton von Freund; the second was the death of his daughter Sophie after an illness of only a few days. Schur (1972) suggests that the writing of *Beyond the Pleasure Principle* and the formulation of the death instinct fulfilled important functions in Freud's inner struggle with the problem of death. Freud himself comments:

> Perhaps we have adopted the belief [that all living substance dies from internal causes] because there is some comfort in it. If we are to die ourselves, and first to lose in death those who are dearest to us, it is easier to submit to a remorseless law of nature, to the sublime *Anangke* [Necessity] than to a chance which might perhaps have been escaped. It may be, however, that this belief in the internal necessity of dying is only another of those illusions which we have created "*um die Schwere des Daseins zu ertragen*" ["to bear the trials of existence"]. (Freud 1920b, 45)

Schur (1972) adds:

> Could it be that uncovering a "death instinct" permitted Freud literally to *live* with the reality of death, especially with the further aid of his simultaneous *creation* of Eros through the sheer omnipotence of thought? . . . Therefore, the formulation of the death-instinct concept—paradoxical as this may seem—may not only have steeled Freud for the sixteen-year ordeal of his cancer, but prepared him for his belief in the supremacy of the ego, of the intellect, of *Logos,* the only force with which he could face *Ananke.* It paved the way for the *Future of an Illusion* and for the formulation of a "scientific *Weltanschauung.*" (p. 332)

As Freud writes to Pfister in 1922, "It is only in old age that one is converted to the grim heavenly pair *logos kai ananke*" (Schur 1972, 333; also in Meng and Freud 1963, 86).

Freud's interest in the occult remains one of the puzzling aspects of his career. After he had passed the critical age of sixty-two and had put *Beyond the Pleasure Principle* behind him, he produced a series of papers dealing with telepathy and occult matters (Freud 1922, 1923b, 1941a). Freud apparently had strong antagonistic feelings about such matters. Freud had to confront these conflicts in the person of Jung, his heir apparent and his hope for a broadening of the scope of psychoanalysis and for its acceptance in a wider range of non-Jewish circles. A critical event occurred in 1909 when Jung and his wife were visiting Freud and his family in Vienna. The two men were heatedly arguing one evening about the meaning of occult experiences. Jung's predilection for the occult and his spiritualist tendencies need little comment; Freud was more skeptical. Jung suddenly experienced strange feelings in his chest, followed immediately by a loud noise from the bookcase which startled the two men and made them leap to their feet in fear that the bookcase was going to fall over on them. When they had recovered their composure, Jung said to Freud, "There—that is an example of a so-called catalytic exteriorization phenomenon." Freud scoffed, but Jung pressed the point, predicting that in another moment there would be a second loud noise. According to Jung's report, the second noise duly followed, and Freud could only stare in amazement. As Jung commented later, "I do not know what was in his mind or what his look meant. In any case, the incident aroused his mistrust of me, and I had the feeling that I had done something against him" (Brome 1978, 113–14).

Freud was obviously troubled. After some weeks had passed, he wrote to Jung about his reactions. The passage is worth quoting at length:

It is strange that on the very same evening when I formally adopted you as eldest son and anointed you—*in partibus infidelium*—as my successor and crown prince, you should have divested me of my paternal dignity, which divesting seems to have given you as much pleasure as I, on the contrary, derived from the investiture of your person. Now I am afraid of falling back into the father role with you if I tell you how I feel about the poltergeist business. But I must, because my attitude is not what you might otherwise think. I don't deny that your stories and your experiment made a deep impression on me. I decided to continue my observations after you left, and here are the results. In my first room there is a constant creaking where the two heavy Egyptian steles rest on the oaken boards of the bookshelves. That is too easy to explain. In the second, where we heard it, there is seldom any creaking. At first I was inclined to accept this as proof, if the sound that was so frequent while you were here were not heard again after your departure—but since then I have heard it repeatedly, not, however, in connection with my thoughts and never when I am thinking about you or this particular problem of yours. (And not at present moment, I add by way of a challenge.) But this

observation was soon discredited by another consideration. My credulity, or at least my willingness to believe, vanished with the magic of
your personal presence; once again, for some inward reasons that I
can't put my finger on, it strikes me as quite unlikely that such phenomena should exist; I confront the despiritualized furniture as the
poet confronted undeified Nature after the gods of Greece had passed
away. (McGuire 1974, 218)

In this same letter, Freud goes on to discuss at length his superstitions
about the ages sixty-one and sixty-two, which he was concerned would
mark the end of his life. His ambivalence was undoubtedly clear to Jung's
eyes: Freud the scientist and rationalist was explaining away phenomena
Jung was convinced were preternatural, while at the same time confessing
somewhat abashedly his own superstitious beliefs.

A further episode bears witness to this unresolved ambivalence in
Freud. Wallace (1978) relates a story told by Fodor (1971) about an
invitation Freud received to join the advisory council of the American
Psychical Institute in 1921. Freud declined, but word got out that he had
made the assertion that if he had his life to live over again, he would have
devoted it to psychical research. When Freud was questioned about this
point, he emphatically and unequivocally denied it. But in fact, when
Freud's letter declining the invitation was uncovered, it was found to
contain the following statement: "If I were at the beginning of a scientific
career, instead of, as now, at its end, I would perhaps choose no other field
of work [than parapsychology] in spite of all the difficulties" (Wallace
1978, 210).

In addition, Jones (1957) recalls that in the years before the First World
War, he conversed with Freud on a number of occasions about occultism
and related subjects. Late into the night Freud would regale Jones with
stories of uncanny experiences with patients, often about misfortunes or
deaths that were realized years after the expression of a wish or prediction.
Jones comments that Freud particularly relished such accounts and seemed
to be strongly impressed by their more mysterious aspects. When Jones
would object to some of these tall tales, Freud would reply with his favorite
quotation: "There are more things in heaven and earth than are dreamt of
in your philosophy." On one occasion Jones pressed him, observing that if
one could believe in mental processes floating in the air, one could very
well go on to believe in angels. To this Freud replied, "Quite so, even *der
liebe Gott.*" Jones (1957) observes, "This was said in a jocular tone as if
agreeing with my *reductio ad absurdum* and with a quizzical look as if he
were pleased at shocking me. But there was something searching also in
the glance, and I went away not entirely happy lest there be some more
serious undertone as well" (p. 381).

There is another curious aspect to all of this. In his office at Berggasse 19
Freud had gathered a unique collection of ancient artifacts, including

numerous pieces of statuary depicting ancient deities and mythological entities. This fascination with antiquity seems to indicate that in exploring the depths of the human mind Freud found it necessary to assemble around him representations of ancient and long-dead deities.

It seems clear that the mystical tendencies in Freud's personality neither can be ignored nor should be underestimated. It is worth noting that the two figures who played predominant roles in Freud's life during periods of creative struggle, first Fliess and later Jung, both professed to be scientists with strong mystical inclinations. Freud was not willing to recognize these tendencies in Fliess in the beginning, but as time wore on they became all too obvious. Nonetheless, Freud's acceptance and encouragement of Fliess's numerology and his frequent involvement in Fliess's elaborations suggest that his attitude was not simply one of toleration. As Jones (1957) and later Schur (1972) point out, Fliess served as a transference object who allowed Freud to personify his own mystical trends by way of externalization.

The same projective device undoubtedly came into play in relation to Jung later on. Jung appeared on the scene in 1906, shortly after Fliess had launched his violent attack on Freud. He too became the object for the displacement of Freud's own mystical tendencies as well as for the ambivalence that loomed in Freud's crumbling relationship to Fliess. In Freud's relationship to Jung the transference interaction took on a father-son quality in which the respective roles frequently alternated, but through which the way was opened for a reenactment of the infantile oedipal conflicts of both men (Shengold 1979). Jung's perception of Freud's reaction to the poltergeist episode was probably not far from the truth. While Freud looked to Jung as his successor with hope and anticipation, he also was distrustful of Jung's mystical intensity and religious fervor. Jung seems to have approached analysis with a crusading zeal that Freud found hard to relate to (McGuire 1974, letter 178J). He saw psychoanalysis as a sort of ideal substitute for the deficiencies of existing religions. Jung's religious instinct must have seemed alien to Freud's agnostic and scientific intentions and must have made Freud feel quite uncomfortable at the thought of turning over psychoanalysis, his creation, to Jung. Freud's letters to Jung during this period have a strongly paternal flavor; we find him advising, admonishing, lecturing, suggesting, recommending, even scolding. It has even been suggested that one of Freud's dreams, about Savonarola, may have been partly determined by Freud's fear of the mystical bent in Jung's character and his apprehension that Jung was a potential religious fanatic (Lehmann 1978).

Another significant thread that surfaces, particularly in relation to Jung, is the series of fainting episodes that Freud experienced. The first such attack occurred in 1906 in Munich, with Fliess; the second took place two years later in the same hotel room, again with Fliess; the third, in 1909, when Freud was in Bremen with Jung; and the fourth and last, in 1912 in Munich, again with Jung. The final episode occurred in the context of the clash between Jung and Abraham. The quarrel came to a head in 1909 at the Salzburg Congress, but by 1912 Freud and Abraham were again at odds over how to deal with Jung. Freud was eager to protect Jung as his hope for the psychoanalytic movement and was suspicious of Abraham's motives in attacking him. In November 1912, Freud gathered five of his inner circle in Munich. Jones (1955) recounts that Freud and Jung went on a long walk during which Freud lectured Jung on his shortcomings. Jung promised to reform, and Freud seems to have felt that he had won Jung back to the cause. At lunch there was a discussion of Abraham's recent paper on Amenhotep. Jung commented that too much had been made of the fact that Amenhotep had erased his father's name from inscriptions: such death wishes seemed of less importance than the task of establishing monotheism. Freud then took Jung to task for recent publications which had ignored the master's own work and *even his name*. As Jung was defending himself, Freud suddenly fell to the floor in a dead faint. Jung carried him to a couch. When Freud revived, his first words were, "How sweet it must be to die."

Jung describes the two fainting attacks of Freud's that he had witnessed. When they were in Bremen in 1909, Jung had been discussing "peat-bog corpses"—that is, bodies of prehistoric men who had been buried in peat marshes in northern Europe, which had been remarkably preserved by a process of natural mummification. The discussion apparently got on Freud's nerves, for he reproached Jung several times for bringing the subject up. At one point, Freud seemed considerably disturbed and suddenly fainted. Jung reports that afterward Freud commented that he felt Jung's insistence on the corpses had reflected his death wishes toward Freud. With regard to the final attack, in Munich in 1912, Jung (1961) recalls that he picked Freud up and carried him into the next room.

> As I was carrying him, he half came to, and I shall never forget the look he cast at me. In his weakness he looked at me as if I were his father. Whatever causes may have contributed to this faint—the atmosphere was very tense—the fantasy of father-murder was common to both cases. (p. 157)

On 8 December, less than a month after this event, Freud wrote to Jones:

> I cannot forget that six and four years ago I suffered from very similar though not such intense symptoms in the *same* room of the Park Hotel. I saw Munich first when I visited Fliess during his illness and this town seems to have acquired a strong connection with my relation to that man. There is some piece of unruly homosexual feeling at the root of the matter. (Jones 1953, 317)

Jones adds to this Freud's recollection that his final quarrel with Fliess had taken place in that same hotel room, although he was not absolutely sure of this point. We recall that Fliess was one of the revenants in the *non vixit* dream, a substitute for Freud's younger brother Julius, who had been the object of Freud's death wishes. Freud himself traced his attacks to the effect of Julius's death. Shengold (1972) remarks:

> Freud's fainting apparently involved both sides of the Oedipus complex. Punishment for death-wishes toward rivals for the exclusive possession of the mother, and homosexuality associated with passive surrender to them—in short, the basic bisexuality of man, here associated with the person whose *name* he had once forgotten in the struggle to claim originality for the discovery of the concept—Fliess. (p. 228)

The conclusion seems inescapable that the same conflicts, together with the same symptomatic expression, were stirred in relation to both Fliess and Jung as revenants associated with little Julius.

RELIGIOSITY AND IDENTITY

Perhaps a key element in the understanding of the religious aspects of Freud's personality lies in his religious identity. It may seem paradoxical to speak of a self-professed agnostic and iconoclastic scientist as having a religious identity. But I think enough has been said already in this discussion to suggest that a picture of Freud as rejecting, negating, and destroying all religious beliefs would be highly oversimplified and would hardly do justice to the complexity of his inner life.

There is little question that Freud's relationship to Judaism was fraught with ambiguity and ambivalence. We have seen that his religious upbringing had been somewhat ambiguous in that although he had been sent to study Hebrew and the Scriptures from the ages of seven to thirteen, he would later claim that he knew no Hebrew and that he was, in fact, unable to understand the inscription in the old Philippson Bible sent to him by his aging father. Freud's grandfather and great-grandfather had probably been Hasidic rabbis in Galicia. While Freud's father seems to have turned to a more secular way of life, he nonetheless was a devoted student of the Torah and the Talmud. Freud's own recollection of his upbringing was that it was quite un-Jewish. We also know that his mother was even less affiliated with the religion of her ancestors. In her declining years, she would invite her children and grandchildren to celebrate feast days with her, but they were always the Christian ones, never the Jewish.

Freud's knowledge of Jewish liturgical practice must have been limited. Jones (1955) recalls that when Freud visited the catacombs in Rome he wrote home that the Jewish graves could be distinguished by the candelabrum carved on them, but he was uncertain whether it was called a *menorah* or not. One would guess that Freud had not spent a great amount of time in the synagogue. He certainly did not think of himself as a religious person. Replying to a query from an American physician, Freud replied:

> As for myself, God had not done so much for me. He had never allowed me to hear an inner voice; and if, in view of my age, he did not make haste, it would not be my fault if I remained to the end of my life what I now was—"an infidel Jew." (Freud 1928, 170)

In the same vein, he asked Pfister, "Incidentally, why have the religiously devout not discovered psychoanalysis, why did one have to wait for a totally Godless Jew?" (Meng and Freud 1963).

It seems clear that while Freud did not strongly adhere to his traditional religious background, he nonetheless valued it for what might seem to be more secular reasons. In his letter to the B'nai B'rith, he remarks:

> It was only to my Jewish nature that I owed the two qualities that have become indispensable to me throughout my difficult life. Because I was a Jew, I found myself free of many prejudices which restrict others in the use of the intellect; as a Jew, I was prepared to be in the opposition and to renounce with the "compact majority." (Freud 1941b, 274)

In the same connection, he writes:

> Nor is it perhaps entirely a matter of chance that the first advocate of psychoanalysis was a Jew. To profess belief in this new theory called for a certain degree of readiness to accept a situation of solitary opposition—a situation with which no one is more familiar than a Jew. (Freud 1925b, 222)

In the preface to the Hebrew edition of *Totem and Taboo* (1912–13), Freud expresses his position in poignant terms:

> No reader of this book will find it easy to put himself in the emotional position of an author who is ignorant of the language of Holy Writ, who is completely estranged from the religion of his fathers—as well as from every other religion—and who cannot take a share in nationalist ideals, but who has yet never repudiated his people, who feels that he is in his essential nature a Jew and who has no desire to alter that nature. If the question were put to him: "Since you have abandoned all these common characteristics of your countrymen, what is there left to you that is Jewish?" he would reply: "A great deal, and probably its very essence." He could not now express that essence clearly in words; but some day, no doubt, it will become accessible to the scientific mind. (p. xv)

One of the fascinating connections in which Freud's ambivalence to his Jewishness expressed itself was his relationship to the great Theodor Herzl. For several years, they lived almost across the street from each other, but it seems that they never actually met or spoke to each other. Yet Freud almost daily read the *Neue Freie Presse,* for which Herzl was a writer and literary editor, and his attendance at Herzl's play *The New Ghetto* in 1898 provoked an important dream. In 1902 Freud sent a letter to Herzl along with a copy of his *Interpretation of Dreams,* more or less asking him to review the book in the *Neue Freie Presse* and expressing his admiration of Herzl as "the poet and fighter for the human rights of our people" (Falk 1977, 7). In the book, however, Freud did not mention *The New Ghetto* as a source for some of his material, nor did he mention Herzl, who was by that time quite famous for this work. Loewenberg (1971) is of the opinion that Freud was trying to avoid being identified with Judaism or Zionism because he was concerned about the universal acceptance and appeal of psychoanalysis and was also afraid that any connection with Zionism would hurt his chances for a professorship in the anti-Semitic climate of Vienna.

Certainly *The New Ghetto,* with its themes of anti-Semitism and the Jewish question, had a strong impact on Freud. The play concerns the position of the Jew who tries unsuccessfully to break out of the invisible walls of the "new ghetto." The theme must have had strong reverberations for Freud. In the dream provoked by the experience of seeing the play, Professor M. of the university staff addresses Freud as "My son, the Myops." This dream was preliminary to a second, in which Freud finds himself in Rome. It becomes necessary to remove the children there to safety because of some danger. Freud is sitting on the edge of a fountain near great double doors that he identified as the Porta Romana at Siena. He is greatly depressed, almost in tears. A female figure brings out two boys and hands them over to their father, who is not Freud, although the elder boy is clearly Freud's eldest son. The woman asks the boy to kiss her goodbye, and Freud notes her red nose. The boy refuses to kiss her but puts out his hand and says *"Auf Geseres"* to her, then *"Auf Ungeseres"* to Freud and presumably to his father.

Freud recognized the relevance of the dream to the Jewish problem, particularly regarding the future of children to whom one could not give a country of their own, and the concern about educating them so that they could move freely across frontiers. Freud's tangle of associations to the dream has led Grinstein (1968) to conclude that the thoughts about the Jewish problem and the future of his children set off by seeing *The New Ghetto* were combined with other thoughts dealing with Freud's sense of freedom and his wish to be free of the bondage of Viennese anti-Semitism. For example, his wish to go to England, where he could feel accepted, was connected with sad memories of leaving Freiburg as a child of three and of the losses he suffered, including that of his old nurse.

This, in turn, was connected with Freud's continuing mourning over the loss of his father. In the dream he weeps over the loss of his eldest son, but may in fact himself have been identified with the eldest son, weeping over the many separations he had suffered, including the death of his father. In the dream Freud thus reassures himself not to make such a *Geseres* over the affliction of his eyes, namely, weeping. *Geseres* stands for a Hebrew word meaning imposed suffering or doom. Freud's associations to it lead to the word pair *gesalzen–ungesalzen* (salted–unsalted), which he connects with the notion of leavening. This is then associated with the flight from Egypt, which the children of Israel celebrate by eating unleavened bread.

However, as Falk (1977) points out, there are additional elements that have to do with Freud's intense and contradictory feelings about the Jewish question, his own Jewishness, and Herzl. These elements are connected to Freud's ambivalence about his father, who is disguised in the dream as Professor M. and the children's father. Falk argues that Herzl played the role of Freud's dead father in Freud's unconscious, as had Fliess before him.

Freud's ambivalence toward his father undoubtedly had many determinants, but a significant role was played by an event that occurred when Freud was a young boy.

I may have been ten or twelve years old, when my father began to take me with him on his walks and reveal to me in his talk his views upon things in the world we live in. Thus it was, on one such occasion, that he told me a story to show me how much better things were now than they had been in his days. "When I was a young man," he said, "I went for a walk one Saturday in the streets of your birthplace; I was well dressed, and had a new fur cap on my head. A Christian came up to me and with a single blow knocked off my cap into the mud and shouted: 'Jew! get off the pavement!'" "And what did you do?" I asked. "I went into the roadway and picked up my cap," was his quiet reply. This struck me as unheroic conduct on the part of the big, strong man who was holding the little boy by the hand. I contrasted this situation with another which fitted my feelings better: the scene in which Hannibal's father, Hamilcar Barca, made his boy swear before the household altar to take vengeance on the Romans. Ever since that time Hannibal had had a place in my phantasies. (Freud 1900, 14)

But the disillusionment with his father had begun even earlier. The family had had to leave Freud's birthplace because of anti-Semitism and the failure of his father's textile business, which had done well until hand-weaving became increasingly obsolete. Like other Jewish factory owners, Jakob Freud became a target for the ire of his Gentile employees over the loss of their jobs. At the same time that he lost financial security, he also apparently lost status within the family, particularly in the eyes of his young son. His father had not stood up to anti-Semitism as Freud seems to have wanted him to. Jakob's place in the affections of his family remained secure, but as Jones (1953) notes, "Freud had described him to Martha as a Micawber-like figure, always hoping for something to turn up" (p. 2). Apparently Freud's repressed oedipal conflicts and ambivalence were reactivated by the recounting of his father's stories.

It is not difficult to discern behind the figure of the woman in the dream Freud's mother and the Catholic nanny he had had as a young child. Jones (1953) describes Freud's mother as a lively and strong-willed woman who adored her *"goldener Sigi."* In a letter to Fliess, Freud (1950a) confesses:

> The "prime originator" of my troubles was a woman, ugly, elderly, but clever, who told me a great deal about God Almighty and Hell and who gave me a high opinion of my own capacities; that later (between the ages of two and two-and-a-half) my libido was stirred up towards *matrem,* namely on the occasion of a journey with her from Leipzig to Vienna, during which we must have spent the night together and I must had the opportunity of seeing her *nudam.* . . . (pp. 261–62)

Not only is Freud's conflict over this experience with his mother manifest in his resorting to Latin vocabulary, but the journey to which he refers took place, in fact, when he was four years old. This might suggest that the memory was a screen for an earlier seduction by the nurse. Undoubtedly, Freud was attached to this woman, and her loss was a great blow to him. She was, as he put it, his "first instructress in sexual matters" (Freud 1954). There is little doubt that in the course of his self-analysis the figure of the nurse from his infancy became fused with that of his beloved mother. Perhaps we can conjecture that Freud's attachment to this old nurse, who taught him about the things of God and took him with her to Catholic services, may have limited his capacity to relate wholeheartedly and unambivalently to the Judaism of his father.

Any doubt over Freud's association of Herzl with his father should be dispelled by an interview between him and Herzl's son, in which Freud supported the young man's wish not to participate in a Zionist Congress. He is reported as saying:

> Your ambitions are poisoning your life. You should finally bury your father within your soul, which is still carrying him alive. . . . It is he [your father], not anyone else, who is appearing to you in your many dreams. . . . Your father is one of those people who have turned dreams into reality. This is a very rare and dangerous breed. It includes the Garibaldis, the Edisons, the Herzls. . . . I would simply call them the sharpest opponents of my scientific work. It is my

modest profession to simplify dreams, to make them clear and ordinary. They, on the contrary, confuse the issue, turn it upside down,
command the world while they themselves remain on the other side of
the psychic mirror. . . . Stay away from them, young man. . . . Stay
away, even though one of them was your father . . . perhaps because
of that. (Falk 1977, 19)

As Falk notes, Freud seems clearly to be talking no less about himself than
about Herzl's son. He could not bury his father either. Falk summarizes
the implications of the Myops dream in the following terms:

Perhaps we can now grasp the full meaning of Herzl to Freud. Herzl
was in part acting out all of Freud's infantile fantasies of becoming a
great political leader like Moses or Hannibal, Massena or Garibaldi.
These fantasies or wishes had been repressed and to some extent
projected onto Freud's father as in the "Father like Garibaldi" dream.
Herzl now took on for Freud the combined meaning in his own
repressed Jewish-political-nationalistic-leadership wishes and fantasies, which he had to ward off, and the father-figure he had struggled
with all his life. This leads us to an expanded interpretation of Freud's
dream "My Son, the Myops . . ." provoked by Herzl's play: Professor M. saying "My Son, the Myops . . ." is indeed Freud's father
saying to Freud: "You are myopic: you do not see the the two sides of
yourself, the masculine and the feminine, the paternal and the maternal, the Jewish and the universal. You are indeed short-sighted and
one-sided, for you are trying to overlook your own fierce attraction to
Jewish nationalism, and to me, and your *preference* for *"Auf Ungeseres"*—the unleavened bread *your* people eat at *Passover."* For
indeed in the dream the boy (which as Grinstein has shown is Freud
himself as well) says *"Auf Geseres"* to the woman, refusing to kiss her,
but *"Auf Ungeseres"* to the father and mother (*or to one of them*), and
this last phrase denotes a preference. The "one of us" can only be the
father, since the boy has already said the opposite to the mother.
Thus, the dream is Freud's attempt to deal with the intense conflict of
bilaterality that he could not resolve within himself—his father on the
one side, his mother and nurse on the other; Judaism on one side,
universality and Christianity on the other. He cannot decide even
whether to say *"Auf Ungeseres"* to both parents or only to his father.
This intense conflict remained with Freud to the end of his days.
(Falk 1977, 20)

Other elements add to the picture. Freud's long-frustrated wish to visit
Rome proved to be a matter of considerable conflict and inhibition for
him. This "Roman neurosis" (Schorske 1973) manifested itself in dreams
in which Rome remains an elusive target: Freud sees the Eternal City, but

it is shrouded in mist. Or he is surprised that the view is so clear, or the train moves on before he can even set foot within city walls (Freud 1900). Between 1895 and 1898, Freud traveled to Italy five times, but on none of these occasions, despite his yearnings, did he manage to reach Rome. He recounts how he overcame this inhibition. On a visit to Italy, he was planning to bypass Rome when a thought came to his mind: "Which of the two, it may be debated, walked up and down his study with the greater impatience after he had formed his plan of going to Rome—Winckelmann, the Vice-Principal, or Hannibal, the Commander-in-Chief?" (Freud 1900, 196). Freud's comments upon remembering this thought are revealing:

> I had actually been following in Hannibal's footsteps. Like him, I had been fated not to see Rome; and he too had moved into the Campagna when everyone had expected him in Rome. But Hannibal, whom I had come to resemble in these respects, had been the favorite hero of my later school days. Like so many boys of that age, I had sympathized in the Punic Wars not with the Romans but with the Carthaginians. And when in the higher classes I began to understand for the first time what it meant to belong to an alien race, and anti-Semitic feelings among the other boys warned me that I must take up a definite position, the figure of the Semitic general rose still higher in my esteem. To my youthful mind Hannibal and Rome symbolized the conflict between the tenacity of Jewry and the organization of the Catholic Church. And the increasing importance of the effects of the anti-Semitic movement upon our emotional life helped to fix the thoughts and feelings of those early days. Thus, the wish to go to Rome had become in my dream-life a cloak and symbol for a number of other passionate wishes. Their realization was to be pursued with all the perseverance and single-mindedness of the Carthaginian, though their fulfillment seemed at the moment just as little favored by destiny as was Hannibal's life-long wish to enter Rome. (Freud 1900, 196–97)

Hannibal's desire had been to conquer Rome, but Winckelmann, the noted art historian, had converted to Catholicism and had made Rome his home. As Bergmann (1976) notes, Freud may well have been struggling unconsciously with two attitudes toward the Catholic church as represented by Rome: either to conquer it, as he ultimately did in his teachings on religion as collective neurosis, or to convert to Christianity, with the attendant advantages of academic advancement. The prohibition against entering Rome symbolized the oedipal taboo. Conquering Rome would have meant becoming victorious over the forces of anti-Semitism and persecution that had beaten down his father; it would have meant outdoing his father and winning the oedipal struggle. His analysis of the Hannibal-

Winckelmann conflict led Freud to discover the crucial childhood memory about the story of his father and the Christian who had knocked off his cap.

The same motifs occur in Freud's experience of derealization on the Acropolis. We have previously touched on the elements of oedipal triumph and its associated guilt. But Freud's discussion of the episode in 1936 was in effect a rebuttal to Romain Rolland. In it, he evaluates the mystical experience, with its attendant alterations of consciousness and disturbances of memory, as a search for bliss by attempting to fill an emotional void with the illusion of a happy memory. Freud's message to Rolland, then, is that what he calls "oceanic feelings" may well provide the basis and springboard of religion—insofar as they are a defense against depression and the memory of a buried wound. As Masson and Masson (1978) conclude, in addressing Rolland, Freud becomes the Hannibal of his fantasy and repudiates the image of his father merely picking up his cap and walking on.

> Behind the inability to face the truth about Romain Rolland lay the rupture in memory ultimately leading back to the humiliation at the hands of a Roman Catholic maid. But Freud did not succumb to the regressive pull of mysticism. That he could not completely free himself from the spell of such idealized figures as Jung and Romain Rolland is a consequence of the repression that overtook the feelings in his memories of early traumata connected with anti-Semitic incidents. (pp. 206–07)

Kanzer (1969) has pointed out the parallels between Rolland and Freud's younger brother Alexander, with whom he climbed the Acropolis. Both were ten years younger than Freud, a coincidence Freud himself notes (1936). Freud expressed a deep bond with Rolland: "I have rarely experienced that mysterious attraction of one human being for another as vividly as I have with you; it is somehow bound up, perhaps, with the awareness of being so different" (E. Freud 1960, 406). The same senti-ment had been directed at Wilhelm Fliess, and the same transference issues were again at work—hostility and ambivalence toward a younger brother, first directed against the dead Julius, subsequently toward the usurper Alexander, and most recently toward Fliess.

Alexander was not altogether unworthy of this role. He had become a recognized authority on tariffs and even threatened to gain the coveted professorship ahead of Sigmund. Was the younger to take precedence over the older? This rivalry resurfaced in the relationship with Rolland, who played the part of a substitute younger brother to Freud, although Freud insisted on the differences between them: Rolland was Catholic, Freud Jewish; Rolland created illusions, Freud had spent his life attempting to destroy them (E. Freud 1960, 341). Rolland was to become one of those "doubles" whom Freud often found among artistic or mystical figures and upon whom he projected a side of himself that he sought to deny but could not resolve. The list of those we can recognize includes Fliess, Jung, Herzl, Zweig, Schnitzler, and Rolland. The same ambivalent wish—to change places with the younger brother, to send him to death while Freud himself gained an additional decade of life, played itself out in relation to each of these screen figures. Behind them all stand the infant brother and the father toward whom Freud's ambivalence and hostile wishes were never resolved.

In 1936, Freud was also occupied in writing *Moses and Monotheism* (1939)—a family romance that he referred to as a "historical novel." In his version, Freud was even compelled to deny the existence of Aaron, Moses' younger brother. The relationship between the older and the younger brother is recapitulated throughout, in the histories of younger brothers who usurp their older brothers' places in maternal affection— Isaac is favored over Ishmael, Jacob over Esau. Behind these stories reverberates Freud's murderous sibling rivalries with Julius, who had replaced him as the youngest and as his mother's favorite, and with Alexander, who had replaced Julius (Kanzer 1976).

All these themes come to a poignant and meaningful focus in Freud's relation to the figure of Moses. Freud's first mention of Moses seems to occur in a letter to Jung in 1908, where he compares Jung to Joshua, who was destined to lead the chosen people into the Promised Land, while Freud, like Moses, could only view it from afar. Schur (1972) tells us that the metaphor of the Promised Land was one of Freud's favorites. It comes up frequently in the Fliess correspondence, and its meaning is not fixed: for a time it is Italy and Rome, the goal that Freud was forbidden to see or conquer (conflating his identifications with both Moses and Hannibal; see Shengold 1966); at other times it is the solution to the riddle of the dream, the understanding of neurosis, or even, toward the end of his life, the publication of *Moses and Monotheism*.

When Freud finally visited Rome in 1901, after he had successfully analyzed his "Rome neurosis," he saw Michelangelo's famous statue of Moses for the first time and became fascinated by it. It seems clear that Freud's interpretation of it has nothing to do with the Biblical account and may have little to do with Michelangelo's vision of the prophet. Instead, it is an account of his own Moses—that is, a projection of his own image of Moses onto Michelangelo's creation.

> Michelangelo has placed a different Moses on the tomb of the Pope, one superior to the historical or traditional Moses. He has modified the theme of the broken Tables; he does not let Moses break them in his wrath, but makes him be influenced by the danger that they will be broken and makes him calm that wrath, or at any rate prevent it from becoming an act. In this way he has added something new and

more than human to the figure of Moses; so that the giant frame with its tremendous physical power becomes only a concrete expression of the highest mental achievement that is possible in a man, that of struggling successfully against an inward passion for the sake of a cause to which he has devoted himself. (Freud 1914, 233)

It is as though Freud sought to elevate Moses above ordinary men and to obliterate his most human characteristic, his wrath (Bergmann 1976). Indeed, Freud may have created a Moses out of his own sense of identification with the prophet whose followers had revolted against him (Shengold 1972). After all, 1914 was the year of his final break with Jung. Freud's Joshua had turned against him, and he needed to create a new Moses in his own image, a Moses who achieves great heights by restraining his disappointment, his sense of loss, betrayal, disillusionment, and his wrath. Indeed, insofar as Freud had broken the "Rome neurosis," it may be that the image of the wrath-conquering Moses reflects a change within Freud himself, allowing closer identification with a less destructive figure of his father. The Moses who restrains his wrath resembles the Jakob Freud who restrained his wrath in the face of insult.

In a sense, Freud's writing of *Moses and Monotheism* was the final attempt to work through and resolve this deep-seated conflict and ambivalence about his father. Jakob had destroyed Freud's image of the omnipotent father, and Freud never forgave him. The work was an act of rebellion and revenge, a rising up against the religion of the father and a smashing of it with the power of the mind. As Freud put it, "A hero is a man who stands up manfully against his father and in the end victoriously overcomes him" (Freud 1939, 18). It is clear that Freud's identification with Moses was powerful and broad. Moses was the leader of his people, the founder of a new nation, the prophet who gave rise to a new religion. The fantasy of the prophet who was without honor in his own country but who ultimately would prevail, whose truth would be universally accepted, was deeply embedded in Freud's mind, although he felt that he was destined never to see his Promised Land.

In Freud's account, Moses fails to reach the Promised Land, not because he dies, but because he is slain by his sons. Freud actually endorses Ernst Sellin's thesis

> that the Jews, who, even by the account in the Bible, were headstrong and unruly towards their law-giver and leader, rose against him one day, killed him and threw off the religion of the Aten which had been imposed on them, just as the Egyptians had thrown it off earlier. (Freud 1939, 60–61)

The subsequent reunification of the tribes takes place at Kadesh, where they take on a new religion, the worship of the volcano god Yahweh.

Wallace (1978) notes that Freud's acceptance of Sellin's rather flimsy and fabricated account must have been based on a strong need to believe, and that it must have derived from Freud's powerful unconscious identification of the figure of Moses with his father and his envisioning of the murder of Moses as an expression of his own unconscious hostility. At the same time, Freud powerfully identified himself with Moses, so that the murder of Moses became a fitting punishment for his parricidal wish and the success he achieved over his father. As Schur (1972) has observed, Freud's Todesangst had been relatively dormant since his formulation of the death instinct, but in the mid-1930s it somehow was revived. This death anxiety, as we have observed, seemed to intensify periodically in Freud's life, particularly at those points when some significant success marked his overcoming of the oedipal father. This anxiety came to a head at the end of Freud's life, both in his conviction that he would die at the age of eighty-one-and-a-half, the age of his father as well as his eldest brother at death, and in the writing of *Moses and Monotheism*. This was the last crescendo of his unconscious ambivalence toward his father. Freud thus identified with the slain Moses-father, a link that was unquestionably intensified by his advanced age and the continuing inroads of his cancer.

There was an interesting parapraxis in connection with the writing of *Moses and Monotheism* that sheds some light on Freud's attitudes. Shengold (1972) calls attention to the fact that Freud omitted from his work any mention of a previous paper by Karl Abraham in which essentially the same thesis is proposed—namely, that Amenhotep IV overthrew the religion of his father, the worship of Amon, and replaced it with the worship of Aten, changing his name to Akhenaten in the process and having his father's name effaced from all the monuments and inscriptions in which it was connected with the name of Amon.* Abraham interprets this act as an expression of the oedipal struggle in which the son seeks to erase his father's identity and to replace him. He further argues that Akhenaten made Aten the one and only God in imitation of the uniqueness of the father. He thereby became the precursor of Moses and his monotheism, in which the one true God reflects the basic features of the patriarchal ruler of the family.

Freud believed that Moses was a follower of Akhenaten and thus declared Moses to be an Egyptian. In so doing, he deprived the Jews of one of their cultural heroes. In the very beginning of *Moses and Monotheism* (1939), he writes:

> To deprive a people of the man whom they take pride in as the greatest of their sons is not a thing to be gladly or carelessly undertaken, least of all by someone who is himself one of them. (p. 7)

---

*It was in connection with the discussion of this paper with Jung that Freud suffered the last of his fainting spells, in November 1912.

But Freud goes on to review the entire story of Amenhotep IV, his rebellion against the god of his father and his establishment of a monotheistic cult of Aten, without any mention of Abraham's paper, which had so impressed him in 1912. Just as he completely omitted the Abraham who had preceded Moses in the history of the Jewish people, he neglected to mention the "Abraham" who had preceded him in the construction of his argument about Moses. For Freud, Moses was a historical figure, while the patriarchs Abraham, Isaac, and Jacob were mere legendary inventions introduced after the time of Moses. It seems that in his parapraxis—his omission of any mention of Abraham's contribution—Freud wished to get rid of all the patriarchs, all the predecessors of Moses, with whom he so strongly identified.

Behind all this lurks the figure of Wilhelm Fliess. As Shengold (1972) recounts, in later years Abraham became acquainted with Fliess and was in fact treated by him. Abraham actually formed a very favorable opinion of Fliess, to which Freud reacted quite negatively. In the last year of his life, Abraham even came to accept some of Fliess's views on periodicity, which Freud had found so appalling and had been forced to reject. Abraham's identification with Fliess set the stage for Freud to erase Abraham's priority in his views about Akhenaten and monotheism, just as he had been forced to erase any recollection of Fliess's priority with regard to theories of bisexuality. Abraham had become another of Freud's both loved and hated ghosts, the revenants of the *non vixit* dream, the victims of his death-wishes, among whom the primary figures were Freud's father and his younger brother Julius. The transference in Abraham's case was accomplished by way of his association and identification with the chief revenant of Freud's adult life, Wilhelm Fliess. As Shengold (1972) comments:

> We know . . . that Freud's family complexes were expressed and lived out in metaphors derived from the Bible and from Egypt. In attempting to write a Family Romance of the Jews, Freud dismissed Father Abraham and his name-sake Karl Abraham. The beloved and lost disciple is forgotten insofar as he is connected with Egypt, the Bible and the oedipal struggle between father and son over the body of the mother that is the essence of the story of Amenhotep IV. (p. 242)

We could almost imagine that Freud is speaking not only of the Jewish religion but, in some displaced projective sense, of himself when he writes the following words:

> Ambivalence is a part of the essence of the relation to the father: in the course of time the hostility too could not fail to stir, which had once driven the sons into killing their admired and dreaded father.

There was no place in the framework of the religion of Moses for a direct expression of the murderous hatred of the father. All that could come to light was a mighty reaction against it—a sense of guilt on account of that hostility, a bad conscience for having sinned against God and for not ceasing to sin. This sense of guilt, which was uninterruptedly kept awake by the Prophets, and which soon formed an essential part of the religious system, had yet another superficial motivation, which nearly disguised its true origin. Things were going badly for the people; the hopes resting on the favour of God failed in fulfillment; it was not easy to maintain the illusion, loved above all else, of being God's Chosen People. If they wished to avoid renouncing that happiness, a sense of guilt on account of their own sinfulness offered a welcome means of exculpating God: they deserved no better than to be punished by him since they had not obeyed his commandments. (Freud 1939, 134)

Freud's own ambivalence played a powerful role throughout the course of his life. His intense disillusionment and disappointment in his father led to a hatred that was almost murderous, except that it was combined with a loving devotion that made it a source of deep internal conflict. And Freud paid the price of this ambivalence in the guilt of the survivor and parricide, which played itself out over and over in the course of his career and never found resolution or surcease. There seems little doubt that in the writing of *Moses and Monotheism* at the end of his long and troubled life, as he was caught in the advancing grip of a painful and ineradicable cancer, Freud made his last attempt to resolve his ambivalence, to absolve his abiding sense of guilt, and either to gain the Promised Land or to resign himself to seeing it only from afar, as in a vision.

Freud also tried to cover his guilt and ambivalence in the illusion that he was chosen to be a savior—a Messiah, another Moses—who would lead his people out of psychological bondage to the freedom of a new religion that provided a new understanding of life and a capacity to deal with its hidden and unconscious forces. But to do this he had to destroy the religion of his fathers and any religion that might have sought to take its place. Let us listen then to the words of the prophet:

I know how difficult it is to avoid illusions; perhaps the hopes I have confessed to are of an illusory nature, too. But I hold fast to one distinction. Apart from the fact that no penalty is imposed for not sharing them, my illusions are not, like religious ones, incapable of correction. They have not the character of a delusion. If experience should show—not to me, but to others after me, who think as I do—that we have been mistaken, we will give up our expectations. Take my attempt for what it is. A psychologist who does not deceive himself about the difficulty of finding one's bearings in this world,

makes an endeavour to assess the development of man, in the light of
the small portion of knowledge he has gained through a study of the
mental processes of individuals during their development from child
to adult. In so doing, the idea forces itself upon him that religion is
comparable to a childhood neurosis, and he is optimistic enough to
suppose that mankind will surmount this neurotic phase, just as so
many children grow out of their similar neurosis. These discoveries
derived from individual psychology may be insufficient, their application to the human race unjustified, and his optimism unfounded. I
grant you all these uncertainties. But often one cannot refrain from
saying what one thinks, and one excuses oneself on the ground that
one is not giving it out for more than it is worth. . . .

. . . We may insist as often as we like that man's intellect is
powerless in comparison with his instinctual life, and we may be right
in this. Nevertheless, there is something peculiar about this weakness.
The voice of the intellect is a soft one, but it does not rest till it has
gained a hearing. Finally, after a countless succession of rebuffs, it
succeeds. . . . Our God, *Logos,* will fulfil whichever of these wishes
nature outside us allows, but he will do it very gradually, only in the
unforeseeable future, and for a new generation of men. He promises
no compensation for us, who suffer grievously from life. On the way
to this distant goal your religious doctrines will have to be discarded,
no matter whether the first attempts fail, or whether the first substitutes prove to be untenable. You know why: in the long run nothing
can withstand reason and experience, and the contradiction which
religion offers to both is all too palpable. Even purified religious ideas
cannot escape this fate, so long as they try to preserve anything of the
consolation of religion. . . .

Education freed from the burden of religious doctrines will not, it
may be, effect much change in men's psychological nature. Our God
Logos is perhaps not a very almighty one, and he may only be able to
fulfil a small part of what his predecessors have promised. If we have
to acknowledge this we shall accept it with resignation. We shall not
on that account lose our interest in the world and in life, for we have
one sure support which you lack. We believe that it is possible for
scientific work to gain some knowledge about the reality of the world,
by means of which we can increase our power and in accordance with
which we can arrange our life. If this belief is an illusion, then we are
in the same position as you. But science has given us evidence by its
numerous and important successes that it is no illusion. (Freud
1927, 53–55)

CONCLUSIONS

I have made no attempt in this discussion to be exhaustive, and the discerning reader will undoubtedly find many loose ends. But I have assembled enough of the fragments that a fairly consistent picture of this rich tapestry begins to emerge.

There can be little doubt that Freud's religious views, which maintained an admirable consistency from his earliest writings on the subject through the final pages of *Moses and Monotheism,* reflected at every step deep psychological forces and unresolved conflicts within his psychic economy. Freud's rationalism and his agnostic disbelief were not free from conflict and clearly rested on powerful underlying motivations. His somewhat superstitious nature and his mystical leanings were matters of significant difficulty for him which he sought to deny and to overcome but clearly was never able adequately to analyze or to resolve.

His Todesangst was perhaps the clearest example of this superstitious trend, but it carried with it a strong mystical bent and a leaning toward superstition that attracted him first to Fliess and later to Jung and at the same time laid the groundwork in both these relationships for the playing out of deep-seated ambivalence and for the eventual development of conflict. In both cases, it seems clear that Freud's unresolved mystical trends were being projected and dealt with in part in an externalized form.

These same conflicts played themselves out in Freud's relationships with the Jewish faith and with his sense of himself as a Jew. Clearly, his ambivalence and his inner conflict in this regard were reflected in innumerable contexts. He could neither embrace nor totally turn his back on the religion of his fathers. The same ambivalence came into play in his "Roman neurosis" and his identification with Hannibal, who set himself to conquer Rome and never achieved it. The figure of Hannibal provided an ideal vehicle for the side of Freud's ambivalence that sought to conquer Catholicism and Christianity as well as for the side that would not succeed in that conquest. But the ultimate expression of that ambivalence and its related conflicts came in Freud's identification with the figure of Moses, who at the same time led the revolt against the religion of the fathers and created a new religion that allowed him to lead his people to the Promised Land.

As we have seen, Freud's interweaving of these complex themes rides on a powerful undercurrent that stems from unresolved infantile conflicts, particularly his ambivalence to his father. Deep in the recesses of his mind, Freud seems to have resolved that his truculent spirit would never yield to the demands of religion for submission and resignation. He would be a Hannibal, a conquistador—and a Moses, a prophet who would find a new religion that would enable him to lead his people to the Promised Land of psychological freedom. But the only way for him to achieve this goal required that he overcome the religion of his fathers and annihilate the very image of the father himself, and in so doing risk the threat of paternal retaliation and the stigma of guilt.

Not only was Freud tainted with the guilt of his murderous oedipal wishes and ambivalence toward his father, but he bore as well the mark of Cain and the guilt of the survivor for his infantile murderous wishes toward the baby Julius (Shengold 1966). Moreover, significantly linked with these oedipal and preoedipal themes was the fusion in his mind between the figures of his mother and his old Catholic nanny, his original seductress, who had introduced him to the mysteries of religion and to the basic tenets of Catholicism, the overpowering mysteries of heaven and hell.

Freud was never able to free himself from these deep-seated entanglements and their associated conflicts, and ultimately what he taught us about religion, religious experience, and faith must be taken in the context of these unconscious conflicts and the role his thinking played in his attempts to deal with them. As we shall see in coming chapters, the Freudian argument about religion must be taken on its own terms. Nonetheless, an equally important aspect of our understanding of the psychoanalytic approach to religion is the forces that helped shape Freud's religious views and the way in which they reflected his inner conflicts and expressed a deep-seated religious identity.

3. THE FUTURE OF AN ILLUSION

We can turn at this point from the man to his work. If Freud's view of religion is rooted in his inner conflicts and ambivalences, we cannot remain satisfied with that perception alone as a basis of understanding. The view of Freud's work from the perspective of his personality and its dynamic forces challenges us to a further task. We must seek to understand the Freudian argument on its own terms. Anything short of that achievement is simpleminded reductionism, a failure to meet the complexity of the issues and the depths of implication embedded in the whole question of religious experience and its psychology.

My purpose in this section is to examine the psychoanalytic approach to religion and to delimit some of its constraints and ambiguities. We will concern ourselves only with the formulation of Freud's thinking about religion, since his approach is essentially the classic psychoanalytic view, which has yet to be substantially modified.

Freud's views on religion first appeared in his brief paper "Obsessive Actions and Religious Practices" (1907), which laid out the basic elements of Freud's theory that were later expanded and substantiated in larger works, among them the analogy between obsessional ceremonials and religious practices. The intention of the analytic argument is to force this analogy into an identity. Indeed, the cluster of resemblances to which Freud points are revealing: the pangs of conscience when the ritual action is omitted, the need to protect the action against external interruption, the conscientiousness regarding detail, and the proclivity of such ceremonials toward increasing complexity and esoteric significance.

But Freud also taught us that such ceremonials have meaning. An unanswered question is whether its meaning is equivalent to the ceremonial itself, and consequently whether the similarity of ceremonial behaviors can be taken as grounds for the identity of their meanings. As Ricoeur (1970) observes, the multiple meanings of the analogs remain in suspense. Freud felt that the meaning of faith could be exhausted by the obsessional analogy; whether it can be so reduced remains an open question. His dictum was intended to bring closure to the issue: "In view of these similarities and analogies one might venture to regard obsessional neurosis as a pathological counterpart of the formation of religion, and to describe that neurosis as an individual religiosity and religion as a universal neurosis" (Freud 1907, 126–27).

But the statement raises problems instead of providing an explanation. Ricoeur comments:

> This statement opens as many things as it closes. It is an astonishing thing that man is capable both of religion and of neurosis, in such a way that their analogy can actually constitute a reciprocal imitation. As a result of this imitation, man is neurotic insofar as he is *homo religiosus* and religious insofar as he is neurotic. The problematic character of the above formula is brought out by another closely related statement: "An obsessional neurosis presents a travesty, half comic, half tragic, of a private religion." Thus religion can be caricatured as neurotic ceremonial. Is this situation due to the underlying intention of religion, or is it the result of its degradation and regression when it begins to lose the meaning of its own symbolism? And how does the forgetfulness of meaning in religious observances pertain to the essence of religion? Does it pertain to a still more fundamental dialectic, the dialectic of religion and faith? These questions necessarily remain as background, even though Freud does not raise them himself. (Ricoeur 1970, 232–33)

Freud's View of Religion

The Freudian supposition relates more specifically to the intrapsychic aspects of religious experience; namely, it implies that all religious behavior and belief is a form of obsessive-compulsive neurosis. The associations to Freud's descriptions are full of implications of infantilism and superstition. We have already seen the extent to which Freud himself was vulnerable to and conflicted about superstitious tendencies (see chapter 2). One sometimes wonders what conception of religion must have held sway in the inner recesses of his mind. Religion is nothing more than a dependence on the sovereign father, according to him. It is an exercise of passivity, compliance, and dependence—essentially a feminine preoccupation. Freud could not conceive of religion on other than emotional grounds. In this regard, he was the heir of Schleiermacher and Feuerbach. Religion signifies an emotional need for authority in the face of the uncertainty and anxieties of existence. Man's helplessness revives the infantile dependencies of his childhood weakness, and religion itself is "born from man's need to make his helplessness tolerable, and built up from the material of memories of the helplessness of his own childhood and the childhood of the human race" (Freud 1927, 18).

There is, of course, no place in all this for consideration of a more mature religious posture—no place for the more masculine exercise of disciplined reason in the search for religious truth. The massive intellectual effort reflected in the religious traditions of Israel and in the entire history of Christendom is eliminated. The history of man's effort to bring the resources of secondary process to the penetration of his more primary religious processes is glossed over. The result could not be other than a caricature of religion—the very charge that Pfister made in reply to Freud (see chapter 4).

The Wolf Man

The lines of Freud's thinking are always most lucid and restrained in his case histories. For this reason, his remarks on the case of the "Wolf Man" (1918) are most informative. The Wolf Man's childhood included several significant episodes. At the age of one-and-a-half, during a bout of malaria, he had witnessed his parents copulating "a tergo," or he may have observed them positioned in such a way as to permit this elaboration of the fantasy later. This incident was followed by a seduction by his sister and then by his nurse's threat of castration. His anxiety dream of wolves on a tree took place at age four and was followed by an animal phobia which persevered until his initiation into religion at age four-and-a-half.

The religious influence came from his mother, and the Biblical narrative was read to him by his pious and superstitious nurse—with an emphasis on the passion of Christ. This introduction gave rise to ruminations and doubts focusing on anal aspects of Christ's life as a man. The threat of castration had led to the suppression of genitality in his developing sexuality and the emergence of sadism and masochism. The religious narrative offered an occasion to sublimate his basic masochism by identification with Christ, an identification facilitated by the fact that his own birthday fell on Christmas Day.

His ambivalent feelings toward his father led him to attack his religion, doubting its dogmatic truth and turning against God. God, the Father, had treated the Son cruelly in allowing him to be sacrificed. Opposing currents of love and hate came together in the Wolf Man's ambivalent struggle over religion.

The upshot of this evolution was a replacement of his anxiety symptoms by obsessional symptoms. His irritability and apprehensiveness gave way to protective rituals and pious practices. Up to this time, he had been having bad dreams, such as the wolf dream. But now, if he kissed all the holy pictures in his room, recited his prayers, and made many signs of the cross on himself and on his bed, he could banish these fears and sleep in peace. Piety had won a victory over sadistic and masochistic sexuality. But the victory was won at the cost of blasphemous thoughts and the obsessive exaggeration of religious ceremonial.

Religion in this case undoubtedly achieved its aims. As Freud (1918) observes:

> It put a restraint on his sexual impulses by affording them a sublima-
> tion and a safe mooring; it lowered the importance of his family
> relationships, and this protected him from the threat of isolation by
> giving him access to the great community of mankind. The untamed
> and fear-ridden child became social, well-behaved, and amenable to
> education. (pp. 114–15)

The motive force lay in his identification with Christ. As Christ he could love God, thus sublimating his homosexual yearnings for his father, and at the same time achieve a sublime satisfaction of his masochistic desires in the Passion inflicted on the Son at the behest of the Father.

While it is immediately apparent that the Wolf Man's obsessive religios-ity was a vehicle for his instinctual pathology, it is not immediately evident that religion need be coextensive with pathological religiosity. Whatever the tenor of Freud's own prejudices may have been, there is a direct line of inference from investigation of the mechanisms underlying this kind of pathological behavior to more grandiose extrapolations regarding the general properties of religious observance. It is an easy transition from documenting the displacement of neurotic ambivalences toward the father onto the figure of God to concluding that the deity is indeed no more than a projected image of the father. In this view, God is the exalted father, and the root of religious belief is a longing for the father.

It is not surprising that a child caught up in the ambivalences of oedipal entanglements should project these ambivalences to the level of the divine. Nor is it surprising that obsessive piety should become a vehicle for transformation and repression of castration anxieties and sadistic impulses. But is this an adequate basis for religious belief? The weight of the argument supports no conclusion further than that religion often serves as a matrix within which the displaced fantasies of infantile residues find expression. It is another matter to say that such projections serve an originative function as well.

The dynamic forces that underlie religious sentiment find their expres-sion in the emergence of religious consciousness and conscience in every human being, as well as in the heritage of belief upon which organized religion is established. The inner dynamics of religious acceptance and commitment are the same in the contemporary believer as they were in the ancient worshippers of the cult of 'El Shaddai. Religion answers basic needs of man, so that, psychologically at least, it is correct to say that its origins are intimately associated with those needs. It strains credibility to envision that which is essentially infantile and neurotic as responding to the most profound human needs. The religious sentiment must have deeper and more viable roots.

Totem and Taboo

The next step in the progression of Freud's argument comes with *Totem and Taboo* (1912–13). Freud bases his argument here on an analogy between the mentality of primitive man and the thought processes of obsessional neurotics. Using anthropological data, he contends that there was a link between primitive totemism and the practice of exogamy. The prohibition, therefore, on sexual intercourse with anyone who belonged to the same totem clan, that is, who was thought to be descended from the same totem animal, laid the groundwork for the prevention of group incest.

The function of such taboos was related to the mysterious and dangerous power inherent in certain objects and attributed to demons and spirits. This fear of demonic powers had the dual aspects of veneration and horror; consequently, taboos were applied in the realm of the sacred as well as in that of the forbidden and unclean. Freud draws an analogy between such primitive taboos and the obsessional prohibitions contained in or compensated by ritual (compulsive) actions. Thus the taboo was rooted in a basic ambivalence toward that which the taboo prohibited. Freud traces the ambivalent aspects of primitive taboos dealing with the treatment of conquered enemies, rulers, and, finally, the dead. Violation of a given taboo called down on the head of the violator the threat of punishment, just as performance of a forbidden act by an obsessional neurotic arouses neurotic guilt and the fear of punishment. Similarly, a neurotic's ambivalent wish that a loved one might die is turned into fear of his own death.

Primitive man's belief in the presence of threatening and demonic powers in his world represented a form of animism based on archaic projections. These were derived from his emotional life, particularly from excessively destructive or hateful wishes that were dealt with by displacement onto the external world. The concept of projection was one that Freud had shortly before applied in his analysis of the Schreber case (1911) to explain Schreber's theocosmological construction, in which he was the submissive and special agent of God destined by serving divine ends to save the world. Submission to the divine will was exemplified by the transformation of Schreber's body into that of a woman. Freud understood the delusion as a displacement of Schreber's repressed homosexual love of his father.

The operation of this paranoid mechanism turns inner mental processes into the outer world, so that feelings are transformed into spirits and demons and threatening powers. Against these threatening and demonic powers, however, the primitive mind can appeal to the protective capacity of the omnipotence of thoughts. Thus primitive man meets his internal processes outside of himself in the form of spirits and demons whom he must then propitiate through the superstitious observance of taboos.

Freud argues that the totem animal was believed to be the ancestor of the tribe, to explain the prohibition against the totem and the requirement of exogamy. From the fact that the totem becomes identified with the tribal ancestor or father, Freud drew the inference that the dual prohibitions, specifically, against killing the totem animal and against a man's having sex with a woman of the same totem clan, are equivalent displacements of the oedipal involvement and expressions of oedipal determinants. What is forbidden as a general rule is permitted in the sacrificial practices of totemic religion. Hence sacramental killing and communal eating become essential elements of religious practice. The derivation of such totemic elements from the oedipal constellation is substantiated by the occurrence of totemism in the experience of children, particularly in the form of animal phobias that serve as displacements for the fear of (murderous wish against) the oedipal father. Freud traced these connections in detail in the case of "Little Hans" (1909a) and later in that of the "Wolf Man" (1918).

Ambivalence toward the totem ancestor with its associated taboos is linked to oedipal ambivalence toward the father and the associated wishes to be rid of the father and to possess the mother—aims equivalent to those prohibited by and symbolized in the taboos of totemic practice. The power of the totem ancestor, with its elements of veneration and fear, undergoes further displacement, ultimately elevating the father figure into a divinity. This translation from prereligious origins is marked by the evolution of the totem meal through sacramental and sacrificial killing of animals and humans to the Crucifixion of Christ and communal eating, culminating in the Christian Eucharist. The totem meal expresses the communion of God and his believers and becomes the point of origin for social organization, moral restrictions, and religion.

The religious element proper in this totem sacrifice is that of guilt, which is derived from the Oedipus entanglement. Here Freud closes the circle of the argument by postulating a myth of a primal horde who kill the primal father. According to the myth, it is the prohibition of sexual contact with the women of the clan that forces the sons to band together and to slay the primal father. The memory of this primordial deed is repressed and thus gives rise to guilt. In order to satisfy the dimensions of the argument, Freud postulates in addition that this guilt is active in the collective mind of all mankind and leads inevitably to remorse for the primal crime. Consequently, religion becomes a series of only partially successful attempts to resolve the unconscious and collective emotional residues created by the murder of the primal father and its corresponding guilt, so that reconciliation with the offended father can be achieved.

But, as Ricoeur (1970) points out, the totem meal and its subsequent religious modifications include not only repentance for but also rehearsal of the filial revolt and triumph by which the religion of the son replaces the religion of the father. In this aspect, Christianity is preeminently the religion of the son who sacrifices his life to redeem his brothers from the stain of original sin. In the sacrifice of the Crucifixion, the two elements of ambivalence come together: the guilt for the killing of the Father is expiated, but in the process the Son himself becomes a god and thus replaces the father religion by a son religion. The ambivalence also finds expression in the revival of the totem meal in the Eucharist: it signifies both a reconciliation with the Father and the substitution of the Son for the Father. The faithful thus consume the Son's flesh and blood in the Eucharist.

In a similar sense, Freud suggests that individual history and the history of mankind are somehow parallel. The consequences of those histories are reflected in neurosis in the individual and in religion in the species. The theory of *Totem and Taboo* is a hypothesis of religious development in which the primal event is the murder of the father by the primal horde. The internecine strife that followed made it necessary for the first forms of social organization and renunciation of instinct to emerge. In this way, the incest taboo and the law of exogamy were established. But the repressed memory of the father lived on in the form of a totem, usually a dreaded animal, which substituted for the father and with which all the ambivalence of feeling formerly directed at the father was associated. Thus the totem represents the most primitive form of religion, which later developments only modified by successively humanizing the totem. Ultimately, out of this process, the omnipotent and unrivaled father-deity reemerges.

Moses and Monotheism

The idea that the powerful and deep impression of monotheism on the Jewish people is based on a repetition of the primal murder of the father carried out on the person of the father-substitute Moses is the thesis Freud elaborates in *Moses and Monotheism* (1939). The murder of Moses is the important link between the forgotten primal murder and its reemergence in the form of monotheism. Guilt over the murder of Moses stimulated the wish for the Messiah, so that Christ became a resurrected Moses and a return of the primal father as well.

As we shall see in greater detail in chapter 5, the argument of the Moses book is seriously flawed by a number of indefensible hypotheses, but it is nonetheless ingenious. Freud tries to establish that Moses was originally not a Hebrew but an Egyptian, in fact a member of the court of Amenophis IV. The young pharaoh had come to the throne in about 1375 B.C., bringing with him sweeping religious reforms that enforced the worship of the one god Aten—perhaps the first true form of monotheism.

It was essentially this religion that Moses communicated to his Jewish brethren in the form of the worship of Yahweh. But the Jews were unable to tolerate this restricted and highly spiritualized religion, so they arose, threw off the intolerable burden, and murdered the prophet-tyrant who had imposed it on them. The tradition lived on, however, so that later, under the need for tribal union and adoption of a common religion, the Israelites returned to the worship of Yahweh. But Yahweh had lost his original character and had taken credit for the deed of liberation from the murdered prophet Moses. Thus, in Freud's words, "The central fact of the development of the Jewish religion was that in the course of time the God Yahweh lost his own characteristics and grew more and more to resemble the old god of Moses, the Aten" (Freud 1939, 63).

Freud undoubtedly satisfied himself that the analogy between neurotic processes and religious events pointed unequivocally to the origins of religion. He also persuaded himself that what he had addressed himself to were not mere psychological necessities but historical actualities. He writes:

> A tradition that was based only on communication could not lead to the compulsive character that attaches to religious phenomena. It would be listened to, judged, and perhaps dismissed, like any other piece of information from outside; it would never attain the privilege of being liberated from the constraint of logical thought. It must have undergone the fate of being repressed, the condition of lingering in the unconscious, before it is able to display such powerul effects on its return, to bring the masses under its spell, as we have seen with astonishment and hitherto without comprehension in the case of religious tradition. And this consideration weighs heavily in favor of our believing that things really happen in the way we have tried to picture them or at least in some similar way. (Freud 1939, 101–02)

Thus there can be no return of the repressed unless a traumatic event has in fact occurred before it. It is one of the ironies of Freud's development that in the twilight of his career he should have returned to a fallacy he had abandoned forty years earlier when he surrendered his hypothesis that neuroses resulted from traumatic seductions in childhood. As in his first struggles with the mysteries of neurosis, in bringing to a close his lifelong struggle with the mystery of religion, Freud again resorts to an appeal to historical actuality instead of to psychological reality and the power of symbolic meaning.

The Future of an Illusion

Perhaps the high point of Freud's thinking about religion and certainly the tour de force of his iconoclasm is *The Future of an Illusion* (1927). In it, Freud addresses an imaginary antagonist, probably his student Oskar Pfister, a Protestant pastor whose correspondence with Freud is a gold mine of information on the psychoanalysis of religion (Meng and Freud 1963). But here we can let Freud speak for himself:

But man's helplessness remains and along with it his longing for his father, and the gods. The gods retain their threefold task: they must exorcise the terrors of nature, they must reconcile men to the cruelty of Fate, particularly as it is shown in death, and they must compensate them for the sufferings and privations which a civilized life in common had imposed on them. (Freud 1927, 17–18)

The argument advances. The gods were originally the lords of nature and were responsible for its existence. Having brought it into being, they could now let it run its course. Only occasionally did they intervene in the form of miracles—making it plain that they had in no way relinquished their power over the universe and its laws. But even though they were the purveyors of destiny, they seemed discouragingly unable to remedy the perplexity and helplessness of the human race. This was their most conspicuous failure.

The more the gods withdrew from nature and the more autonomous it became, the more intensely did human expectations of the deities become focused in the third area of divine operation: morality became their primary and true domain. Now their tasks became to regulate the evils of civilization, to attend to human suffering, especially the anguish men inflict on each other, and finally to supervise the precepts of civilization, which were observed more in the breach than in fact. To such laws and precepts a divine origin was attributed, elevated beyond human concerns and needs. Freud comments:

And thus a store of ideas is created, both from man's need to make his helplessness tolerable and built up from the material of memories of the helplessness of his own childhood and the childhood of the human race. It can be clearly seen that the possession of these ideas protects him in two directions—against the dangers of nature and Fate, and against the injuries that threaten him from human society itself. Here is the gist of the matter. Life in this world serves a higher purpose; no doubt it is not easy to guess what that purpose is, but it certainly signifies a perfecting of man's nature. (p. 18)

Thus the course of events on earth follows the intentions and direction of a superior intelligence whose ways are mysterious to our limited understanding. Nonetheless, we are assured that it is a benevolent intelligence that watches over and protects each one of us from harm and orders all for the best. If Providence is stern and judging, it is only for our own good—to save us from becoming helpless victims of the overpowering and pitiless forces of nature. It even removes the sting of death:

Death itself is not an extinction, is not a return to inorganic lifelessness, but the beginning of a new kind of existence which lies on the path of development to something higher. . . . In the end all good is rewarded and all evil punished, if not actually in this form of life then in the later existences that begin after death. In this way all the terrors, the sufferings and hardships of life are destined to be obliterated. Life after death, which continues life on earth just as the invisible part of the spectrum joins on to the visible part, brings us all the perfection that we may perhaps have missed here. And the superior wisdom which directs this course of things, the infinite goodness that expresses itself in it, the justice that achieves its aim in it—these are the attributes of the divine beings who also created us and the world as a whole, or rather, of the one divine being into which, in our civilization, all the gods of antiquity have been condensed. (p. 19)

Such religious ideas are specifically teachings, not products of reason or precipitates of experience. They are illusions, wish-fulfillments that respond to the oldest, strongest, and most urgent of human desires and needs. Their strength derives from the strength of those underlying impulses. They answer to the terrifying sense of helplessness in childhood, which gives rise to the powerful need for protectors, primary among whom is the father. The perdurance of this sense of helplessness and vulnerability throughout the course of life makes it necessary to cling to the father and his substitutes—in this case, to the belief in an all-powerful and lovingly protective father.

Thus, our inherent fear of the dangers of life gives rise to our belief in the benevolent rule of divine Providence. Establishing and securing a moral world order gives us hope for the fulfillment of justice that is so sadly neglected in human affairs. The extension of existence beyond human life provides a framework within which these wish fulfillments can take place. In this way a great burden is lifted from the individual psyche; the conflicts of childhood that derive from the father complex and have never been resolved are projected on a universal level and thus may be brought to a satisfactory resolution.

Freud's imaginary opponent, however, objects that such illusions are necessary. Freud responds:

I must contradict you when you go on to argue that men are completely unable to do without the consolation of the religious illusion, that without it they could not bear the troubles of life and the cruelties of reality. That is true, certainly, of the men to whom you have instilled the sweet—or bitter-sweet—poison from childhood onwards. But what of the other men, who have been sensibly brought up? Perhaps those who do not suffer from the neurosis will need no intoxicant to deaden it. They will, it is true, find themselves in a difficult position. They will have to admit to themselves the full extent of their helplessness and their insignificance in the machinery of the universe; they can no longer be the center of creation, no longer the object of tender care on the part of a beneficient Providence. They will be in the same position as a child who has left the parental house where he was so warm and comfortable. But surely infantilism is destined to be surmounted. Men cannot remain children forever; they must in the end go out into "hostile life." We may call this "*education to reality*." Need I confess to you that the sole purpose of my book is to point out the necessity for this forward step? (p. 49)

Then Freud, the man of science and reason and at heart a staunch representative of nineteenth-century materialistic scientism, offers an illusion of his own.

You will not find me inaccessible to your criticism. I know how difficult it is to avoid illusions; perhaps the hopes I have confessed to are of an illusory nature, too. But I hold fast to one distinction. Apart from the fact that no penalty is imposed for not sharing them, my illusions are not, like religious ones, incapable of correction. They have not the character of a delusion. If experience should show—not to me, but to others after me, who think as I do—that we have been mistaken, we will give up our expectations. . . . The idea forces itself upon him [the psychologist] that religion is comparable to a childhood neurosis, and he is optimistic enough to suppose that mankind will surmount this neurotic phase, just as so many children grow out of their similar neurosis. These discoveries derived from individual psychology may be insufficient, their application to the human race unjustified, and his optimism unfounded. I grant you all these uncertainties. But often one cannot refrain from saying what one thinks, and one excuses oneself on the ground that one is not giving it out for more than it is worth. . . .

. . . We may insist as often as we like that man's intellect is powerless in comparison with his instinctual life, and we may be right in this. Nevertheless, there is something peculiar about this weakness. The voice of the intellect is a soft one, but it does not rest till it has gained a hearing. Finally, after a countless succession of rebuffs, it succeeds. This is one of the few points on which one may be optimistic about the future of mankind, but it is in itself a point of no small importance. And from it one can derive yet other hopes. The primacy of the intellect lies, it is true, in a distant, distant future, but probably not in an *infinitely* distant one. (p. 53)

And then a last word:

If this belief is an illusion, then we are in the same position as you. But science has given us evidence by its numerous and important successes that it is no illusion. . . .

No, our science is no illusion. But an illusion it would be to suppose that what science cannot give us we can get elsewhere. (pp. 54–56)

So runs the Freudian argument. I will make no extensive attempt to evaluate or criticize it here, since my main concern at this juncture is to make the lines of the argument clear and concise. My point is that Freud's ingeniously elaborated position has inherent validity and therefore requires no particular refutation.

THE BASIS FOR A RESPONSE

To acknowledge the validity of Freud's treatment is not to say that it is invulnerable to criticism or debate. Freud argues on the basis of an analogy from the pathological realm, particularly that of obsessional neurosis, to the broader realm of the economy of religious phenomena. The inherent assumption is that all religious behavior and belief is a form of obsessive-compulsive neurosis. There is no place in this view for the more disciplined exercise of reason and intellect in the search for religious truth—the Augustinian *intellectus quaerens fidem.*

But the argument rests on an analogy. What of this analogy? What in fact does it mean? With his customary lucidity, Ricoeur (1970) takes up this question. He argues that psychoanalysis has no access to this question, no resources for determining the validity of an answer. The analytic approach illumines the aspect of religious experience that goes by the name of the "birth of idols." It cannot determine whether the worship of idols occupies the limits of religious experience or faith. But is the function of religious ritual in its origins and primary significance no more than obsessional ritual? Is faith no more than consolidation of a childhood pattern of credulity and wishful fantasy? Ricoeur comments:

> Analysis can reveal to the religious man his caricature, but it leaves him the task of meditating on the *possibility* of not resembling his distorted double. For it is truly a matter of distortion, and of self-understanding through distortion: distortion of the infantile, distortion of the neurotic, distortion of the primitive (or the so-called primitive person, himself interpreted as the analogue of the neurotic and the child). (Ricoeur 1970, 533)

To point out the limits of the analogy, however, does not prove it invalid. The critical question is whether the dynamism of religious belief has an inherent capacity to supersede its own archaisms. An investigation of the instinctual substrate of religion can hope to provide no more than a partial answer. In Freud's use of the analogy, religion is taken to be a repetition of its own origins. Such repetition is a vehicle of archaism. The repressed returns in the form of a repetition—the Eucharist repeats the totem meal; the death of Christ repeats the death of Moses, itself a repetition of the killing of the father by the primal horde. This emphasis on repetition and the return of the repressed amounts to the exclusion of possible epigenetic dimensions of the affective quality of religious experience. Freud's refusal to consider them derives not only from theoretical exigencies and convictions but also from his personal unbelief.

Ricoeur argues that the originative and primal fantasies Freud postulates do not stand by themselves. Rather, they are the material with which human intelligence forms, intends, and interprets, through a progressive hermeneutic, meanings of another order that transcend the constraints of the originative fantasies and become signs and symbols of the sacred. A philosophic reflection can do little more than acknowledge these symbols at the horizon of its emerging intentionality, which arises out of the fantasies and interprets them symbolically in terms of their relevance to lost origins, lost archaic objects, or the "lack inherent in desire." Thus "What gives rise to the endless movement of the interpretation is not the fullness of memory, but its emptiness, its openness" (Ricoeur 1970, 540).

In these terms, then, the father figure cannot be divorced from its mythopoetic function: it provides a prototype for the deity throughout the history of polytheism and, finally, monotheism. Its projective quality is not to be denied, but it is left relatively unanalyzed as such. Freud seems here to take a great deal for granted and to choose not to worry this bone as he does others. His formulation of the critical displacements of the father imago onto the totem animal and the totem god is too easy; he does not push the inquiry far enough. He seems to think that his appeal to an analogy with animal phobias (in "Little Hans" and the "Wolf Man") and paranoia (in Schreber) dismisses him from any further responsibility for perplexity or complexity.

An argument based on analogy and repetition fails to carry the full weight of religious experience. The critical issue centers on the poetic relationship between levels of symbolic organization and expression—between sacred and archaic symbolism. Ricoeur focuses on the heart of the dilemma:

> Is not the father-figure as much "denied and overcome" as it is "repeated"? What have I understood when I have discovered—or divined—the father-figure in the representation of the deity? Do I understand both of them better? But I do not know what the father means. . . .
>
> But if symbols are fantasies that have been denied and overcome, they are never fantasies that have been abolished. That is why one is never certain that a given symbol of the sacred is not simply a "return of the repressed"; or rather, it is always certain that each symbol of the sacred is also and at the same time a revival of an infantile and archaic symbol. The two functions of symbol remain inseparable. The symbolic meanings closest to theological and philosophical speculation are always involved with some trace of an archaic myth. This close alliance of archaism and prophecy constitutes the richness of

religious symbolism; it also constitutes its ambiguity. "Symbols give rise to thought," but they are also the birth of idols. That is why the critique of idols remains the condition of the conquest of symbols. (Ricoeur 1970, 541, 543)

Other recent psychoanalytic attempts have come closer to the mark. The thesis that religion and the impulse to belief are born out of the fear of death has been advanced. Religious belief, according to this formulation, has its roots in man's restitutive effort to compensate for the ultimate loss implicit in death (Rochlin 1965). Analytic material, anthropological evidence, and evidence provided by children as young as three years of age converge in the hypothesis that the religious impulse is a response to the impending sense of loss that every man feels in facing the prospect of his own finitude and ultimate loss of life. The sense of loss, then, sets in motion powerful forces that are rooted in narcissism. Their function is preservation of self beyond the impenetrable wall of death through belief in the continuity of life guaranteed by the power of the deity.

Restitution and loss, however, do not have the same roots. The sense of loss is a derivative of our basic narcissism. The cathected object becomes valued through identification and thus becomes psychologically part of the self. The heightened significance of what is lost is a reflection of our investment of it with narcissistic interest. Restitution, on the other hand, serves the aims of narcissism but is not simply a derivation of it. Restitution calls upon the inner resources of the ego to provide environmental manipulations or symbolic representations that serve to gratify wishes and to restore what is wanting.

The implications of this formulation should not be overlooked. Underlying the simple cycle of loss and restitution is the realization that in those human tragedies we call loss—the loss of love and dread of abandonment, the inevitable human fabric of failure, disappointment, deprivation, and impoverishment, and ultimately the depletion of death—is occasion for man's most sublime achievements. Rather than capitulate to the inexorability of fate and destiny, the human restitutive response at its best is a creative impulse to restore loss and to reconstitute the structure of the shattered self.

Religion is undoubtedly one of the most sublime of man's creative achievements. It is so in the history of the race and should be so in the history of the individual. There is, however, a world of psychological difference between religious faith seen as an obsessive expression of repressed infantile wishes and religious faith seen as a restitutive inspiration of man's creative resources. It is the difference between a conception of man as neurotically captive to his infantile needs and wishes and a conception of man as capable of autonomous and genuine creativity in achieving mastery, competence, and integrity in the vicissitudes of tragedy in life.

The relation of man's religious inspirations to the fear of death is undoubtedly complex. It is probably an oversimplification to relate the origins of religion only to this dimension of human anxiety. But it is nonetheless a facet of man's existence that has profound implications. Freud very clearly distinguished fear of death from realistic (object) anxiety and neurotic libidinal anxiety. From the vantage of his structural theory, he describes the mechanisms of the fear of death in terms of the ego's relinquishing its narcissistic libidinal cathexis. It appears under conditions analogous to those in which other anxieties arise—namely, in external danger and in an internal process like depression. In the latter case, the ego surrenders its narcissistic investment because it feels itself hated, rather than loved, by the superego. To live is to be loved by the superego; not to be loved by the superego is to be deserted by all protecting forces and to die. The fear of death, then, can be reduced to nothing more than the fear of castration (Freud 1923a).

It is clear, however, that this interpretation of the fear of death as reductively equivalent to castration anxiety is false, as Freud himself was aware. What can safely be asserted is that all later situations of loss probably establish an inner association with the narcissistic injury involved in the failure of oedipal wishes and their replacement by fears of castration. Thus, oedipal wishes and oedipal failure can be conceived as intimately related to the psychology of loss.

While the fear of death thus intimately involves castration anxiety, the two are by no means identical. The fear of death is an issue with children too young for oedipal conflicts. It is also the one fear that confronts men with increasing insistence until, inevitably, it becomes a reality. The realization of mortality is something other than instinctual aggression directed against the ego by an unloving superego. The concept is problematic for psychoanalysis, as Freud (1923a) acknowledged. He thought of death as an abstraction lacking unconscious correlates. But it seems, nonetheless, that death poses very real danger to the ego. It is not a present reality, but it is inevitably a future one. The only question is when, an uncertainty that makes death an ever-present possibility.

Even the more ego-oriented conceptual framework of loss and restitution cannot entirely carry the weight of explaining the origins of religious belief. It is difficult to point to specific empirical evidence that might direct the argument. There is no need, however, to insist either that man's religious instincts are completely derived from the narcissistic injury of loss or that they are inevitably a function of the sadism of the superego. In other words, religion need not be regarded as a psychologically defensive posture. Considered as a creative posture of the ego, religious belief need not be seen as solely reactive or compensatory; it can also represent a constructive aspect of ego functioning.

The religious enterprise is in many respects a quest, a striving within the ego to define an ultimate meaning, a personal significance, for oneself in the broader context of existence. The success of this enterprise is a function of the degree of autonomy and conflict-free resources the ego can bring to bear. The ability to ask and in some measure to resolve such questions is directly related to the ego's capacity to mobilize its resources of intellect and self-determination without becoming entangled in infantile ambivalences or fundamental anxieties. The rigors of the undiluted enterprise are not for the weak. But for those who can brave them is the prize of emergence of the ego on the higher level of integration and identity that is loosely called "spiritual." This noble autocreativity in which man most fully becomes himself is the ideal of religious existence.

Psychologically, however, the enterprise of spiritualization does not occur independently of certain laws. Growth and regression are complementary aspects of the dynamism by which the ego becomes ego. The search for a broader context of personal meaning cannot proceed without returning to and reviving inner sources of trust. It is this inner dimension of the religious enterprise that Freud's genius has enabled us to understand better. For, although religion is not adequately described as a return of infantile dependencies, an authentic religious enterprise cannot achieve meaningful integrity without reviving the psychological roots that establish the possibility of trust on a higher level of spiritual maturity.

4. THE ILLUSION OF THE FUTURE

When Freud wrote *The Future of an Illusion* (1927), he directed his argument against a fictive antagonist, who for all practical purposes was embodied in the person of his disciple Oskar Pfister. Pfister took up the challenge in a spirit of friendly contention and shortly after published a counterargument in the form of a lengthy article, "The Illusion of the Future" (1928). The interchange was, in fact, the high point of a dialogue between Freud and Pfister that spanned more than thirty years of their productive lives (Irwin 1973b). My purpose in reviewing that debate here is to bring into focus some of the divergences and tensions in points of view that have set the terms for the psychoanalytic discussion of religious experience and its meaning since.

THE RELATIONSHIP BETWEEN FREUD AND PFISTER

Oskar Pfister was born in 1873 and spent the early part of his career becoming a pastor of some distinction within the Lutheran church. In 1908 he was offered a chair of systematic and practical theology at Zurich. He declined the offer, however, apparently because he had, even by that time, turned from the study of philosophy and theology to a concern with the spiritual and social sufferings of the souls whom he encountered in his pastoral work. He was struggling to find a new way "to understand the phenomena of faith and the strange mutations which it has undergone" and "new means to cure the defects of religious and ethical life and to implant Christian love where hitherto I had failed" (Pfister 1948, 22).

Not long after Pfister refused the professorship, he discovered what he was looking for in the psychoanalysis of Sigmund Freud. Pfister's enthusiasm knew no bounds. He would later write:

> I tried forthwith to apply these discoveries to my ministry, and found to my joy that I could now discover facts and render help in a way which since then has not failed. . . . What caused my analytic labours

to become the fulfillment of a long-standing dream was that while they dealt with real life they were also connected with my task as a pastor. In hundreds of instances which I had attacked in vain by methods grappling directly with the conscious—in vain because the religious-ethical conflict was situated and did its work in the unconscious—I now achieved the cures which I had so long desired. (Pfister 1948, 23; cited in Irwin 1973a, 190)

Pfister went on to practice his psychoanalytic-pastoral ministry for over thirty-seven years as pastor of the Predigerkirche in Zurich. Despite occasional difficulties with ecclesiastical superiors due to his espousal of psychoanalysis and the turmoil surrounding Freud's sexual theories, Pfister continued to be an effective pastor and an enthusiastic proponent of the cause of psychoanalysis among the clergy, educators, and the general public.

The relationship between Freud and Pfister spanned nearly three decades of unbroken and mutual respect and friendship. Freud's relationship to Pfister was quite unusual among those he had with people who professed and espoused religious convictions. Something in their relationship allowed Pfister to escape the stigma of the unresolved ambivalence that Freud directed at those revenants and doubles who became repositories for his conflicts. It may well have been Pfister's spiritual simplicity, honesty, sincerity, and unquestioning loyalty to Freud and psychoanalysis that allowed him to avoid the fate of Fliess and Jung. Pfister was always the loyal disciple, nothing more. His discipleship was intelligent, questioning, at times even confrontational, but never in a spirit of envious acrimony or hostility—and Freud must have sensed this.

Pfister's regard for Freud was genuine and deep, and inevitably, in a man of his religious sentiments, it led him to try to recast Freud in a religious image. In the face of Freud's protest that he was a godless Jew, Pfister wrote:

Finally you ask why psycho-analysis was not discovered by any of the pious, but by an atheist Jew. The answer obviously is that piety is not the same as genius for discovery and that most of the pious did not have it in them to make such discoveries. Moreover, in the first place you are no Jew, which to me, in view of my unbounded admiration for Amos, Isaiah, Jeremiah, and the author of Job and Ecclesiastes, is a matter of profound regret, and in the second place you are not godless, for he who lives the truth lives in God, and he who strives for the freeing of love "dwelleth in God" (I John 4:16). If you raised to your consciousness and fully felt your place in the great design, which to me is as necessary as the synthesis of the notes is to a Beethoven symphony, I should say of you: A better Christian there never was. (Meng and Freud 1963, 63)

Pfister frequently spoke to Freud in this vein (Meng and Freud 1963, 138). The high point of his canonization of Freud came in the opening pages of his reply to *The Future of an Illusion*:*

> Your book was an act of inner necessity for you, an act of honesty and courageous self-revelation. Your titanic lifework would have been impossible without the destruction of idols, whether in universities or in churches. That you yourself serve science with the reverence and dedication that transforms your study into a temple is well known by anyone who has the pleasure of associating with you. I shall speak frankly: I have the definite suspicion that you struggle with religion— but out of a sense of religion. Schiller extends to you the warm hand of brotherhood; are you going to reject it?
>
> And from the point of view of faith I see no basis for me to lend my voice to the clamoring of a few watchers of Zion. Anyone who has struggled so powerfully for the truth and fought so courageously for the redemption of love as you have is, whether he admits it or not, a true servant of God according to scripture; one who through the creation of psychoanalysis has fashioned an instrument through which suffering souls find their shackles broken and the gates of their prison open, so that they can rush into the sunshine of a life-giving faith, is not far from the kingdom of God. . . . Will you be angry with me for seeing you as bathed in the brilliant rays of eternal light and consumed in a struggle for truth and human love despite your professed disbelief, as closer to the throne of God than many a churchman who murmurs prayers and performs rituals, but in whose heart there is no glimmer of desire for knowledge and human welfare? And since everything for the gospel-oriented Christian depends on doing God's will (not crying "Lord! Lord!"), can you understand how I might envy you? (Pfister 1928, 149–50)

Freud tolerated such Christianization well. In a friendly demur, he wrote to Pfister:

> I do not believe that I behave as if there were "one life, one meaning in life"; that was an excessively friendly thought on your part, and it always reminds me of the monk who insisted on regarding Nathan as a thoroughly good Christian. I am a long way from being Nathan, but, of course, I cannot help remaining "good" towards you. (Meng and Freud 1963, 129)*

Freud's attitude toward Pfister was always remarkably friendly and accepting. In the earliest letter of their correspondence we have, Freud expresses satisfaction that a minister of religion has taken an interest in

---

*The translations from *Die Illusion einer Zukunft* are my own; however, I am indebted to Miss Elfriede M. Banzhaf for her invaluable assistance.

psychoanalysis (Meng and Freud 1963, 15). Soon after, Pfister's gift of a replica of the Matterhorn prompted the following reply:

> It reminds me of a remarkable man who came to see me one day, a true servant of God, a man in the very idea of whom I should have had difficulty in believing, in that he feels the need to do spiritual good to everyone he meets. You did good in this way even to me. . . . But for your visit and your influence, I should never have managed it; my own father complex, as Jung would call it, that is to say, the need to correct my father, would never have permitted it. (Meng and Freud 1963, 24)

Pfister was an occasional visitor to the Freud household, and the quality of his presence there is reflected in some comments by Anna Freud in her preface to the Freud-Pfister correspondence:

> In the totally non-religious Freud household, Pfister, in his clerical garb and with the manners and behaviour of a pastor, was like a visitor from another planet. In him there was nothing of the almost passionately impatient enthusiasm for science which caused other pioneers of analysis to regard time spent at the family table only as an unwelcome interruption of their theoretical and clinical discussions. On the contrary, his human warmth and enthusiasm, his capacity for taking a lively part in the minor events of the day, enchanted the children of the household, and made him at all times a most welcome guest, a uniquely human figure in his way. To them, as Freud remarked, he was not a holy man, but a kind of Pied Piper of Hamelin, who had only to play on his pipe to gather a whole host of willing young followers behind him. (Meng and Freud 1963, 11)

FREUD'S AND PFISTER'S CONTRASTING ATTITUDES TOWARD RELIGION

The two men differed radically in their assessment of and attitudes toward religious experience and belief. Freud's views on religion are well known and are discussed at length elsewhere in this work (particularly in chapter 3). His conviction that religious beliefs were forms of illusion (if not delusion) and that religious experience and practice were universal forms of neurosis are familiar by now. Freud set himself against religion and devoted the best part of his long career to its destruction. In his relationship with Pfister, he continually emphasized the differences he saw between himself and the Lutheran pastor. He continually presented himself as an unbeliever, an atheistic pagan, a "godless Jew." Reflecting on a religious experience, he writes:

> As for myself, God had not done so much for me. He would never have allowed me to hear an inner voice; and if, in view of my age, he

did not make haste, it would not be my fault if I remained to the end of my life what I now was—"an infidel Jew." (Freud 1928, 170)

But Freud also consistently stressed the differences he saw between psychoanalysis and religion. For example, he notes that the young people with whom Pfister worked were drawn to him by a personal attraction and could thereby be influenced by religion as a form of sublimation. The vehicle of success is the same as that in analysis, namely, an erotic transference to the influencing figure. But Freud goes on to say:

> But you are in the fortunate position of being able to lead them to God and bringing about what in this one respect was the happy state of earlier times when religious faith stifled the neuroses. For us, this way of disposing of the matter does not exist. . . . Thus our patients have to find in humanity what we are unable to promise them from above and are unable to supply them with ourselves. Things are therefore much more difficult for us, and in the resolution of the transference many of our successes come to grief. (Meng and Freud 1963, 16–17)

Moreover, the analytic method cannot influence the course of therapy by either granting or refusing an illusory emotional satisfaction. The analyst cannot set himself up in the analysand's mind as a substitute for God and Providence. If the analysand seeks such satisfaction, he must be left either to overcome his impulse after an explanation has been provided or to find ways of satisfying it in some sublimated fashion, religious or otherwise. At the same time, Freud observes in a moment of concession, the analyst might make a technical mistake if he gave the impression of belittling this emotional demand for illusory satisfaction. He cannot require everyone to overcome a piece of infantilism; only a few may be capable of doing so (Meng and Freud 1963, 118).

The analytic insistence on the resolution of all elements of the transference, as opposed to the dependence of religion on transference phenomena, was a central issue in Freud's assessment of religion. Upon receipt of Pfister's reply to *The Future of an Illusion,* Freud replied:

> The rift, not in analytic, but in scientific thinking which one comes on when the subject of God and Christ is touched on I accept as one of the logically untenable but psychologically only too intelligible irrationalities of life. In general I attach no value to the "imitation of Christ." In contrast to utterances as psychologically profound as "Thy sins are forgiven thee; arise and walk" there are a large number of others which are conditioned exclusively by the time, psychologically impossible, useless for our lives. Besides, the above statement calls for analysis. If the sick man had asked: "How knowest thou that my sins are forgiven?" the answer could only have been: "I, the Son of God,

forgive thee." In other words, a call for unlimited transference. And
now, just suppose I said to a patient: "I, Professor Sigmund Freud,
forgive thee thy sins." What a fool I should make of myself. To the
former case, the principle applies that analysis is not satisfied with
success produced by suggestion, but investigates the origin of and
justification for the transference. (Meng and Freud 1963, 125–26)

Yet, even though he saw the matter of transference and sublimation as a
central issue between psychoanalysis and religion, clearly Freud envied the
power of religion. In an earlier letter to Pfister he writes: "As for the
possibility of sublimation to religion, therapeutically I can only envy you.
But the beauty of religion certainly does not belong to psycho-analysis. It is
natural that at this point in therapy our ways should part, and so it can
remain" (Meng and Freud 1963, 63).

We can observe from our late vantage point that Freud's envy must have
run deep indeed. We know that in some unconscious and repressed part of
his personality Freud harbored an identification with the prophetic figures
who held the charismatic power to move men's souls. This identification
was particularly powerful with Moses, who led his people to the Promised
Land (see above, chapter 2). We can suggest, therefore, that in contending
with the issue of suggestion and unanalyzed transference in the religious
sphere, Freud was contending with repressed, unresolved, and ambivalent
aspects of his own psychic functioning.

Yet with Pfister, Freud's attitude was frequently less harsh and rejecting
and more conciliatory. At times he would play down their differences, as,
for example, in an early letter to Pfister:

I conclude with great pleasure from your letter that our differences
begin only at the point at which influencing the thought process by
emotional stimuli becomes permissible, and thus amount to no more
than a useful variation. (Meng and Freud 1963, 19)

On another occasion, discussing Pfister's work, Freud's tone is much more
balanced and impartial:

In itself, psycho-analysis is neither religious nor non-religious, but an
impartial tool which both priest and layman can use in the service of
the sufferer. I am very much struck by the fact that it never occurred
to me how extraordinarily helpful the psycho-analytic method might
be in pastoral work, but that is surely accounted for by the remoteness
from me, as a wicked pagan, of the whole system of ideas. (Meng and
Freud 1963, 17)

Or again, Freud expresses pleasure at the prospect of Pfister's proposal to
present an argument in opposition to *The Future of an Illusion*:

The prospect of your making a public stand against my pamphlet gives me positive pleasure, and it will be refreshing in the discordant critical chorus for which I am prepared. We know that by different routes we aspire to the same objectives for poor humanity. (Meng and Freud 1963, 112–13)

Needless to say, Pfister's view of the role and function of religion is diametrically opposite that espoused by Freud. For Pfister, religion is the repository of the noblest striving and highest ideals of human nature. But the demands of Christian humanism correspond to a higher conception of human nature than that which arises from the lower level of instinctual demand. Rather, it expresses an idealistic realism that is achieved only with difficulty and strives toward the highest ideals. Yet whereas Freud seems to emphasize the differences between himself and Pfister, Pfister on his part tends to minimize them. At various points, he attempts to reduce the ethical distance between Freud's outlook and his own (Meng and Freud 1963, 18). In 1922, he writes to Freud: "In matters of ethics, religion, and philosophy there remain differences between us which neither you nor I regard as a gulf" (Meng and Freud 1963, 85). Again, while preparing his reply to Freud's pamphlet, he comments:

I have been using the rest chiefly to write my friendly criticism of you. I have been doing so with the greater pleasure because in it I do battle for a cause that is dear to me with an opponent who is the same. There is not much danger of your turning up for baptism or of my descending from the pulpit, but among the points that bring us closer to each other there are some which are very important, and when I reflect that you are much better and deeper than your disbelief, and that I am much worse and more superficial than my faith, I conclude that the abyss between us cannot yawn so grimly. (Meng and Freud 1963, 121–22)

In Pfister's mental vision there was no necesary opposition or contradiction between psychoanalysis and religion. In approaching his debate with Freud, he writes:

And yet I turn decisively against your judgment on religion. I do so with the opposition that suits a disciple, but also with the sense of joy with which one defends a holy and beloved matter, and with the earnest seeking for the truth that your teaching demands. But I do so also with the hope that many who have been frightened away from psychoanalysis by your denial of religious belief can be drawn back again through the insight gained from a methodical summary of experience. And so, I would prefer to write not against you but for you, since whoever takes a stand for psychoanalysis fights for you. I am also fighting on your side since you are devoted, as I am, to the conquering of illusion through truth. Whether you come closer to the ideal with your *Future of an Illusion* or I with my "Illusion of the Future" will be decided by a higher tribunal. Neither of us has donned the prophet's mantle, but rather we are satisfied with the more modest role of the meteorologist; but then even meteorologists can make mistakes. (Pfister 1928, 150)

And again, at the end of the "Illusion," Pfister returns to the theme of common elements between Freud and himself:

I am delighted to say that Freud himself and I seem to be striving for basically the same goal, he from the viewpoint of a scientific genius, and I with my own simple means. He is driven by his God, Logos, by which he understands the intellect, "apparently" toward the goal of human love and the diminution of human suffering; my God is also Logos, but one which, based on the first chapter of the Gospel of St. John, I regard as divine wisdom and love. (Pfister 1928, 183–84)

One of the themes that continually recurs throughout the long course of their association is the stark contrast between Freud's pessimism on the one hand and Pfister's optimism on the other. In 1918, Freud writes:

One thing I dislike is your objection to my "sexual theory and my ethics." The latter I grant you; ethics are remote from me, and you are a minister of religion. I do not break my head very much about good and evil, but I have found little that is "good" about human beings on the whole. In my experience most of them are trash, no matter whether they publicly subscribe to this or that ethical doctrine or to none at all. That is something that you cannot say aloud, or perhaps even think, though your experience of life can hardly have been different from mine. If we are to talk of ethics, I subscribe to a high ideal from which most of the human beings I have come across depart most lamentably. (Meng and Freud 1963, 61–62)

Again in 1922, he observes: "Complete objectivity requires a person who takes less pleasure in life than you do; you insist on finding something edifying in it. True, it is only in old age that one is converted to the grim heavenly pair *logos kai ananke* [reason and necessity]" (Meng and Freud 1963, 86). And again in 1930, after Freud had declared his devotion to this grim pair, he writes:

If I doubt man's destiny to climb by way of civilisation to a state of greater perfection, if I see in life a continual struggle between Eros and the death instinct, the outcome of which seems to me to be indeterminable, I do not believe that in coming to those conclusions I have been influenced by innate constitutional factors or acquired emotional attitudes. I am neither a self-tormentor nor am I cussed and, if I could, I should gladly do as others do and bestow upon mankind a rosy future, and I should find it much more beautiful and consoling if we could count on such a thing. But this seems to me to be yet another instance of illusion (wish fulfilment) in conflict with truth. The question is not what belief is more pleasing or more comfortable or more advantageous to life, but of what may approximate more closely to the puzzling reality that lies outside us. . . . Thus to me my pessimism seems a conclusion, while the optimism of my opponents seems an *a priori* assumption. I might also say that I have concluded a marriage of reason with my gloomy theories, while others live with theirs in a love-match. I hope they will gain greater happiness from this than I. (Meng and Freud 1963, 132–33)

By contrast, we are constantly confronted with Pfister's optimism, his ability to find the good and the hopeful, however obscurely mingled with the tares of evil and destruction. The contrast to Freud is evident in matters great and small. With regard to therapy, Pfister had an initial reaction to *The Future of an Illusion*:

Thus remains between us the great difference that I practice analysis within a plan of life which you indulgently regard as servitude to my calling, while I regard this philosophy of life, not only as a powerful aid to treatment (in the case of most people), but also as the logical consequence of a philosophy that goes beyond naturalism and positivism, is well-based on moral and social hygiene, and is in accordance with the nature of mankind and the world. (Meng and Freud 1963, 116)

And again, reflecting on the gloomy pronouncements of Freud's *Civilization and Its Discontents* (1930) on the broader stage of history Pfister observes:

In instinctual theory you are a conservative while I am a progressive. As in the biological theory of evolution, I see an upward trend . . . in which the laborious ascent of the gods continues, in spite of obstacles and reverses and occasional slipppings back. . . . I see civilisation as full of tensions. Just as in the individual with his free will there is a conflict between the present and the future to which he aspires, so it is with civilisation. Just as it would be mistaken to regard the actual, existing facts about an individual as the whole of him, ignoring his aspirations, it would be equally mistaken to identify with civilisation its existing horrors, to which its magnificent achievements stand out in contrast. (Meng and Freud 1963, 131)

The contrasting attitudes and spirit of the two thinkers provided the

omnipresent background that subtly but inexorably influenced the course
and tenor of their debate.

THE GREAT DEBATE

The Preliminaries

In October 1927, Freud wrote to Pfister announcing that his recently
completed pamphlet on the subject of religion was to appear. Freud's
phrasing in the letter makes it clear that his continuing discussion with
Pfister, which by then had extended over a score of years, was one of the
primary sources of stimulation for writing the pamphlet. It also allows us to
conjecture that the personage to whom the argument of the pamphlet is
addressed may also have been Pfister:

> In the next few weeks a pamphlet of mine will be appearing which has
> a great deal to do with you. I had been wanting to write it for a long
> time, and postponed it out of regard for you, but the impulse became
> too strong. The subject-matter—as you will easily guess—is my com-
> pletely negative attitude to religion, in any form and however attenu-
> ated, and, though there can be nothing new to you in this, I feared,
> and still fear, that such a public profession of my attitude will be
> painful to you. When you have read it you must let me know what
> measure of toleration and understanding you are able to preserve for
> the hopeless pagan. (Meng and Freud 1963, 109–10)

Pfister's reply displays an attitude of "so what else is new?"

> A powerful-minded opponent of religion is certainly of more service
> to it than a thousand useless supporters. . . . I have been unable to
> imagine that a public profession of what you believe could be painful
> to me. . . . You have always been tolerant towards me, and am I to be
> intolerant of your atheism? If I frankly air my differences from you,
> you will certainly not take it amiss. Meanwhile my attitude is one of
> eager curiosity. (Meng and Freud 1963, 110)

Pfister not only was curious but responded to Freud's challenge by offering
to write a refutation of Freud's arguments against religion. The prospect
delighted Freud (Meng and Freud 1963, 112–13).

When Pfister finally had a chance to read *The Future of an Illusion* the
following November, he found little in it that was unexpected. He sent his
initial objections to Freud and soon after set about writing his refutation.
Freud, on his part, found no surprises in Pfister's reaction and emphasized
that he welcomed Pfister's initiative in undertaking a criticism, particularly
since it came from an old friend whose loyalty to analysis was unshaken
(Meng and Freud 1963, 117). With Pfister's manuscript finally in his

hands, Freud expressed satisfaction at the outcome but at the same time some reservations about Pfister's arguments. Almost in a pique of impatience, he unveiled what may have been the ultimate sticking point for him: "And finally—let me be impolite for once—how the devil do you reconcile all that we experience and have to expect in this world with your assumption of a moral world order? I am curious about that, but you have no need to reply" (Meng and Freud 1963, 123). And when Pfister expressed his appreciation for the tolerant and open-minded attitude of the staff of the *International Journal,* Freud brushed this aside with an almost scoffing comment: "Such 'tolerance' is no merit" (Meng and Freud 1963, 125).

The Argument

The argument of *The Future of an Illusion* (1927) is fairly straightforward. Freud begins by setting civilization in opposition to nature. Civilization embraces "all those aspects in which human life has raised itself above its animal status and differs from the life of beasts—and I scorn to distinguish between culture and civilization" (pp. 5–6). This definition includes "all the knowledge and capacity that men have acquired in order to control the forces of nature and extract its wealth for the satisfaction of human needs" and "all the regulations necessary in order to adjust the relations of men to one another and especially the distribution of the available wealth" (p. 6). Civilization thus exacts a heavy price from the individual, so that in his natural state he is virtually its enemy. And civilization consequently has to defend itself against the individual by regulations, institutions, and commands.

One of the prices and burdens of civilization is instinctual renunciation. Here the Freudian view becomes almost Platonic in character, recalling the *Republic*:

It is just as impossible to do without control of the mass by a minority as it is to dispense with coercion in the work of civilization. For masses are lazy and unintelligent; they have no love for instinctual renunciation, and they are not to be convinced by argument of its inevitability; and the individuals composing them support one another in giving free rein to their indiscipline. It is only through the influence of individuals who can set an example and whom masses recognize as their leaders that they can be induced to perform the work and undergo the renunciations on which the existence of civilization depends. (pp. 7–8)

In addition to these prohibitions and privations, which may be imposed externally or internally, by the superego, a culture sets before its participants certain ideals, which are proposed as its highest achievements, greatly to be valued and striven for. The satisfaction such ideals offer is basically narcissistic and rests on pride in achievement. Every culture thereby elevates and proclaims its own ideals and disparages those of other cultures. The narcissistic satisfaction provided by these ideals is one of the forces that checks man's basic hostility to culture. It allows the lower, suppressed classes to identify with the upper classes who rule and exploit them and, in spite of their underlying hostility, to find in the upper classes an embodiment of their ideals. It is only when such narcissistic forces are at work that it is possible for civilizations to survive in spite of the justifiable hostility of a large portion of their membership.

What is the role of religious ideas in this unending struggle between civilization and the forces of nature? Religion serves the principal task of civilization, that is, the defense against nature. As Freud (1927) writes: "Nature rises up against us, majestic, cruel and inexorable; she brings to our mind once more our weakness and helplessness, which we thought to escape through the work of civilization" (p. 16). The "slings and arrows of outrageous fortune" inflict severe injuries on man's natural narcissism. What defense does he have against the superior powers of nature and fate that constantly threaten him? Civilization seeks to answer this need. But civilization itself imposes privations on him and fills his life with suffering. "Man's self-regard, seriously menaced, calls for consolation; life and the universe must be robbed of their terrors; moreover his curiosity, moved, it is true, by the strongest practical interest, demands an answer" (p. 16).

In his hopelessness man turns the forces of nature into gods with whom he can associate on relatively human terms. But this transformation follows the prototype of the original infantile state of helplessness in relation to one's parents. The gods thus are transformed into fathers. There was, to be sure, reason to fear fathers, but they could also be looked to as a source of protection against unknown dangers. Freud sums up the argument in the following terms:

> And thus a store of ideas is created, born from man's need to make his helplessness tolerable and built up from the material of memories of the helplessness of his own childhood and the childhood of the human race. It can clearly be seen that the possession of these ideas protects him in two directions—against the dangers of nature and fate, and against the injuries that threaten him from human society itself. Here is the gist of the matter. Life in this world serves a higher purpose; no doubt it is not easy to guess what that purpose is, but it certainly signifies a perfecting of man's nature. It is probably the spiritual part of man, the soul, which in the course of time has so slowly and unwillingly detached itself from the body, that is the object of this elevation and exaltation. Everything that happens in this world is an expression of the intentions of an intelligence superior to us, which in the end, though its ways and byways are difficult to follow, orders everything for the best—that is, to make it enjoyable for us. Over

each one of us there watches a benevolent Providence which is only seemingly stern and which will not suffer us to become a plaything of the over-mighty and pitiless forces of nature. Death itself is not extinction, is not a return to inorganic lifelessness, but the beginning of a new kind of existence which lies on the path of development to something higher. And, looking in the other direction, this view announces that the same moral laws which our civilizations have set up govern the whole universe as well, except that they are maintained by a supreme court of justice with incomparably more power and consistency. In the end all good is rewarded and all evil punished, if not actually in this form of life then in the later existences that begin after death. (Freud 1927, 18–19)

Religious ideas, therefore, are in essence illusions. They are enunciated as dogmatic teachings rather than as the product of experience or of argument and proof. As Freud proclaims:

They are illusions, fulfilments of the oldest, strongest, and most urgent wishes of mankind. The secret of their strength lies in the strength of those wishes. As we already know, the terrifying impression of helplessness in childhood aroused the need for protection—for protection through love—which was provided by the father; and the recognition that this helplessness lasts throughout life made it necessary to cling to the existence of a father, but this time a more powerful one. Thus the benevolent rule of a divine Providence allays our fear of the dangers of life; the establishment of a moral world-order ensures the fulfilment of the demands of justice, which have so often remained unfulfilled in human civilization; and the prolongation of earthly existence in a future life provides the local and temporal framework in which these wish-fulfilments shall take place. (Freud 1927, 30)

Even the basic prohibitions and regulations that order human living are attributed to God. The prohibition against murder, for example, is clearly based on the need to preserve some social order and is promulgated in the interest of protecting and preserving communal existence. The explanation is practical and rational, but the religious view asserts that this prohibition has been issued by God himself. Thus, the cultural prohibition is invested with a special solemnity, whose force nonetheless depends on our belief in God's existence. As far as Freud is concerned, such sleight of hand carries with it certain advantages, but too many disadvantages. We would be much better off if we could leave God out of it altogether and simply admit that the prohibitions have a purely human origin. The prohibitions would lose their assumed sanctity and solemnity but also their rigidity and immutability. People would begin to understand that such prohibitions are to their advantage and instead of developing a hostile and destructive attitude toward them might even aim for their promotion and improvement.

The persistence of such wish fulfillments and illusions and the preservation of the infantile model that underlies religious belief and practice provide the basis for Freud's conclusion that religious phenomena are essentially neurotic. Just as an individual child may pass through certain developmental phases of neurosis in the course of growing up, so too, Freud argues, the human race in its development has passed through stages that are analogous to the neuroses. The reason for this neurotic course is the same for the race as for the child—"namely, because in the times of its ignorance and intellectual weakness the instinctual renunciations indispensable for man's communal existence had only been achieved by it by means of purely affective forces" (p. 43). But the residues of the repressive forces have persisted throughout the history of civilization. Consequently, religion, like obsessional neurosis in childhood, becomes a universal obsessional neurosis of humanity and, like neurosis in childhood, arises out of the oedipus complex, specifically out of relationship to the father.

Freud realized that his analogy had only partial validity, but in qualifying his argument he leans even more heavily on the pathological implications:

> Our analogy does not, to be sure, exhaust the essential nature of religion. If, on the one hand, religion brings with it obsessional restrictions exactly as an individual obsessional neurosis does, on the other hand it comprises a system of wishful illusions together with a disavowal of reality, such as we find in an isolated form nowhere but in amentia, in a state of blissful hallucinatory confusion. But these are only analogies, by the help of which we endeavour to understand a social phenomenon; the pathology of the individual does not supply us with a fully valid counterpart. (Freud 1927, 43)

The obvious conclusion of the argument is that if religious ideas have such a nature, we may be better off without them:

> Our knowledge of the historical worth of certain religious doctrines increases our respect for them, but does not invalidate our proposal that they should cease to be put forward as the reasons for the precepts of civilisation. On the contrary! Those historical residues have helped us to view religious teachings, as it were, as neurotic relics, and we may now argue that the time has probably come, as it does in an analytic treatment, for replacing the effects of repression by the results of the rational operation of the intellect. . . . In this way our appointed task of reconciling men to civilisation will to a great extent be achieved. We need not deplore the renunciation of historical truth when we put forward rational grounds for the precepts of

civilisation. The truths contained in religious doctrines are after all so distorted and systematically disguised that the mass of humanity cannot recognize them as truth. (Freud 1927, 44)

The Counterargument

Pfister wastes no time in getting down to the essentials of the argument. He challenges Freud's identification of civilization with culture. Rather than adopting Freud's negative view, he emphasizes aspects of human cultural achievement as a positive force in human affairs.

> I must confess that in my opinion there is much that is infamous and destructive included in what elevates man above the animals; knowledge and abilities, goods for the satisfaction of human needs, the regulation of social interactions and the distribution of wealth, all seem to me to be highly permeated with cruelty, injustice, all sorts of poisonous seeds, so that religion really has no reason to exert itself to maintain this state of affairs. War, the spirit of Mammon, the search for pleasure, the misery of the masses, exploitation, suppression, and countless other evils point to the necessity for distinguishing between what is good and worthy of protection, which we call culture, and the evil that must be fought against. So it seems to me that Christianity worthy of the name must strive for profound changes in our culture, which has become superficial and stunted in inner values, especially affective values; and the study of psychoanalysis has confirmed me in this viewpoint. (Pfister 1928, 168)

Rather than seeing culture as somehow opposed to human nature, Pfister views it as a natural development and extension of that nature. Pfister could hardly agree with Freud's view of the function of religion as equivalent to policing or controlling culture. "Religion has more important things to do than to watch over the mixture of sovereignty and abomination which is today called culture," he observes (p. 168).

> Religion should be for us not a restraining police force, but a guiding light leading us from our pseudo culture to a true culture. It seems to me also that the task Freud assigns to religion is unworthy of it—that of providing consolation for the suppression of drives required by nature and, in a certain sense, of providing muzzles and handcuffs for the asocial masses. The subduing of animalistic instincts (insofar as they are detrimental to man's well-being and self-esteem) should be only the other side of the coin for the achievement of a positive goal: that religion should unleash the highest mental and spiritual forces; foster the highest achievements in art and science; fill the lives of everyone, even the poorest, with the greatest goods of truth, beauty, and love; help conquer realistic needs of living; initiate new forms of

social living that are more substantial and genuine; and thus call into existence a higher, spiritually enriched mankind, corresponding better to the true demands of man's nature and ethics than our much-praised unculture, which Nietzsche described as the thin skin of an apple covering a glowing chaos. (pp. 168–69)

Pfister challenges Freud's view that religion is based on the renunciation of instincts. The drives, he argues, have no separate existence; abstracting them from the broader context of human reality can only lead to serious misconceptions. Rather, the drives must be conceived in a broad organic context that relates them to other aspects of human functioning. Undoubtedly, Freud is correct in pointing to the negation or denial of drives as playing an important role in the development of religious ideas, but the understanding of religious phenomena cannot rest on that basis alone. Moreover, Freud's view of religion as somehow absorbing neurotic impulses, or even protecting against neurosis, seems overgenerous and not well supported by the facts. Neurotic manifestations are, in fact, generously distributed among pious believers. But by the same token, Pfister suggests, a genuine and free evangelism can prove an indispensable protection against the danger of neurosis (p. 181).

Pfister takes particular aim at Freud's view of religious ideas as wish fulfillments—as "illusions, fulfillments of the oldest, strongest and most urgent wishes of mankind" (Freud 1927, 30). Freud was not the first to advance this idea; he follows the lead of Feuerbach, who regarded theology as a disguised form of anthropology and related religious ideas to dreams. Freud's contribution was to define the argument in specifically psychological terms. There is no denying that unconscious wishes, derivatives of the oedipal situation, and even suppressed sadism and masochism play a definite role in the development of religion. But Pfister then takes the argument a step further:

Is all religious thinking explained by this? And is this intermingling of desire and reality characteristic only of religion? Or should not religion and science, yes, even art and morality, strive for the suppression of wishful thinking by realistic thinking, and the mobilization of real thinking through wishful thinking, as an ideal toward which mental development gropes, optimistically yet always with painful disappointment? (Pfister 1928, 157)

He goes on to observe that theologians could meet Freud halfway, just as they were able to meet Feuerbach halfway. The fact that behind the fatherhood of God lurks a very human father should not come as any surprise, although Freud's argument gives this association a new clarity. By the same token, it does not come as a startling revelation that the other world of the Eskimo is filled with whales, or that the happy hunting ground of the Indian is well stocked with game: such beliefs reflect the wishes and desires of their authors. Even those who would deny God are often led by wishful thinking. Nor is it an uncommon experience for the analyst to find that behind the unbelief of the atheist lies an ambivalence toward the father.

What, then, does Pfister say about the motivation for religious beliefs?

> And now let us take a closer look at the desires that lead to religion. It is agreed that initially they were largely narcissistic. Is it any different in science? Can one expect from primitive man a disinterested thirst for knowledge? Even in so-called natural man we see that there is a moral need expressed in cult and belief, as, for example, the need for redemption after wrongdoing (for example, in the death-wish against the father). With moral development, religion also matures. The selfish wishes retreat more and more into the background, even though there may be lapses into egoistic thinking; this only proves that wild and primitive elements are difficult to eradicate from human nature. (Pfister 1928, 158)

In fact, Pfister explains, the religion of Jesus demands the direct opposite of narcissism:

> The gentleness and humility, the self-denial and rejection of riches, the sacrifice of his own life for the highest moral values—in short, the entire standard of life that the crucified of Golgotha demands of his followers—is diametrically opposed to the lusts of primitive nature. Yet, this also corresponds to a higher conception of human nature, which certainly could not arise from lower instinctual demands, but only from an idealistic realism that can be achieved only with severe difficulties. (Pfister 1928, 158–59)

Pfister's argument follows a similar format regarding the question of obsessional and compulsive components of religion. Just as forms of wish fulfillment operate in religious cognition yet do not account for its full range, so also the obsessional and compulsive elements of religion can be seen to form a part of some religious practices without necessarily constituting the essence of religion itself. Pfister again takes a position diametrically opposed to that of Freud. While the compulsive element admittedly characterizes certain lower forms of religious involvement, Pfister insists that the same does not apply to mature forms of religious development; in fact, they run counter to neurotic compulsion. The forms of neurotic compulsive nominalism that involve rigid ceremonialism and literal belief systems are counteracted by Christ's essential commandment to love. Jesus put love in the center of his religion and its view of life, but a love that was morally pure and

morally complete. The Christian idea of the father is completely freed
from the shackles of the oedipal tie, as Pfister points out:

> What is expected of the human being is nothing more than what
> corresponds with his being and his true destiny, promotes well-being,
> and—in order to make room for the biological viewpoint—promotes
> maximal health both individually and collectively. It is a major confu-
> sion to understand Jesus' basic commandment, "Thou shalt love God
> with thy whole heart and thy neighbor as thyself" (Matt. 22:37ff.), as
> if it were a law in the Mosaic sense. The form of the imperative is
> retained, but who does not see the fine irony in which the content,
> love, an act only to be given freely, suspends the quality of legal
> imperative? (Pfister 1928, 154)

Thus, the Christian idea of God as father is free of all elements of
oedipal hatred, in the sense that God is not to be appeased by sacrifices but
is to be loved in one's brother.

> We can remind ourselves that brotherly love, in its deepest and
> broadest sense, is the sign and center of Christian teaching. We can
> also recall that the goal and the highest good of all striving and longing
> lie not in personal satisfaction but in the kingdom of God—that is, in
> the sovereignty of love, truth, and justice for the individual as well as
> for the universal community of man. (Pfister 1928, 155)

Pfister then faults Freud for his limited view of religion, particularly his
focus on the more neurotic and pathological aspects of religion without
adequate consideration of the broader religious perspective:

> It is unfortunate that Freud ignores precisely the noblest utterances of
> religion. In terms of the history of its development, it is not true that
> religion creates compulsions and holds man fast in neurosis. It is more
> that prereligious life creates neurotic compulsions, which then lead to
> corresponding religious images and rites. The magic that precedes
> religion is not yet religion. But this element may remain submerged
> within even the greatest religious tradition—the Judeo-Christian—
> where it encompasses consistently religious insights, which include
> ethical and also sociobiological ones, and ultimately gives rise to a
> religious inspiration that strives to renounce compulsion and to create
> freedom, until, under conditions that no one understands better than
> the analyst, it creates new bonds, which an even more developed reli-
> gious conception will be called upon to dissolve. (Pfister 1928, 155–
> 56)

In sum, then, Pfister clearly rejects Freud's essential notion that religion
is a form of universal obsessive-compulsive neurosis. He attempts to refute
the basic arguments Freud advances to support his position. In Pfister's

eyes Freud's emphasis falls upon a limited and pathological aspect of religious experience that in no sense encompasses its range and cannot be identified with what is essential in it.

The Epistemological Argument

The debate was also carried on in more strictly epistemological terms. Freud insists on an empirical form of verification that we can call the "Constance test." If one wishes to verify that the town of Constance lies on the Bodensee, as geography teaches, he has only to go there and see for himself. Any teaching, then, that demands belief must produce empirical grounds for verification of the claim. Further, the ultimate basis for verification lies in sensory experience of some kind. Pfister counters by challenging the epistemological assumption on which Freud's position rests. He questions the very existence of a purely objective perceptual experience that can serve as the basis for such a verification:

> "Pure" experience is in my view a fiction in any event, and if we look at the history of the sciences we see how doubtful is the reality hidden behind our so-called experience. And even this mixture of illusion and truth that we call "experience" we acquire only with the aid of trans-empirical assumptions. . . . In my view there can be no such thing as a pure empiricist, and a man who sticks rigidly to the data is like a heart specialist who ignores the organism as a whole and its invisible laws, divisions of function, etc. (Meng and Freud 1963, 114)

To Freud's further charge that religious doctrines have no claim to belief because they are "full of contradictions, revisions and falsifications, and where they speak of factual confirmations they are themselves uncon-firmed" (Freud 1927, 27), Pfister answers that contradictions exist, but that it is the continuing goal of theology to overcome and resolve them. And while such efforts have not been completely successful, one may ask whether there is any area of human thinking in which contradictions cannot be found. Even the natural sciences cannot claim to lack contradic-tions. Scientists have learned by bitter experience to be more modest in what they regard as adequately proven, and, since it is unfair to demand of other disciplines what one cannot accomplish within one's own, the natural scientist ought not to accuse the theologian of contradiction. Even Freud proposes proofs of his theoretical statements with reservations. But in following his tack of argument, Pfister complains, Freud pays no attention to those defenders of religion who not only bring out these contradictions even more sharply than Freud himself but also attempt to resolve them in meaningful philosophical-religious contexts (Meng and Freud 1963, 115).

Freud contends that the teachings of religion violate the principles of reason and thereby forego any claim to acceptance.

When we ask on what their claim to be believed is founded, we are met with three answers, which harmonize remarkably badly with one another. Firstly, these teachings deserve to be believed because they were already believed by our primal ancestors; secondly, we possess proofs which have been handed down to us from those same primaeval times; and thirdly, it is forbidden to raise the question of their authentication at all. In former days anything so presumptuous was visited with the severest penalties, and even today society looks askance at any attempt to raise the question again. (Freud 1927, 26)

This statement is such a profound distortion of the claims of religion and the bases of belief that we can readily imagine Pfister's astonishment at reading it. Certainly, he admits, such bizarre claims may have been advanced from time to time, but no informed Christian of his day would tolerate such a short-circuiting of religious understanding. In taking such a position Freud completely ignores Biblical criticism, theological reflection, and even the science of apologetics. Even if one rejects the efforts of theological reasoning philosophically, or regards it in Freudian terms as rationalization, an essential part of them still demands respect.

Pfister addresses the assumptions of Freud's theory of knowledge directly, claiming that Freud presents us with the results of a theory of knowledge without considering the theory itself:

He [Freud] takes it for granted that we are dealing only with the world of appearances. But does not the essence of science everywhere consist of dissolving this world of appearances and imposing abstractions on it which mediate our understanding of sense experience? . . .

We have to be clear, however, that the "perceiving psychic apparatus," which according to Freud every investigation of the world has to take into account, is not at all an unambiguous structure protected from deception. Can I measure temperatures with a thermometer without being sure of the dependability of the instrument? Is one allowed to ignore the recent history of philosophy, in which we find Descartes proposing absolute skepticism, Hume destroying the illusion of certain causality, Kant overthrowing the illusion of empirical knowledge of the world in itself, and, in their most recent work, even the natural sciences conjuring up a real dawn of idols? Have we not yet admitted into what sort of scientific labyrinths one stumbles if one frivolously takes the terms of epistemology and metaphysics and tries to apply them to natural science? Have we forgotten how the natural sciences deceived us with their understanding of the natural laws, the atoms, the ether, the formula of LaPlace, and so forth?

There is no natural science without metaphysics, never has been, and never will be. (Pfister 1928, 173–74)

Pfister goes on to argue that one cannot think about such matters as a critique of religious ideas without a critique of knowledge. Anyone who is afraid to abstract or infer conclusions from the data of experience had best stay clear of the sciences. Philosophy endeavors to extend man's knowledge beyond the limits of his experience; therefore anyone who does not intend to deal seriously with philosophical problems will only confuse matters by approaching technical matters from a layman's position. In short, there can be no human experience without subjectivity. Insofar as Freud bases his convictions on the assumption of a form of objective experience that can serve as a valid basis for our knowledge of reality, his approach is philosophically naive and misguiding.

Religion versus Science

Freud's polemic against religion is cast in the form of a radical opposition between natural science and religion. His argument is essentially that religion has failed to achieve its objectives. Although it has held sway over men's minds for thousands of years, it has not succeeded in making the majority of men happy or, for that matter, in bringing them to a more moral condition of life. The major result of its efforts has been to keep the mass of men submissive to religious beliefs and practices. This view is congruent with his more general statements on the role of religion in civilization and with his basic view of man's nature as hostile to the demands, prohibitions, and regulations of culture.

To Freud's mind, the decline of religion is due to the rise of natural science in recent centuries. He observes:

> Let us consider the unmistakable situation as it is to-day. We have heard the admission that religion no longer has the same influence on people that it used to. (We are here concerned with European Christian civilization.) And this is not because its promises have grown less, but because people find them less credible. Let us admit that the reason—though perhaps not the only reason—for this change is the increase of the scientific spirit in the higher strata of human society. Criticism has whittled away the evidential value of religious documents, natural science has shown up the errors in them, and comparative research has been struck by the fatal resemblance between the religious ideas which we revere and the mental products of primitive peoples and times. (Freud 1927, 38)

Anticipating the grim vision that he would later enunciate in *Civilization and Its Discontents* (1930), Freud described the dire consequences of the weakening of the influence of religion on the mass of men:

> But it is another matter with the great mass of the uneducated and

oppressed, who have every reason for being enemies of civilisation. So long as they do not discover that people no longer believe in God, all is well. But they will discover it, infallibly, even if this piece of writing of mine is not published. And they are ready to accept the results of scientific thinking, but without the change having taken place in them which scientific thinking brings about in people. Is there not a danger here that the hostility of these masses to civilisation will throw itself against the weak spot that they have found in their task-mistress? If the sole reason why you must not kill your neighbor is because God has forbidden it and will severely punish you for it in this or the next life—then, when you learn that there is no God and that you need not fear His punishment, you will certainly kill your neighbor without hesitation, and you can only be prevented from doing so by mundane force. Thus either these dangerous masses must be kept down severely and kept most carefully away from any chance of intellectual awakening, or else the relationship between civilisation and religion must undergo a fundamental revision. (Freud 1927, 39)

The answer, of course, is to replace religion with science. Since religion has proven so deceitful, misguided, untrustworthy, and oppressive, mankind is obviously better off without it. Moreover, man can do without illusions, argues Freud, and the sooner he abandons his dependence on such infantile illusions, the better off he will be.

Thus I must contradict you when you go on to argue that men are completely unable to do without the consolation of the religious illusion, that without it they could not bear the troubles of life and the cruelties of reality. That is true, certainly, of the men into whom you have instilled the sweet—or bitter-sweet—poison from childhood onwards. But what of the other men, who have been sensibly brought up? Perhaps those who do not suffer from the neurosis will need no intoxicant to deaden it. They will, it is true, find themselves in a difficult situation. They will have to admit to themselves the full extent of their helplessness and their insignificance in the machinery of the universe; they can no longer be the center of creation, no longer the object of tender care on the part of the beneficient Providence. They will be in the same position as a child who has left the parental house where he was so warm and comfortable. But surely infantilism is destined to be surmounted. Men cannot remain children forever; they must in the end go out into "hostile life." (Freud 1927, 49)

Moreover, men who abandon these childish illusions are not without resources or assistance. Their scientific knowledge, which is increasing every day, gives them power to deal with and control their environment, to face the demands of harsh reality more effectively. And, Freud says, "as for the great necessities of Fate, against which there is no help, they will learn to endure them with resignation" (Freud 1927, 50).

A central question in the discussion centers around the extent to which religious illusions are essential for man's well-being. Freud anticipates Pfister's counterargument by putting some of the key objections into the mouth of his opponent. A race of men capable of renouncing all illusions and thus of making their existence on earth tolerable is itself, he objects, an illusion. Freud pins his hopes on "the possibility that generations which have not experienced the influence of religious doctrines in early childhood will easily attain the desire to primacy of the intelligence over the life of the instincts. This is surely an illusion: in this decisive respect human nature is hardly likely to change" (Freud 1927, 51). If one wishes to dispel the illusions of religion, this can be done only by substituting another system of illusions that will, in effect, take over the psychological characteristics of religion—that is, a similar sanctity, rigidity, intolerance, and prohibition of thought, as a matter of necessity.

Pfister would in fact have gone this far, but Freud goes further, in effect setting up a straw man whom he can easily demolish. He has his opponent argue for the preservation of imposed religious doctrinal systems as providing a necessary basis for human education and communal life, by preparing children for their place in civilization. Religion is best suited to this purpose precisely because of its wish-fulfilling and consoling power, which reflects its illusory character. And religion has the added advantage of allowing for a refinement and sublimation of ideas that let it divest itself of the residues of primitive and infantile thinking. What is left is a body of ideas "which science no longer contradicts and is unable to disprove. These modifications of religious doctrine, which you have condemned as half-measures and compromises, make it possible to avoid the cleft between the uneducated masses and the philosophic thinker, and to preserve the common bond between them which is so important for the safeguarding of civilization" (Freud 1927, 52).

Freud's reply to this imagined argument seems to lack conviction. Certainly, he says, no one has to tell him about the difficulty of avoiding illusions, and perhaps his own hopes are illusory too. But at least his illusions are not, like religious ones, incapable of correction, he contends. To that extent, they are not delusions, as religious convictions would be. Finally, he holds out some optimism that man can overcome and free himself from his neurotic entanglements.

The weakness of Freud's position does not, however, strengthen that of his opponent, against whom Freud stakes his modest claim for the superiority of man's intellect to his religious beliefs:

> I think you are defending a lost cause. We may insist as often as we like that man's intellect is powerless in comparison with his instinctual

life, and we may be right in this. Nevertheless, there is something peculiar about this weakness. The voice of the intellect is a soft one, but it does not rest until it has gained a hearing. Finally, after a countless succession of rebuffs, it succeeds. This is one of the few points on which one may be optimistic about the future of mankind, but it is in itself a point of no small importance. And from it one can derive yet other hopes. The primacy of the intellect lies, it is true, in a distant, distant future, but probably not in an infinitely distant one. It will presumably set itself the same aims as those whose realization you expect from your God (of course within human limits—so far as external reality, "Ananke," allows it), namely the love of man and the decrease of suffering. (Freud 1927, 53)

Pfister summarizes the Freudian viewpoint in one trenchant sentence: "The God, Logos, hurls the God of religion from the throne and reigns in the realm of necessity, about whose meaning we, in the meantime, do not know the least" (Pfister 1928, 172). Then he answers Freud in words that seem almost prophetic:

We can also now take issue with Freud's prognosis for scientific knowledge. We cannot speak of such a rosy-fingered Eos as he offers us. Freud is far too serious and honest to make promises that from lack of conviction he cannot keep. Man will, with the help of science, widen the scope of his powers—how far, we do not know—and he will learn to endure the great necessities of fate with resignation. This is all, everything. But hasn't Freud already said too much? Couldn't culture collapse soon? Hasn't the decline of the West been prophesied for us by a man whose rich knowledge is recognized everywhere? Is it really unthinkable that a culture guided only by science will succumb to wild passions, after the World War has shown us the barbarism that lurks in the depths of people? Do not Eduard von Hartmann and many others assure us that growth of the sciences only increases our miseries? Is it so certain that scientific progress has thus far enlarged the total sum of human pleasures of life; and if it has done so thus far, is it certain that it will do so always? . . . What will become of the greatest achievements of technology if they are put at the disposal of human greed, cruelty, and an infrahuman lust for pleasure?

Freud's prognosis for science rests merely on an argument from analogy, which I do not consider as certain. It states: Because scientific progress has brought advantages to mankind thus far, it shall do so in the future also. Or, in better words, in the background there is a faith in science the basis of which Nietzsche saw clearly with his eagle eye and expressed in these words: "One must understand . . . that there is always a metaphysical faith on which our faith in science rests

—that we sophisticated people of today, we atheists and antimeta-physicists, still draw our fire from the flame of a thousand-year-old faith, the Christian faith, which was also the belief of Plato, that God is truth, that truth is divine. . . . But what if just this became more and more incredible. . . ?"

Do we know, by an oracle, that knowledge will always contribute to the increase of human happiness, especially when evil passions may decide the issue? Byron laments: "The tree of knowledge is not the tree of life!" Can exact knowledge refute him? And when a Faustian burning desire for knowledge glows within us, can natural science and medicine (philosophy and theology excluded) satisfy us, or will even the Faust of today have his heart almost burned? . . .

Is it not possible that behind Freud's belief in the final victory of the intellect there is only another wish, and that his prediction about the end of one illusion includes the marshaling up of a new one, namely, a scientific illusion? That the parade does not take place with marching bands and waving flags, but with muted sounds and groping steps speaks for his humility; but I cannot follow this path, precisely because the reality principle stands in my way, urging caution. (Pfister 1928, 175–76)

After reading Freud's draft for the first time, Pfister had written to him in a similar vein:

Your substitute for religion is basically the idea of the eighteenth-century Enlightenment in proud modern guise. I must confess that, with all my pleasure in the advance of science and technique, I do not believe in the adequacy and sufficiency of that solution of the problem of life. (Meng and Freud 1963, 115)

In the face of Freud's optimism about the future of science and the primacy of the intellect, Pfister retreats in skepticism:

As joyfully and enthusiastically as I follow Freud along the marvelous paths of his science, here it is impossible for me to keep step with him. Freud's illuminating mind aspires to an intellectualism that, intoxi-cated with its successes, forgets its limits. We human beings are not only thinking apparatuses, we are living, feeling, desiring beings. We need values, we have to have something that satisfies our hearts and souls, that vivifies our desires. Even thinking has to give us values, logical as well as otherwise. In analysis, do we not often have to deal with clear-thinking people who drive themselves almost to starvation and despair with their thinking? . . . It is assumed that intellect can-not value. The sharpest mind cannot determine whether a symphony of Mahler or a painting by Holder is beautiful. The cleverest human being might welcome, without any sense of contradiction, common treason and ridicule the death of a hero for the sake of truth. A heartless scoundrel can dispose of clear-thinking intelligence, and a mentally retarded person can be indignant about perfidy. Science lacks the ability to appraise esthetic and ethical greatness. . . .

It is only natural that Freud has to find a place somewhere for the values of heart and soul of which his own life demonstrates such wonderful riches, in his scientific constructions. But I do not find that place in his understanding of science. (Pfister 1928, 177)

Thus, Pfister totally rejects Freud's attempt to substitute natural science for religious belief. To do so, he argues, would be to destroy much of what is finest and noblest in human nature and achievement. Moreover, it would undercut and destroy any realistic basis for ethics and morality. He sums up his argument in the following terms:

Religion is the sun which gave rise to the most splendid flowering of art and the richest harvest of moral convictions. Every great and powerful work of art is a prayer and a sacrifice before the throne of God. God, who for the religious philosopher is the foundation of all ideals, is for us, the pious, the basis of his true creativity, the Pentecostal spirit who leaps upon the earth in tongues of fire, the revealer whose "Let there be light!" brightens the darkness of man's spirit with dazzling clarity. Anyone who would destroy religion would be sawing through the tap roots of art that unveil the deepest meaning and the noblest forces of life.

And we also see religion as the main foundation of morality. We do not fail to notice that pious faith has encompassed deep moral insight and continues to do so, as, for example, the history of Christianity teaches us. But we also do not forget that the most courageous and splendid ethical progress could happen only in terms of religion. We owe the great progress in ethics to religious pioneers, not to scientists. Even Kant, whose elimination of love signifies a serious retreat from the ethics of Jesus, is basically the only learned spokesman for Protestantism who has diverged into the puritanical.

Natural science, therefore, leaves us in the lurch concerning the formation of ethical concepts. And, what is more important, the genesis of moral life has never yet been achieved with lean theories and clever concepts. To fail to recognize this would be pedantry of the worst sort. Religion, with its partly sublime, partly attractive symbols, with its poetic splendor and its shattering interpretations of reality, with its overpowering personalities who by their heart-warming deeds and sufferings charm people, and by their faults and weaknesses warn yet inspire the fallen person with courage to aspire to his ideal with new strength—religion is an educator that science with its theories certainly cannot replace. Religion, with its enormous metaphysical background and future perspectives, with its divine sanctioning of moral law and its message of forgiveness, anticipating some of the most important achievements of psychoanalysis, with its insistent attempts to overcome all resistance of the experiential world through the certainty of higher obligations and commitments—in short, this whole world of ideals, which is an expression only of the certainty of a higher, indeed the highest reality, and which with ease can absorb all gifts of science, yet can add to them an unheard-of abundance of other treasures, of ideals and vital powers, is an educator which science with its theories certainly cannot replace. But even if such faith were to be false, we would have to fight for it in spite of its results. It is better to go to hell with the truth than to heaven for the price of lies! (Pfister 1928, 179–80)

Then Pfister advances the argument to the point that Freud does not reach, bringing into focus not only the basis of morality but also the role of religion in forming and maintaining values and value systems.

However, this by no means exhaustively indicates the scope of religion. Religion cannot be defined as enthusiasm for art or morality, or as buffering against neurosis. Some other components have to be added. Religion concerns itself with the meaning and value of life, with the singular drive of reason toward a universal view of the world encompassing both being and obligation, with the yearning for home and peace, with the impulse toward mystical union with the absolute, with the chains of guilt, with the thirst for freedom and grace, with the need for a love that is removed from the unbearable uncertainties of earthly life, and with innumerable other anxieties which, if not relieved, can choke and disquiet the soul but through religious harmony can lift the life of man toward radiant mountain heights with indescribably joyous vistas, can strengthen the heart, and by the imposition of heavy moral obligations in the spirit of love can elevate the value of existence. The irreligious man cannot feel this, just as the unmusical man cannot appreciate a composition of Brahms. Religion is, however, not nearly as aristocratic an art as science. It is a stream in which lambs can swim and elephants drown. But the fact of the matter is still just as the New Testament says: "Faith is not every man's thing" (2 Thess. 3:3). Faith, however, implies not merely a concept of man but a laying-hold of the entire inner life of man.

How meager science seems to us in relation to such abundance, of which we have been able to indicate only a very small part, because we do not have space for greater detail; even so, words cannot express that which is inexpressible! It is no surprise that some of the greatest scientists thought of their work as service to God and that some of the greatest artists and poets humbly laid down their laurel wreaths before the altar of God. (Pfister 1928, 181–82)

The Question of Lay Analysis

In the course of the discussion over *The Future of an Illusion*, Freud raised an important issue that was peripheral to the central argument but nonetheless reflected in a practical sense the tension between the outlooks of the debaters. In November 1928 Freud writes to Pfister:

I do not know if you had detected the secret link between the *Lay Analysis* and the *Illusion*. In the former, I wished to protect analysis from the doctors and in the latter, from the priests. I should like to hand it over to a profession which does not yet exist, a profession of *lay* curers of souls who need not be doctors and should not be priests. (Meng and Freud 1963, 126)

Allied to this position is Freud's previous objection to the use of any illusory emotional satisfaction in the analysis, as he thought might be the case if one were to introduce religious concepts into the analytic work (Meng and Freud 1963, 118). In a similar vein, he had decried the apparent dependence of religious approaches on unresolved transference (Meng and Freud 1963, 125).

Pfister was not slow to take up the challenge. In the following February he writes to Freud:

Please allow me to return to your remark that the analysts you would like to see should not be priests. It seems to me that analysis as such must be a purely "lay" affair. By its very nature it is essentially private and directly yields no higher values. In innumerable cases I have done nothing but this negative work, without ever mentioning a word about religion. The Good Samaritan also preached no sermons, and it would be tasteless to have a successful treatment paid for in retrospect by religious obligations. Just as Protestantism abolished the difference between laity and clergy, so must the cure of souls be laicised and secularised. Even the most bigoted must admit that the love of God is not limited by the whiff of incense. . . . If no priest should analyse, neither should any Christian or any religious or morally deep-thinking individual, and you yourself emphasize that analysis is independent of philosophy of life. Disbelief is after all nothing but a negative belief. I do not believe that psycho-analysis eliminates art, philosophy, religion, but that it helps to purify and refine them. Forgive a long-standing enthusiast for art and humanitarianism and an old servant of God. Your marvelous life's work and your goodness and gentleness, which are somehow an incarnation of the meaning of existence, lead me to the deepest springs of life. I am not content to do scientific research on their banks, but have to drink and draw strength from them. . . . At heart you serve exactly the same purpose as I, and act "as if" there were a purpose and meaning in life and the universe, and

I with my feeble powers can only fit your brilliant analytical discoveries and healing powers into that gap. Do you really wish to exclude from analytical work a "priesthood" understood in this sense? I do not believe that that is what you mean. (Meng and Freud 1963, 126–28)

To this rebuttal, Freud answers with a grudging concession. Within the week, he writes to Pfister as follows:

My remarks that the analysts of my fantasy of the future should not be priests does not sound very tolerant, I admit. But you must consider that I was referring to a very distant future. For the present I put up with doctors, so why not priests too? You are quite right to point out that analysis leads to no new philosophy of life, but it has no need to, for it rests on the general scientific outlook, with which the religious outlook is incompatible. . . . [The] essence [of religion] is the pious illusion of providence and a moral world order, which are in conflict with reason. But priests will remain bound to stand for them. It is of course possible to take advantage of the human right to be irrational and go some way with analysis and then stop, rather on the pattern of Charles Darwin, who used to go regularly to church on Sundays. (Meng and Freud 1963, 128–29)

Second Thoughts

There are, of course, points in the debate with Pfister at which Freud seems to give ground or at least to reconsider the force of his argument. He does not seem at such points to concede, but the force of his convictions about the nature and value of religion seems to wane and to leave at least a glimmer of a possibility that they might not be as compelling as at first. In the course of the debate that followed in the wake of *The Future of an Illusion,* he writes to Pfister:

Of course it is very possible that I might be mistaken on all three points, the independence of my theories from my disposition, the validity of my arguments on their behalf, and their content. You know that the more magnificent the prospect the lesser the certainty and the greater the passion—in which we do not wish to be involved—with which men take sides. (Meng and Freud 1963, 133)

Even in the course of writing *The Future of an Illusion,* he seems to have second thoughts:

But I will moderate my zeal and admit the possibility that I, too, am chasing an illusion. Perhaps the effect of the religious prohibition of thought may not be so bad as I suppose; perhaps it will turn out that human nature remains the same even if education is not abused in order to subject people to religion. I do not know and you cannot know either. . . . Should the experiment prove unsatisfactory I am ready to give up the reform and to return to my earlier, purely descriptive judgement that man is a creature of weak intelligence who is ruled by his instinctual wishes. (Freud 1927, 48–49)

At times, he even seems to draw back to a more neutral or open-minded position that views analysis as not at all antithetical to religion but rather as a more neutral and impartial instrument. In presenting his essay to Pfister, he notes that analysis might even be used to reach conclusions quite opposite his own:

Let us be quite clear on the point that the views expressed in my book form no part of analytic theory. They are my personal views, which coincide with those of many non-analysts and pre-analysts, but there are certainly many excellent analysts who do not share them. If I drew on analysis for certain arguments—in reality one argument—that need deter no-one from using the non-partisan method of analysis for arguing the opposite view. (Meng and Freud 1963, 117)

And even in the work itself, he comments in the same vein:

An outcry of this kind will really be disagreeable to me on account of my many fellow-workers, some of whom do not by any means share my attitude to the problems of religion. But psycho-analysis has already weathered many storms and now it must brave this fresh one. In point of fact psycho-analysis is a method of research, and an impartial instrument, like the infinitesimal calculus, as it were. . . . Nothing that I have said here against the truth-value of religions needed the support of psycho-analysis; it had been said by others long before analysis came into existence. If the application of the psycho-analytic method makes it possible to find a new argument against the truths of religion, *tant pis* for religion; but defenders of religion will by the same right make use of psycho-analysis in order to give full value to the affective significance of religious doctrines. (Freud 1927, 36–37)

Even on the question of the destruction of illusions, Freud at points seems to tread more cautiously. To the objection of his opponent that it is a cruelty to deprive men of their illusions, he replies:

On another point I agree with you unreservedly. It is certainly senseless to begin by trying to do away with religion by force and at a single blow. Above all, because it would be hopeless, the believer will not let his belief be torn from him, either by arguments or by prohibitions. And even if this did succeed with some it would be cruelty. A man who has been taking sleeping draughts for tens of years is naturally unable to sleep if his sleeping draught is taken away from him. (Freud 1927, 49)

Even in the context of analysis illusory emotional satisfactions cannot be completely outlawed; the analyst cannot "call on everyone to overcome a piece of infantilism which only a few are capable of overcoming" (Meng and Freud 1963, 118).

The End of the Debate

In December 1939, after Freud had finally succumbed to cancer, Pfister wrote a charming letter to Frau Freud in London. He reminisced about the years of their friendship and the good times he had shared with Freud and his family. His final words make a fitting close to the debate between these two great thinkers:

> Your husband's letters are among my most cherished possessions. As long as I live I shall always have them by my side. . . . I am working on a number of projects in which, with my feeble powers, I continue your husband's method of work. Though the unfavorable times are more willing to strike up a dance for the devil of lies than to listen to symphonies of truth, I believe with your husband: *la vérité est en marche.* (Meng and Freud 1963, 147)

5. FREUD AND THE RELIGION OF MOSES

THE ARGUMENT

In his monumental and provocative last major work, *Moses and Monotheism* (1939), the founder of psychoanalysis tries to establish, first of all, that Moses was not really a Hebrew but an Egyptian—in fact, that he was an Egyptian aristocrat and a member of the court circles of Pharaoh Amenophis IV. This young pharaoh came to the throne in about 1375 B.C., bringing with him sweeping religious reforms. He enforced the worship of a single god, Aten, perhaps the world's first true monotheism. It was this religion that Moses communicated to the Jewish people in the form of the worship of Yahweh. The Jews, unable to tolerate this highly restrictive and spiritualized religion, arose, threw off this intolerable burden, and savagely destroyed the tyrant who had imposed it on them.

But the tradition lived on. Later, in need of tribal union and a common religion, the Israelites returned to the worship of Yahweh. Credit for their liberation passed from Moses, the murdered prophet, to Yahweh, the all-powerful deity. As Freud (1939) saw it, "the central fact of the development of the Jewish religion was that in the course of time the God Yahweh lost his own characteristics and grew more and more to resemble the old god of Moses, the Aten" (p. 63).

The Freudian view, then, is that the idea of a single god and its amalgam of ethical demands and prohibitions against magical ceremonial were, in fact, Mosaic doctrines. They were effectively ignored for a time but then came into their own. The delay in their acceptance has its intrapsychic parallel in the individual's resistance to new knowledge that contradicts his wishes and convictions. In the history of the Jewish religion, then, there was a long period of latency after the breaking away from the religion of Moses, during which the monotheistic idea was submerged. While it remained alive in the oral tradition of the Hebrews, the factions responsible for its codification wanted to deny the earlier religion and its teachings, so that the written and the oral traditions began to diverge, the latter

An earlier version of this chapter was published in *Journal of Religion and Health* 6 (1967): 269–79 and 7 (1968): 43–60, 151–63.

preserving what had been deleted from the former. The latency period, then, came about because the official written history tried to suppress facts that were never really lost.

Instead of weakening with the passage of time, the Mosaic traditions were preserved over the course of centuries and found their way into much later codifications. Ultimately they became the decisive influence on the thought and character of the Jewish people. The Jews had turned their backs on Mosaic monotheism to embrace the worship of Yahweh, who differed little from the Canaanite Baalim. But the persisting Mosaic tradition succeeded at last in transforming Yahweh into the Mosaic God. The transformation brought with it the ethical demands and prohibitions against magic that were derived from the cult of Aten.

The Neurotic Analogue

To give a better understanding of this process, Freud employs an analogy from the genesis of neurosis. Its significant point is that early childhood impressions of traumatic experiences become inaccessible to memory. They belong to the period of infantile amnesia that is penetrated only by isolated, fragmentary screen memories. These impressions are either sexual or aggressive, or they involve injuries to narcissism. Human sexuality, then, blossoms early, is suppressed during the latency period, and finally reemerges at puberty. An early trauma has both positive and negative effects. The former are represented by "fixations" to the trauma and by "repetition compulsions." The latter are more defensive reactions, which aim at keeping the trauma unremembered and unrepeated. Both aspects contribute significantly to the formation of character. The symptoms of the neurosis constitute an uneasy compromise in which these positive and negative effects are continually in conflict.

All these phenomena display a characteristic compulsiveness that isolates them from the demands of reality and logical thinking. An inner psychic reality takes control of perceptions of the outer world and establishes the grounds for neurotic conflict. The formula, then, is early trauma, defense, latency, outbreak of neurosis, and partial return of the repressed.

Freud then takes a giant step. He suggests that individual history and the history of mankind are parallel. The consequences that are reflected in neurosis in the individual are reflected in religious phenomena in the species. Basing his argument on the formulations of *Totem and Taboo* (1912–13), Freud advances his theory of religious development. Again, the primal event is the murder of the father by the horde. The internecine strife that followed made it necessary for the first forms of social organization and renunciation of instinct to emerge, which evolved into the incest taboo and the law of exogamy. The memory of the father lived on in his substitute, the totem, with which all the ambivalence of feeling formerly directed toward the father became associated. The totem represented the most primitive form of religion. Later developments modified it only by humanizing the totem. Ultimately, however, the all-powerful, one and only father-deity reemerged.

Freud here goes on to say that the deep impression of the monotheistic idea on the Jewish people is based on a repetition of the primal murder of the father carried out on the father-substitute Moses. The murder of Moses, then, is the link between the forgotten primal murder and its reemergence in monotheism. Guilt for the murder of Moses stimulated the wish for the Messiah. Christ then became a resurrected Moses and a returned primal father as well.

Freud undoubtedly satisfied himself that the analogy between neurotic processes and religious events pointed unequivocally to the origins of religion. He remarks:

A tradition that was based only on communication could not lead to the compulsive character that attaches to religious phenomena. It would be listened to, judged, and perhaps dismissed, like any other piece of information from outside; it would never attain the privilege of being liberated from the constraint of logical thought. It must have undergone the fate of being repressed, the condition of lingering in the unconscious, before it is able to display such powerful effects on its return, to bring the masses under its spell, as we have seen with astonishment and hitherto without comprehension in the case of religious tradition. And this consideration weighs heavily in favor of our believing that things really happened in the way we have tried to picture them or at least in some similar way. (Freud 1939, 101–02)

It must be admitted that the force of the argument rests on a tissue of probabilities or, more exactly, possibilities. Yet in spite of the fact that the argument is suspect at multiple points, it carries us forward to a number of critical considerations that have far-reaching implications for the understanding of man's religious experience and, pari passu, his inner reality.

In considering Freud's fascinating argument, we must keep in mind certain suppositions on which it rests. The first is that the religion of Israel underwent a historical evolution from a more primitive and animistic nature worship to a more sophisticated monotheism. In Freud's view, the intervention of Moses with his unique form of Egyptian monotheism was decisive in determining the course of this evolution. His second important supposition is that the practice of religion is inherently neurotic and obsessive-compulsive; and his third, that there is a parallel between the mechanisms of individual and group behavior. The implications of these suppositions are far-reaching for both the understanding of religious behavior and the understanding of human psychology. Some examination of them may prove rewarding.

HISTORICAL ASPECTS

The Influence of Hegel and Wellhausen on Freud's Historicism

Freud's understanding of the history of Israelite religion was based on the brilliant formulations of Julius Wellhausen. Wellhausen's brilliant synthetic reconstruction of the evolution of the Israelite religion appears for the first time in his *Prolegomena,* published in 1878. It represents the full development of the influence of Hegelianism in biblical research. Hegel had proposed as a cornerstone of his philosophic system the notion of a "dialectic" comprised of thesis, antithesis, and synthesis. Every concept or experience, he claims, necessarily involves the existence of an opposite. Thesis and antithesis are thus thrown into inevitable conflict, to be resolved by the subsequent synthesis, which comprehends both thesis and antithesis and subsumes them into a higher complex. Hegel applies the principles of dialectic to nearly the whole of human experience, in a sweeping formulation. In the historical process, he distinguishes three major phases. The first, the phase of thesis, took place in China, India, and the Near East. This was a phase of absolute monarchy and absolute political subjection of the individual. Man was in his infancy, dominated by nature rather than spirit. The second, antithetic phase took place in the Mediterranean; it was represented by the flowering of the classical cultures of Greece and Rome. The revolt against political absolutism that carved a place for human freedom began here. The final phase, synthesis, would be realized by the triumph of Germanic culture, in which man would become conscious of his freedom yet freely will the submergence of the individual in the universal idea.

The impact of these views on biblical studies was immense. F. C. Baur, founder of the Tübingen school, was an ardent Hegelian. His reconstruction of New Testament history saw the origins of Christianity in the conflict between the thesis, a Jewish parochial gospel proposed by Jesus and his disciples, especially Peter, and the antithesis of Pauline universalism. The Pauline doctrine was considered only in those Pauline epistles that Baur considered authentic, namely, Galatians, 1 and 2 Corinthians, and Romans. The synthesis came in the Synoptics and the Gospel of John, which Baur placed at about 160 A.D. This dating is no longer tenable, and Baur's reconstruction has fallen into disrepute, but he put a Hegelian stamp on New Testament scholarship that persists more than a century later.

Wellhausen was the founder of a school of Old Testament studies to which nearly every Old Testament scholar of any standing belonged in the early decades of this century. Albright (1957) describes various ways in which this school's approach reflected a Hegelian background:

> in the division of Old Testament religion into three phases, animism (polydemonism, etc.), the prophetic stage (henotheistic), the nomistic stage (monotheistic); in the chronological arrangement of Hebrew literature in the order, early poetry, prophetic writings, legal codes; in the unilateral theory of evolution and in the Hegelian view that the fully developed religion of Israel unfolded gradually from primitive naturalism to lofty ethical monotheism. (p. 88)

The great extent to which Freud's reconstruction reflects the suppositions of the Wellhausen school is not surprising. These views were overwhelmingly dominant in biblical scholarship at the time Freud was writing. Indeed, it would have been strange for him to have taken any other approach. It remains true, however, that contemporary developments have surpassed the Wellhausen view, which must now be regarded as unacceptable. Dissatisfaction with the Wellhausen view has generally been based on its telescoping of the evolutionary process into an incredibly brief period, on its dating of many critical events considerably later than is supported by available sources, and on its tendency to reject or ignore key biblical accounts that did not support the evolutionary hypothesis.

In general, the archeological discoveries of the past generation have brought about a significant change in the attitudes of biblical scholars. Rapidly accumulating data from archeological digs give impressive support for the substantial historicity of the patriarchal tradition contained in the biblical accounts. Wellhausen and his school tried to reconstruct the pre-Yahwistic stage of Israelite religion by sifting the early, but still fully Yahwistic, sources for primitive features. The primitive character of these sources was determined in terms of an a priori Hegelian typology of religious ideas. Alt ([1929] 1953), who initiated the modern discussion of patriarchal religion, recognized that such procedures succeed only in isolating the superstitions of Israelite religion at any stage of its development. At the same time, it was becoming clear that the archeological data relevant to the second millennium gave a different picture of early Israelite religion from that painted by older historians (Cross 1962).

Since the dependence of the Freudian fable on the Wellhausen orientation is so marked, it would repay a psychoanalytic investigation to attempt to reassess the argument from a more contemporary and more authentically historical perspective. Freud was able to advance an ingenious reconstruction on the basis of a historical account that has so altered in the intervening years that it is no longer tenable. We must ask, then, whether the updated account of the origins of Israelite monotheism offers grounds for new insights relevant to the understanding of man's religious stance and its psychic significance. After examining a few of the issues at stake, I propose to review some of the important historical material to discern its significance for the dynamics of religious thought and experience.

The Problem of Faith and Reason

Our immediate purpose, then, is to survey the broader aspects of the argument provided by Freud's reconstruction. Let us then return to his second major supposition, that religious behavior is inherently neurotic and obsessive-compulsive. Freud was particularly impressed by two elements in religious rites and doctrines: fixations on the ancient history of the family and revivals of the past with the return of what has been forgotten.

> What has returned from oblivion asserts itself with peculiar force, exercises an incomparably powerful influence on people in the mass, and raises an irresistible claim to truth against which logical objections remain powerless: a kind of "credo quia absurdum." This remarkable feature can only be understood on the pattern of the delusions of psychotics. We have long understood that a portion of forgotten truth lies hidden in delusional ideas, that when this returns it has to put up with distortions and misunderstandings, and that the compulsive conviction which attaches to the delusion arises from this core of truth and spreads out onto the errors that wrap it round. We must grant an ingredient such as this of what may be called *historical* truth to the dogmas of religion as well, which, it is true, bear the character of psychotic symptoms but which, as group phenomena, escape the curse of isolation. (Freud 1939, 85)

Freud's position is unequivocal, but it is nonetheless a staggering appraisal of a basic human commitment. This is an essential aspect of his understanding of religious behavior to which we must return later. Here I wish only to underline the place of his supposition in the argument and to consider, although briefly, the implications of a shift in viewpoint.

The claim of religious dogma to infallible truth is indeed irresistible, but it is a distortion of theological thinking to describe its power as against the claims of logic. The problem here is a perennial one that has been subsumed under the rubric of "faith and reason." But it is a violation of both faith and reason to argue that because faith does not arrive at the same conclusions as reason it is therefore opposed to reason and ipso facto psychotic. If one surveys the history of theology from the beginnings of man's conscious reflection on religious experience down to the contemporary theological scene, what emerges with considerably greater force than anything else is the continual and progressive engagement of the human intellect with the understanding of religious truth. The "fides quaerens intellectum" is far more impressive than the "credo quia absurdum." Rather than rejecting reason and logic, faith finds its true dynamism in exploiting the logical and rational resources of man's intellect to achieve an ever-deepening understanding of religious belief and dogma.

To adopt this conclusion, however, neither resolves the problem of faith and reason nor illumines the paradoxical position of religious belief. One must remember that faith is a response to revelation. The challenge to faith and, therefore, to reason is that revelation conveys a content that eludes human understanding. The agony of faith is thus the agony of reason. The "credo quia absurdum" must remain operative to fill the vacuum between the faltering of "fides quaerens intellectum" and dogma. But this faltering of reason is totally removed from a rejection of, or a flight from, reason. The former marks the limits of human capacity; the latter is psychotic. The important point, however, is that faith operates from the initiation of the quest for understanding to its uttermost limits and then takes the leap into the dark.

The Character of Religious Belief

Faith is thus a human response to divine revelation. If one presupposes that there is no revelation and no revealing god, faith becomes totally meaningless and bizarre. But these presuppositions are themselves without convincing validity. If they are insecure, the supposition resting on them must also be questionable. Hence we are again pushed to consider the alternative. If we presume a revealing god and revelation with a dogmatic content that resists the efforts of rational understanding, what can we conclude about the inner meaning of religious belief and its implications for man's psychological life?

It is apparent that Freud attributed the "compulsive conviction" attaching to religious beliefs to the return of the repressed. As I have tried to suggest, the label "compulsive conviction" does not reflect the true character of religious belief. This is not to say that the neurotic mind cannot be compulsive about religious belief. This is common enough, but does not concern us at the moment. The question is whether religious belief itself is compulsive: Is religious behavior made compulsive by an associated neurosis, or is it of itself necessarily and intrinsically neurotic? At this point, I will only suggest that further investigation may not support the intrinsic neuroticism of religious belief and behavior. An affirmation such as Freud's must remain a supposition.

His supposition, however, raises a further important question. If we consider for the moment the alternate supposition, that religious behavior need not be compulsive and neurotic, we are left with a major concern: What is it that motivates man to religious belief? The question is a psychological one; it is not answered by theological appeals to absolute truth or to the veracity of the revealing god. In short, once we strip the argument to the bone we are left with the core problem, faith.

Faith and Tradition

But the problem of faith, while it is primarily a phenomenon concerning the relation between the individual and the revealing god, is not wholly restricted to the intrapsychic realm. It is concurrently a phenomenon in the social order, involving the community of believers and the organized structure of religious groups. Freud presupposes that the social aspect of religious belief can be understood by analogy with intrapsychic dynamics. To structure the historical data in terms of this hypothesis is tantalizing but still leaves the supposition open to question. If we do question it, we are pressed to provide an alternate approach to understanding the social aspect of religious belief. If we cannot simply extrapolate from our understanding of the psyche to the social order, it is nonetheless apparent that these two levels are not entirely unrelated. But merely to project intrapsychic mechanisms onto the social level tends to oversimplify the problem and distort reality. While Freud believed the mass neurosis of the community to be based on a prior racial repression, his formulation must postulate too many hypothetical entities to preserve scientific perspective. For such a theory to make sense, the community must acquire dynamisms and psychic agencies proper to itself, over and above the psychic structure of its participating members, and it must create some mechanism for preserving the mutative effects of communal experiences in order that these experiences may achieve contact with current communal practices and experiences.

Freud certainly recognized that the transfer of terms could not be univocal. In reference to the "return of the repressed" he remarks:

> Here I am not using the term "the repressed" in its proper sense. What is in question is something in a people's life which is past, lost to view, superseded and which we venture to compare with what is repressed in the mental life of an individual. (Freud 1939, 132)

In the development of a tradition or culture, particularly in the early stages, the oral forms of preserving tribal or cultic traditions are predominant. While the line between the oral and the presumably later written traditions is not very precise, there is no doubt that the oral tradition has specific characteristics and follows fairly specific laws. In the process of transmission, the tradition is selective in proportion to the predominance of oral over written techniques. The question Freud raises is whether what is lost in the transmission of a tradition can rightly be thought of as "repressed" and whether the mechanism of selectivity can rightly be compared to the process of repression.

The Presumptive Analogy

If repression as an analogy has any place in the argument, one must raise the question what represses what—as well as out of what and into what. Given the presumption of repression, it is difficult to avoid the inference of inheritable unconscious elements. Freud (1939) goes on to say:

> We cannot at first sight say in what form this past existed during the time of its eclipse. It is not easy for us to carry over the concepts of individual psychology into group psychology, and I do not think we gain anything by introducing the concept of a "collective" unconscious. The content of the unconscious, indeed, is in any case a collective, universal property of mankind. For the moment, then, we will make shift with the use of analogies. The processes in the life of peoples which we are studying here are very similar to those familiar to us in psychopathology, but nevertheless not quite the same. We must finally make up our minds to adopt the hypothesis that the psychical precipitates of the primaeval period became inherited property which, in each fresh generation, called not for acquisition but only for awakening. (p. 132)

It becomes abundantly clear that Freud's supposition permitted him to deal with historical materials on the basis of an analogy derived from individual psychopathology. While this is a legitimate form of speculation, it is nonetheless a speculation based on certain presumptions that can and should be questioned. If we permit ourselves to be properly suspicious of these presumptions, we allow ourselves a second look at the available evidence, which is more abundant and more secure than what was available to Freud. Once we have reexamined the historical processes by which traditional material is transmitted, we may or may not find Freud's analogy justified. We may also find that data from modern historical research into the biblical tradition offer us more meaningful insight into the psychological processes that gave form and substance to the social structure of the religious community.

RECENT HISTORICAL EVIDENCE AND ITS IMPLICATIONS

The pattern of argument sketched out above has focused on three issues central to Freud's discussion that demand further examination: the historical emergence of the concept of monotheism, the nature of religious belief and practice, and the process of selection and transmission of the religious tradition. Examination of the history of the emergence of Israelite monotheism and the transmission of Israelite religious traditions depends on the insights available from modern biblical research. It is to be hoped that a more empirically developed approach to these processes will offer better grounds for the psychoanalytic understanding of a significant aspect of man's existence. I have been concerned here only with the preamble to a more thoroughgoing analysis of the pertinent data. A cursory presentation would do injustice to the substance of the issues at stake; they deserve more mature consideration and reflection. For the insights they provide ultimately promise significance for our understanding of the involvement of man's psychic life in his specifically religious experience.

It is important, however, to recognize that it was part of Freud's genius to recognize those critical issues to which psychoanalytic inquiry might address itself in seeking a deeper understanding of man's psychic life. That he came to these issues with various suppositions is after all a secondary matter. Returning to these same concerns after a half century of development in archaeological and biblical research, we cannot employ the same presumptions. But it is important in any such undertaking that we sort out such presumptions from authentic intellectual insight. This has been our present objective. It remains to move on to the more difficult task we have set ourselves, recognizing that we may in fact only be exchanging one set of suppositions for another. We can hope, though, that by planting our feet on more secure historical ground, we may gain an understanding that comes closer to the reality of things.

The argument as outlined indicates that one of the major suppositions behind Freud's understanding of the evolution of monotheism and, therefore, of religious behavior is that the doctrine of the one true god, supreme and omnipotent, evolved out of a more primitive religious matrix. Freud endeavors to show that the notion of one god came not directly from the primitive religious traditions of Israel but from Egypt, through the agency of Moses. In this, Freud shared the suppositions of the vast majority of biblical scholars of his time. Their dominant influence, as we have seen, was that of Wellhausen and his school, who extended the philosophy of Hegel into biblical research.

The wealth of archeological data derived from strata in Palestine contemporary with the patriarchal and prepatriarchal eras has completely revolutionized the thinking of biblical scholars about these periods. While the biblical accounts had previously been thought to be unreliable and highly edited renditions actually reflecting much later religious views, recent archeological evidence supports the validity and historicity of the biblical accounts.

Hebrew Traditions and Mesopotamian Origins

The Hebrew traditions, as distinct from other ancient national traditions, preserve a clear impression of their tribal and familial origins. Nothing comparable can be found in Egypt, Babylonia, Assyria, Phoenicia, Greece, or Rome. The traditions of the Jews preserve a record of simple beginnings, multiple migrations, and vicissitudes that brought them from a position of favor under Joseph to bitter oppression in the time of Moses. These accounts were long regarded as artificial productions of Israelite scribes from the period of divided monarchy. Genesis 11–50 was regarded as a late invention, or at least as a retrojection of events under the monarchy into a past that had been lost in the obscurity of history.

The traditions of Genesis indicate that the ancestors of the Jews were nomadic and seminomadic peoples who wandered in and around the Middle East toward the close of the third and the first centuries of the second millennia B.C. Recently excavated inscriptions of Ur support this hypothesis. According to the Genesis account, the ancestors of the Israelites came from Mesopotamia. Abraham's father, Terah, migrated from Ur-Kasdim, the region of the early Babylonian city of Ur, to the region of Harran in northwestern Mesopotamia. The excavations at Ur have yielded cuneiform documents proving that Ur was at the height of its prosperity from about 2070 to 1960 B.C., when it was destroyed by the Elamites. The city of Ur was partially restored in the eighteenth century but was again utterly devastated in the early seventeenth century, this time not to be heard of for centuries. The date of Terah's migration from Ur to Harran will probably never be fixed with certainty, but sometime in the third quarter of the twentieth century B.C. would fit the historical data quite well (Albright, 1949).

The Hebrew tradition was undoubtedly correct in tracing patriarchal origins back to the Balikh valley in northwestern Mesopotamia. The references are explicit to cities like Harran and Nahor, which were flourishing in the nineteenth and eighteenth centuries B.C. This origin is also indicated by personal, tribal, and divine names. The data indicate that the Hebrew ancestry in Mesopotamia was a mixture of Accadian, Hurrian, and Amorite influences. The Nuzian documents from the fifteenth century B.C. indicate that the customary law found in the patriarchal narratives fits better with the framework of Nuzian social and legal practice than with either that of later Israel or that of Babylonia in the nineteenth century. The discovery of the Mari documents and related ones from the eighteenth century has added striking parallels.

Of particular importance are the cosmogonic narratives of Genesis 1–11. They are significant in that they bear a close similarity to material in Assyrian and Babylonian tablets and show little relation to what is known of Canaanite cosmogony. This cosmogonic material is inexplicable without the supposition that it was brought from Mesopotamia by Hebrew ancestors before the middle of the second millennium. The now extensive data on Canaanite beliefs and legends reveal nothing comparable to the Genesis account. Nor is there anything like it in Egyptian literature. The Mesopotamian parallels, however, are striking (Albright 1957).

The evolution of the Mesopotamian religion reflects the deepest human concerns in the course of Mesopotamian history and culminates in the patriarchal traditions of Israel (Jacobsen 1963). In the fourth millennium, Mesopotamian economy was based on artificially irrigated crops and therefore subject to drought, famine, and other disasters. Mesopotamian deities were correspondingly gods of agriculture and nature, and their cult had the intention of insuring that these deities provided fertility, produce, and food. In the third millennium, the advance of civilization added a new fear to the fear of starvation: the fear of war and destruction. Protection against this new danger was sought in great walls surrounding cities, in collective institutions of security, and in the emergence of kings invested with awesome powers to defend against outside foes and to right wrongs within the community. The element of power and majesty was transferred to the gods, who became powers not only in nature but in human affairs. At the beginning of the second millennium, the concerns of the individual worshipper began to emerge. His private fortune and misfortune and anxieties in disease and suffering came to the fore and added a personal dimension to his relation with the divine. By personal fault, he could estrange himself from the favor of his personal god, but by confessing guilt before his god, he could gain forgiveness. The insight that the divine stood for a moral law that was realized by human responsibility was born. When Israel emerged in the transition from the second to the first millennium, therefore, the concept of a divinely sanctioned morality had already been achieved. It was possible for man to enter into a covenant with God under which he could live collectively in social justice and individually in moral responsibility. To this extent, Israel stood as heir to the religious history of the preceding millennia.

Evidence has accumulated suggesting that the early Hebrews were related to the "Apiru" who appear in the cuneiform records of the nineteenth and eighteenth centuries B.C., as well as in the Nuzian, Hittite, and Amarna documents of the fifteenth century. They were landless soldiers, freebooters, captives, and slaves of varied ethnic origins. Later on, in Canaanite sources of the fourteenth century, they are described as rebelling against Egyptian authority, often in alliance with Canaanite princes. The question is by no means decided, but an "Apiru" origin would be consistent with many details of traditional Hebrew history.

The Egyptian Connection

Albright (1957) remarks that these multiple corroborations have led to the rejection of the old critical theory, according to which the patriarchal narratives were thought to be retrojections from the ninth to the eighth century. However, we cannot rely too heavily on the present forms of the tradition, since conflicting versions appear in documents derived from different sources. But the various traditions are so close in form and content that they must reflect different recensions of a common national epic handed down from the patriarchal age. The Egyptian sojourn is an essential part of the tradition and must have lasted for a long period. The adoption of Egyptian names presumably reflects this influence. This was possibly the case even for Moses' name. The Joseph episode and its subsequent history may in fact have its historical nucleus in the Hyksos movement.

The Fifteenth Dynasty was followed by a weak foreign dynasty, against which the Theban princes revolted. The revolt persisted until the fall of Avaris under Amosis I in 1560 B.C. The designation "Hyksos" is apparently a corruption of a phrase meaning "chiefs of a foreign country" and is often applied to Palestinian and Syrian chiefs and princes in the literature of the Middle Empire. The Israelites were, in fact, settled in the area of the Hyksos capital Avaris or Tanis. Canaanite place names there in the time of the New Empire bear witness to a long period of Semitic occupation. In addition, many of the Hyksos leaders bore Semitic names. Albright (1957) concludes: "In short, it must be considered as practically certain that the ancestors of part of Israel, at least, had lived for several centuries in Egypt before migrating to Palestine" (p. 243).

Pre-Mosaic Religion

In the pre-Mosaic religion of the Hebrews, the chief god of the patriarchs was Shaddai. Later patriarchal generations recognized a deliberate choice of God, a basic and very ancient principle that is demonstrated by Alt to be central in shaping the religious traditions. Personal names of the early Hebrews, incorporating appellations of the deity, reflect the influence of divine worship. Such names were common in pre-Accadian Semitic documents and are relatively abundant in the Old Accadian documents from the twenty-fifth to twenty-third centuries. They are more apparent in Old Assyrian records (twentieth to ninetenth centuries) and are often found in Amorite nomenclature between 2100 and 1600 B.C. In general they became less frequent over time. Such names contain a vow or invocation to God, usually uttered by a parent or other authoritative person at the child's birth. Thus Ya'qobh (Jacob) is a short form of Ya'qobhi'el, "May El protect."

The evidence suggests, first, that the principal deity of the pre-Mosaic patriarchs was a mountain god or a god cloaked with mountain imagery. 'El Shaddai was "the god of the mountain." Second, the Hebrews, like their Semitic ancestors, had a keen sense of relationship between a patriarchal group and its deity. The deity was actually a member of the clan and could be addressed as "father" or "brother." Albright (1957) has rejected the notion of an El monotheism among early Western Semites. El was probably a father-god in early Hebrew popular tradition. A son, Shaddai, appears in the form of a storm god. Whether the distinction between El and Shaddai was sharply drawn is questionable. The divine appellations of Genesis 14–35 that incorporate the appellation "El" are certainly pre-Israelite. The primary names are 'El 'olam, 'El 'elyon, and 'El Shaddai.

Cross (1962) has reviewed the data pertaining to these names and draws the following conclusions:

1. It is highly likely, if not certain, that the biblical epithet 'El 'olam must be interpreted as a liturgical title of 'El meaning originally "El, lord of Eternity" or "El, the Ancient One." Such names are also characteristic designations of the god 'El in Canaanite myths and liturgies.
2. 'El 'elyon must mean "creator of heaven and earth" in Genesis 14:18 and may be construed as "the god 'Elyon, creator." 'El was the creator god of Ugarit and Canaan, and the origin of this appellation must be sought in the cult of the Canaanite El.
3. Exodus 6:2 explicitly identifies the god of Abraham, Isaac, and Jacob as 'El Shaddai. The Shaddai element seems to mean "the mountain one" and to be related to other Western Semitic divine epithets known from Ugaritic sources. It also seems to refer to the cosmic mountain. Shaddai may be an epithet of Ba'l-Hadad, but this makes it difficult to understand the identification in Israelite tradition of 'El Shaddai with Yahweh, because of the opposition between the gods of the Canaanites and the god of the patriarchs. It cannot be established whether Shaddai was an old Amorite deity, brought to Palestine by the patriarchs and early identified by them with the Canaanite 'El, or whether Shaddai was originally a cultic epithet for the Canaanite 'El.

Patriarchal Tradition

The biblical traditions regarding the God of the Fathers actually represent pre-Mosaic religious ideas. The names derived from the earliest sources, "God of Abraham," "Kinsman of Isaac," and "Champion of Jacob" in particular are of authentic patriarchal origin. Each patriarch is represented as choosing his god for himself and in so doing, selecting a different manifestation of Yahweh, later God of Israel. This individualistic perspective and the belief in the relationship between the clan and its god were primary features of the religion of the patriarchs.

The name "Yahweh" is identified in both the Elohistic and Priestly traditions with the god of the patriarchs and specifically with 'El Shaddai in the Priestly tradition (Exodus 6:2). The relationship between Yahweh and 'El remains a problem. Certainly the 'El epithets continued to be used throughout the history of Israel as proper names of Yahweh at the same time that a ferocious antagonism was being directed toward Ba'al, the primary deity of Syria in the first millennium B.C. The cult of 'El was popular in the Semitic communities of Sinai, Egypt, and Seir. Further, the rapid unification of cults in the formation of the twelve-tribe league suggests some prior form of cultic unity between the Palestinian descendants of the patriarchs and the disparate elements invading Canaan from the desert. Further evidence for the relation of the Canaanite 'El and the

Israelite Yahweh is found in the fact that traits and functions of 'El appear also as those of Yahweh in the earliest Israelite traditions (Cross 1962).

The Pentateuch

The appearance of Moses in this religiocultural background was undoubtedly an event of great significance. In all the pentateuchal traditions, Moses stands as a dominant figure. The tradition, including Christian tradition, credited the composition of the entire Pentateuch to Moses. But modern scholarship has revealed variations in style, disruptions of sequence, and narrative repetitions that argue against a single author. Following Wellhausen, modern scholars have regarded the Pentateuch as an amalgam of four documents, all written much later than the time of Moses. There were initially two narrative sources, the Yahwistic (J), which uses the divine name (Yahweh) that was given to Moses, and the Elohistic (E), which uses the common name for God, Elohim. J was written in Judah in the tenth century B.C., and E followed a little later in Israel. After the fall of the Northern Kingdom (following the fall of Samaria in 722 B.C.), J and E were combined. After the period of Josiah, the Deuteronomic (D) source was added; the Priestly Code (P), made up of laws for the most part, with a smattering of narrative, was joined to the existing compilation (JED) after the exile. The redactional steps by which the Deuteronomic and Priestly traditions were later joined to JE are still matters of scholarly debate, but it is clear that the entire Pentateuch had reached its present form by the period of the exile or shortly thereafter. It has also become apparent from our growing archeological data that many of the pentateuchal laws and institutions had nonbiblical counterparts long before the dates assigned to these documents. There can be little question that the basic substance of the Pentateuch, its recorded traditions and legislation, goes back to the origins of Israel. Moses was the organizing spirit, the primary legislator and leader of the movement, and the events surrounding his emergence compose the substance of the national epic.

There is little to support Freud's premise that Moses was an Egyptian, although his name is Egyptian. Most biblical scholars agree that in all probability he was a Hebrew born and raised in Egypt. Here again, our increased knowledge of topography and archeology have lent considerable support to the historicity of the Exodus account. Even the date of the exodus can be fixed within reasonable limits. In 1937, an inscription dating from 1221 B.C. was discovered in the ruins of the latest Canaanite Lachish; it proved that the town fell to the Israelites at around that time. The stele of Marniptah, dated at 1219 B.C., also proves that the Israelites were in western Palestine in some force. Allowing for the "generation" that Israelite tradition demands, the date of the exodus cannot be later than 1250 B.C. Allowing for the occupation of eastern Palestine and the move westward, Albright argues for a date early in the thirteenth century, probably around 1280 B.C. (Albright 1957).

The God of Moses

The god of Moses was Yahweh. The name has been variously interpreted but seems best to carry the somewhat abstract connotations of existence and/or causality—"he who is," "he who causes to be." The name may in fact be no name—Yahweh was above naming and beyond understanding. In any case, the Israelites certainly regarded him as the source and creator of all things. Moreover, he was unique in that he stood alone, without family connections. Nor was he restricted to any dwelling place. He was lord of all cosmic forces who dwelt, if anywhere, in heaven and could appear or manifest himself anywhere. The theophany of Exodus 19 was probably influenced by recollections of volcanic eruptions combined with the memory of thunderstorms in the mountains of northwestern Arabia or Syria.

A fundamental aspect of early Israelite traditions and the Mosaic religion was their anthropomorphic conception of Yahweh. Yahweh is always referred to in human form, although this form is always hidden in his "glory" (Kabod). He also has a very human psychology—he loves and is angered, feels revenge and remorse. To be sure, such concepts reflect the primitive and perhaps polytheistic origins of the Israelite religion (see, for example, Genesis 18 and 19). On the other hand, it seems reasonable that this anthropomorphism had a functional aspect as well. If Yahweh was to be a god of the individual Israelite as well as of the community, it was essential that he be a god to whom the individual worshipper could look for understanding and sympathy, a god whom he could both love and fear. As Albright (1957) remarks:

> It was precisely the anthropomorphism of Yahweh which was essential to the initial success of Israel's religion. Like man at his noblest the God of Israel might be in form and affective reactions, but there was in Him none of the human frailties that make the Olympian deities of Greece such charming poetic figures and such unedifying examples. All the human characteristics of Israel's deity were exalted; they were projected against a cosmic screen and they served to interpret the cosmic process as the expression of God's creative word and eternally active will. (p. 265)

Another striking characteristic of the cult of Yahweh was the prohibition against his representation in any visible or tangible form. Presumably this rigid aniconism was calculated to separate the cult of Yahweh from the iconistic cults of other gods in neighboring nations. It also had the force of underlining the immediacy of the relationship between Yahweh and the people of Israel.

The Mosaic Religion

One of the important problems in understanding the origins of the Mosaic religion has been the derivation of the ethical, civil, and ceremonial laws attributed in the later tradition to Moses. Alt's monumental work (1934) distinguishes between two forms of pentateuchal legislation, apodeictic versus casuistic law. Casuistic laws—Exodus 21–23, for example—are legal codes similar to the Code of Hammurabi or the Hittite and Assyrian laws. They derive their form from Sumerian jurisprudence of the third millennium B.C. The apodeictic laws, however, are unique and originate in Israel. They do not appear in other parts of western Asia. Best illustrated by the Ten Commandments, these apodeictic laws have a striking categorical character that sets them apart from their closest parallels, the Egyptian Negative Confession and the Babylonian Shurpu. The Israelites are commanded to avoid sin simply because this is the will of Yahweh; moreover, their apodeictic laws reflect a more advanced standard of conduct than the extrabiblical counterparts.

The assumption that the original teaching (*torah*) of Moses may have contained Egyptian elements is entirely consistent with his origins and social position in Egypt. However, the absence of direct documentation and the complex pattern of borrowing from Egyptian sources make any conclusions somewhat speculative and uncertain. Certain elements do suggest a possible relationship to the worship of Aten. One such element is the concept of a god who is the sole creator of all things. Another is the emphasis on one god and the recognition that such a deity must necessarily be international, cosmic, and universal. However, there is no agreement among scholars that such a theology is essentially monotheistic, or, for that matter, that the teaching of Moses was actually a form of monotheism. On the other hand, it is clear that the religion of Israel violently rejected almost every other aspect of Egyptian religion—the complex iconography, the preoccupation with magic, the materialistic conception of the afterlife.

There seems to be good reason, on the other hand, to believe that there were other strong influences on the religion of Moses that were common throughout the Near East and presumably Mesopotamian in origin. Still other elements may reflect a Canaanite derivation. Which of these influences were actually accepted by Moses, as opposed to what was later introduced into Yahwism from older traditions after his death, will remain a mystery. Hebrew influences can clearly be discerned in the notion of a close association between deity and worshipper, the contractual chracteristics of the relationship between the deity and his people (illustrated primarily in the notion of the covenant), the association of the deity with such natural manifestations as storms and volcanic eruptions, and the identification of Yahweh with 'El Shaddai and with the god of Abraham, Isaac, and Jacob.

Monotheism

While there is obviously much in the foregoing reconstruction that is speculation rather than demonstrable historical fact, the picture of emergent monotheism is quite different from that required by the suppositions of Wellhausen and Freud. It seems more than likely that the religion of the patriarchs had its origins in the milieu of Mesopotamian religious thought. The migration to Palestine brought many of the finest inspirations of Mesopotamian religion with it. The patriarchs evolved a highly personalistic, clan-oriented, and family-based form of religion. The deities who emerged from this unique matrix were the gods of Abraham, Isaac, and Jacob, and especially 'El Shaddai. The worship of 'El in the pre-Israelite tradition seems to reflect strong influences of the Canaanite worship of 'El. While this evolution reflects uniquely Semitic characteristics, nowhere in this tradition can an unequivocal monotheism be demonstrated. Even the Yahwistic formulas, which were introduced with a Mosaic reformulation, cannot be interpreted in any stronger sense than the concept of 'El with whom Yahweh was identified.

The later formulas reveal hardly any more convincing demonstration of the monotheistic inspiration as the development of the Mosaic religion progressed. In the formulas of the Yahwistic (J) tradition shortly after the time of Moses, the explicit monotheism of the Israelite religion seems less than secure. The subsequent development of the tradition reflects its continuity with earlier strata. At this point in our knowledge, however, we cannot be certain that the teaching of Moses, however influenced by the cult of Aten, was monotheistic in the same unequivocal sense as was the later tradition. As Albright (1957) remarks:

> If . . . the term "monotheist" means one who teaches the existence of only one God, the creator of everything, the source of justice, who is equally powerful in Egypt, in the desert, and in Palestine, who has no sexuality and no mythology, who is human in form but cannot be seen by the human eye and cannot be represented in any form—then the founder of Yahwism was certainly a monotheist. (pp. 271–72)

Religious Development

With this panorama of religious development spread before us, let us try to see a little more deeply into its psychic significance. To begin with, the origins of the religious tradition lie buried deep in the prehistorical era. At the most primitive levels of this tradition that are known to us, the gods were forces of nature with which man endeavored to ally himself. Out of a welter of nature gods evolved a theology in which history and human events also became objects for divine guidance and intervention. The nation, the tribe, the clan, and the family served as basic units of identification. Each had a relation to a deity who served its collective interests. For the seminomadic clans of the desert, of whom the Apiru and perhaps the Hebrew patriarchs are representative, the deity preserved a special relation to the clan or family. He was addressed in terms of kinship and by reason of this relationship was specially charged with providing for the prosperity and welfare of his clan.

This primitive animism gave way to anthropomorphism. While the religion of the Hebrews preserved certain special elements derived from its Mesopotamian origins, it shared this pattern of evolution with the religions of surrounding nations and divinities. An important feature of this evolution is that the participation of the god in the life of the clan was based on kinship, which meant, of course, that the god bore characteristics common to the clan, not foreign to it. This made it possible for an individual clan member to allay his fears and anxieties by securing the active protection of the father-god of his clan.

On another level altogether, and in all probability evolving pari passu with the increasing socialization of tribal life, man became increasingly aware of another source of anxiety and destructiveness: his own instinctual drives. The upsurge of libido and aggression provoked anxiety, even at a much more primitive level of man's existence than we are now considering. These anxieties must have become increasingly pertinent as developing technological and agricultural skills gave man greater control over his environment. The conflict with nature had diminished in urgency by the time of the patriarchs. There was still conflict with other hostile nations, and in this regard the gods who supervised the destiny of the clan were extremely important. But there was undeniably another force at work in the operation of religious behavior.

Origins of Monotheism

By the time the biblical record begins, the religion of the Hebrews had evolved to quite a sophisticated level. Out of Mesopotamia had come the fundamental conceptions of individual responsibility and guilt, together with the essential association of the moral code with the deity. Except for occasional hints of prebiblical polytheism (Genesis 18–19), the written records indicate a concentration on a single deity. At each stage of the tradition, the patriarchal tradition endorses and takes as its own a single deity. It is not at all clear that at the earliest levels of the tradition this single deity was always the same. There is a residual diversity in the tradition that is at once consistent with later theological formulations and capable of monotheistic interpretation. Yet, it is clear that these early patriarchal traditions are not unequivocal and do not provide their own claims to represent theological monotheism.

It is also plain, however, that the post-Mosaic tradition did interpret the

early texts and traditions in a monotheistic sense. Apparently, the patriarchs who migrated into western Palestine brought with them a concept of
one god who was peculiarly theirs. The overtones of this belief made it
possible for the Hebrews to identify their own Shaddai with the Canaanite
'El. 'El is primordially the patriarchal deity who reflects the structure of
nature and the order of patriarchal social organization. Cross (1973)
summarizes his predominant characteristics:

> We see 'El as the figure of the divine father. 'El cannot be described as
> a sky god like Anu, a storm god like Enil or Zeus, a chthonic god like
> Nergal, or a grain god like Dagon. The one image of 'El that seems to
> tie all of his myths together is that of the patriarch. Unlike the great
> gods who represent the powers behind the phenomena of nature, 'El is
> in the first instance a social god. He is the primordial father of gods
> and men, sometimes stern, often compassionate, always wise in
> judgment.
>
> In Akkadian and Amorite religion as also in Canaanite, 'El fre-
> quently plays the role of "god of the father," the social deity who
> governs the tribe or league, often bound to league or king with kinship
> or covenant ties.
>
> His characteristic mode of manifestation appears to be the vision or
> audition, often in dreams. This mode stands in strong contrast to the
> theophany of the storm god whose voice is the thunder and who goes
> out to battle riding the cloud chariot, shaking the mountains with
> stormy blasts of his nostrils, striking the enemy with fiery bolts. Ba'l
> comes near in his shining storm cloud. 'El is the transcendant one.
> (pp. 42–43)

The relationship between 'El and Shaddai is quite complex and fluid, but
it seems adequate to say that a certain amount of syncretism must have
taken place through the close association of the Hebrews and the people of
Canaan. Such amalgamation was all the more likely in view of the greater
advancement and stability of Canaanite culture in comparison with that of
the Hebrews. In any case, out of these interlocking influences emerged a
belief in one god, the god of the Fathers. Thus Yahweh, the god of the
Israelites, was originally a cultic name of 'El, the divine father of gods and
men. The later traditions identified Yahweh with 'El, the god of the
patriarchs. As Cross concludes:

> Our interests have been directed toward the continuities between the
> god of the Fathers and Yahweh, god of Israel. We have agreed with
> Alt to this extent, that Patriarchal religion had special features: the
> tutelary deity or deities entered into an intimate relationship with a
> social group expressed in terms of kinship or covenant, established its

justice, led its battles, guided its destiny. This strain entered Yahwism.
Yahweh was judge and war leader of the historical community. He
revealed himself to the Patriarch Moses, led Israel in the Conquest; he
was the god who brought Israel up from the land of Egypt, her savior.
There is also the second strain which entered Israel's primitive religion, that of the high and eternal one. 'El the creator of heaven and
earth, father of all. (p. 75)

This was at best an ambiguous monotheism. The term "henotheism" has
been proposed to describe this stage of the development of Israelite
religion, suggesting that the choice of one god as having special reference
to the nation had been made, but that other gods were not denied.

The syncretistic process involved here was extended and deepened by
the intervention of Moses and the revelation of Yahweh through him.
Yahweh was identified with 'El Shaddai. The questionable monotheism of
'El Shaddai cast a parallel doubt on the monotheism of Yahweh. The
deliverance from the bondage of Egypt and the return to the Promised
Land were the works of Yahweh through his servant Moses. The cult of
Yahweh was not a replacement for the pre-Mosaic religion but, rather, a
revision that subsumed previous religious belief into a new synthesis. The
new revelation specified that Yahweh was the source and creator of all
things, but this new formulation was neither a rebuttal to nor a rejection of
the patriarchal formulas. It was precisely this continuity within reformulation that made it possible for later theological reflection to identify Yahweh
with the god of Abraham, Isaac, and Jacob.

The Transmission of Tradition

What we are describing is a process of theological reflection and elaboration. The reflection consists in turning back to the content of the tradition
in an effort to find its continuities and thereby the origins of contemporary
belief. The revelation of Yahweh took place in a *Sitz-im-Leben* that might
not have permitted the understanding or appreciation of an explicit monotheism. Theological reflection, however, at a remove of several centuries
in the evolution of belief, can look back to the most primitive levels of
extant traditions and find there the origins of its belief. Within a theological perspective, the earliest formulations are then seen as obscure, primitive, and somehow dense prehensions that find expression in the context of
human culture and understanding as mediated by fractional and fragmented symbols. The density and obscurity of these symbols serve as a
seedbed for the later fertilization by a deepened awareness. The fruit of
such fertilization is both a clarification of belief and a deepened understanding of the prior obscurities. The evolution of culture and history at

each step in the historical process provides a new *Sitz-im-Leben* and a renewed understanding of the revelation.*

Needless to say, while much of the work of theological elaboration is carried on at a conscious level, much is effected at an unconscious level as well. The process involves preserving certain elements of the tradition and allowing other elements to fade into the obscurity of history. In ancient cultures the selection and transmission were primarily oral. This was certainly the case in the early patriarchal traditions, since it was not until the beginning of the first millennium B.C. that the tradition assumed written form. The point has often been made that writing in antiquity served as a crutch for memory rather than as a substitute. The Greeks committed Homer to memory, and the Romans, Virgil. The practice of memorizing traditional texts has always been prominent in the East, even in very recent times. The Talmud was not committed to writing until nearly the Middle Ages, and the Koran was transmitted orally until well after Mohammed's death. The Rig-veda, of course, was composed in the second millennium and transmitted by oral means alone until at least the fifth century B.C. and may not actually have been put in writing until the fourth century A.D., when Sanskrit literature enjoyed a renaissance.

Usually the style of the medium was poetic, again as a mnemonic aid, but there were also certain legal and liturgical codes in prose. Legal corpora tended to take a formulary style—for instance, the Hebrew Book of the Covenant, the Ten Commandments, the Code of Hammurabi, and the laws of Sumeria and Assyria. It is probable that a period of prose transmission usually preceded translation into verse. Despite its usual poetic form, oral tradition had a decidedly didactic character. This was especially true of legal and liturgical transmissions, but it was also a prominent feature of poetical songs and tales. Oral literature, as demonstrated in the poems of Hesiod, the didactic poems of Mesopotamia, Aesop's fables, the parables of Jesus, or the rabbinical Haggadah, had a directly pedagogical intention. Thus, superfluous elements tended to disappear, and only elements that served some positive pedagogical function, in terms of either emotional appeal or intellectual understanding, were retained.

There is no doubt that the oral tradition tended to include elements of folklore. Every noteworthy figure—king, warrior, or prophet—had an accretion of legends about him. Frequently, the accumulation of folklore obscures the nucleus of historical truth. Fortunately, the data from com-

---

*It is important to note that the process of theological elaboration is distinct from that of faith, although in fact the former presupposes the latter. The problem of faith, however, does not concern us here. Theological elaboration pertains to a revelation accepted in and through faith. Faith, then, justifies it, but with or without faith our psychological understanding of it should not change.

parative mythology, philological and linguistic analysis, and archeological investigation make it possible to distinguish legend from history. The circumstances for establishing the historicity of the traditions in early Israel are quite good. The Israelite traditions belonged to an established nation with strong tribal, familial, and cultic ties that would have demanded that oral documentation be validated. Further, writing was known throughout the patriarchal period, and it is well known that the reliability of oral tradition in times when writing and written documents exercised control over transmission is considerably greater than in situations in which the influence of writing was slight. The discovery of many inscriptions in the Phoenician alphabet in Palestine, Syria, and Cyprus dating between 1200 and 900 B.C. indicates the currency of this script among the early Israelites. Other inscriptions suggest that the same alphabet was known in Palestine as early as 1700 B.C. In addition to proto-Canaanite script, Accadian and Ugaritic cuneiform were known to Palestinian sedentary Canaanites and nomads of the fifteenth century B.C.

Selection in the Tradition

The transmission of the tradition into written form was an exceedingly complex process. It is apparent from study of the earliest written sources of Israelite religious traditions that they are essentially conservative. Ancient Oriental scribes tended to compile rather than to eliminate divergent material in their various sources. The documents issuing from this approach, J and E, were thus additive rather than subtractive. They certainly show some significant divergences, but these reflect maximum variation. Some of the more striking differences undoubtedly reflect divergent traditions, both of which were incorporated, first into J and E respectively, and later into the compilation. As a result, oral transmission tends to be more consistent and logical than written transmission, in that by constantly refining and sifting its material it includes and transmits only that which is consistent with the main body and ideology of the tradition.

The influences that select and control the content of the tradition in the course of its evolution are complex. Unquestionably, part of the process is carried on at unconscious levels. It would be arbitrary to suggest that significant events are repressed out of the evolving tradition, in the absence of any supporting evidence and in the face of demonstrable tendencies in the opposite direction. At the same time, there is an apparent selectivity of the material of the tradition and a cathectic reinforcement of the content that serves as the object of belief. It is striking in surveying the history of Israelite traditions how frequently and consistently Yahweh is cast in the role of protector, guide, liberator, and father. He does battle on behalf of Israel and protects her from her enemies. Perhaps the dominant themes of the religion of Israel center on the liberation from Egypt and the subsequent desert experience. It was the hand of Yahweh that freed Israel from bondage and miraculously guided and protected her through the wanderings of the desert years. These events pervaded the consciousness of the Jewish people and won their peculiar psychic force by reason of their intense resonance with deep and in large part unconscious motivations. The complex events of the exodus responded to very central needs in the soul of Israel. If we extrapolate from the inner significance of the bondage and the desert wanderings, they symbolize the ever-present threats of loss, deprivation, separation, and abandonment. They stand for and call forth the most profound and powerful anxieties of human existence, at a thinly veiled remove from the *Angst zum Tode*. To think of these fundamental anxieties only as forms of castration anxiety is at once insufficiently penetrating, overly reductive, and precariously theoretical. The classical analytic appraisal of castration anxiety is probably related to this level of human experience, but the experience itself transcends that conceptualization and calls for additional and more penetrating understanding.

Yahweh

Beyond all doubt, Yahweh stands forth as the preeminent safeguard against such anxieties. In the desert, he guided and fed the people. In the struggle for survival, he became the warrior god—the wars of Israel were the wars of Yahweh. Perhaps a decisive influence in the evolution of monotheism was the idea of a god who was not tied to one place, like the gods of Canaan, but moved from place to place with the tribe in its nomadic wanderings. For the patriarchs, God was attached to the people; he was "God of the Fathers," with whom a special covenant had been formed. He was thus different from the proliferation of pagan gods which Israel knew at every stage of its existence. For the patriarchs the question of the existence of a single deity beyond whom there were no others was not relevant. Even the more abstract and generalizing tendency of Mosaic formulation and revelation of the name of Yahweh does not bring with it the full sense of unequivocal monotheism. Only in the prophets do the previously ambiguous monotheistic themes become unconditional. Elias puts the power of the living god to the test against the impotence of the Ba'al (3 Kings 18); Amos proclaims Yahweh as the god of all nations (Amos 1:3–15); and Deutero-Isaiah proclaims the unity and the universality of the deity (Isaiah 41–45). In this evolution, it is important to recognize that the deepened awareness of later theological reflection was able to return to earlier formulations and to find within their ambiguity elements that would support more evolved concepts. In this manner, an inner consistency developed within the evolving patterns of realized belief.

Thus, the evolution of the Israelite concept of monotheism stems from a multiplicity of influences: the unconscious needs and anxieties of the people of Israel, the complex aspects of their peculiar economic and social existence, the determinants of the matrix of human values that constituted their unique culture, and the patterns of historical interaction that swirled about them, setting off the powerful forces at work in preserving their integrity as a nation from the cultural and military onslaughts of neighboring peoples.

It has been my primary concern in this chapter to explore the historical aspects of the evolution of monotheism. I suggest that the religious awareness of Israel went through a process of continuous evolution, dating from the earliest recognizable strata of prehistory. The concept of pure monotheism was not self-consciously asserted until the age of the prophets. The Mosaic revelation must be regarded as a significant point in this progression. It represents a significant discontinuity within continuity, as frequently occurs in human noetic evolution. In Teilhard's (1959) terms, it represents a point of conjunction of complexification and convergence.

The interesting point, of course, is the extent to which Moses himself was a contributor to or a determiner of this evolution toward a higher and more sophisticated religious apperception. The question is difficult in that later historical attribution of religious teaching to Moses was a literary device for expressing or asserting the religious authenticity of the teaching. It seems likely that much of so-called Mosaic doctrine is a later redaction of pre-Mosaic Hebrew tradition that was attributed to Moses to mark its acceptance as authentic tradition. We can assume that in some degree Moses brought new insight and a new synthesis. At the same time, there is real doubt as to precisely what the Mosaic contribution may have been. Even the relatively lucid texts of Deuteronomy must be regarded as a much later redaction and much later in origin. The Mosaic synthesis was only questionably an advance toward unequivocal monotheism. In terms of theological awareness, it is almost a secondary issue that the role of Yahweh was not much different from that of the "God of the Fathers, 'El Shaddai." It is likely, indeed, that the influences of Egyptian monotheism were at work in some fashion, but they seem relatively remote. It is also clear that the theology of Yahweh is not that of Aten. In addition, the Egyptian influences were much more diversified than might have been anticipated if they had been spread through the efforts of one man—even a Moses.

Specifically in terms of Freud's historical suppositions, our review of the evolution of Israelite religious traditions suggests that his hypothesis—that a pure Egyptian monotheism was imposed on the Jewish people as a replacement for their primitive polytheism, which was subsequently repressed and later emerged as the worship of Yahweh—cannot be maintained in the face of contemporary views of biblical history. A more realistic view suggests that the seminomadic Hebrews derived their religious traditions from Mesopotamian roots, evolving the worship of a specific deity by each clan from a polytheistic matrix of belief. The emergence of Moses on this scene was a brilliant moment of religious insight and perhaps revelation. But the monotheism of Moses remains ambiguous and presents itself as continuous with the extant context of Hebraic belief. Moreover, the moral code that accompanies the Yahwistic formulas of Mosaic doctrine has stronger parallels in non-Egyptian sources. It is important to note, however, that these formulas are consistent with the explicit and unambiguous monotheism that is expressed in later redactions of the tradition.

The upshot of these reflections is that a divergence between oral and written tradition cannot realistically be maintained. Freud supposed that the people of Israel rejected the strict monotheism of Moses and repressed it in a period of historical latency, only to have the repressed return later. By this account, the authors of the written tradition were anxious to deny earlier religious doctrine, but it remained vital in the oral tradition. All the relevant historical indices contradict this formulation. It seems, rather, that the written tradition was overly conservative and operated so as to preserve the essential historicity and validity of the tradition.

PSYCHIC ASPECTS

The concept of the one and only god who created and ruled the universe was the product of a long and complex evolutionary process with multiple determinants. Those significant to a psychological perspective derive from the interaction of intrapsychic aspects of individual belief with the societal forces that shape and control the individual's response to the demands of religious commitment. The process has both intrapsychic and sociocultural components that must be understood in order to grasp the dynamic significance of the evolution of the Israelite religious tradition.

The inner workings of this process, it should be clear, are quite independent of its religious or theological significance. Within the context of belief, they represent the intervention of divine action in human history and the revelation of divine wisdom in human thought. Their story is the *Heilsgeschichte,* the record of Yahweh's saving presence among his people. In this context, they represent the most sublime reach of human experience and realization. With or without belief, they demand a profundity of understanding commensurate with their sublime reality.

Israelite Belief as Superego Projection

We have already had occasion to note that the Israelite community of the patriarchal era was heir to religious concepts that emerged from the Mesopotamian milieu. By the end of the second millennium B.C. the conception of a personal relationship between God and man was well established. This relationship was intricately involved with notions of personal responsibility, personal fault, and personal guilt. The divinity was

the proponent of a moral order and a moral law. Further, the character of
the divine-human relationship was a function of the individual's adherence
to the prescriptions of the moral code. By personal fault, he estranged
himself from God. Only by confessing his guilt before God could he be
reinstated in divine favor. The injunction to obey the laws rested specifically
on an appeal to the will of Yahweh, a feature unique to Israelite morality.

That Yahweh thus became the guarantor of a moral order tempts us to
consider him as a projection of the superego. The emergence of the
superego as an operative intrapsychic structure is essential to civilization
and is part of the mechanism of renunciation of instinct that is implicit in the
evolution of culture. As Anna Freud ([1937] 1973) has pointed out, the
superego emerges as an ally of the ego in the ego's defensive struggle with
instincts. The upsurge of libidinal and aggressive instincts is a constant
threat to the integrity of the ego and is the common human peril—modified
and modulated by the accretion of adaptational demands implicit in the
evolution of culture, perhaps, but a real component of human existence at
all phylogenetic levels. The threat is a challenge to the integrity of the ego,
for the emergence of instinct bespeaks a regression equivalent to the
dissolution of ego-organization.

The existence of a divine being who incorporates and represents the
demands of instinctual renunciation and restraint gives the ego a powerful
ally indeed. Dynamically, then, the character of Yahweh can be seen not
only in relation to threats of loss and abandonment but also in relation to an
entirely different set of anxieties that are endogenous, stemming from the
most basic human drives.

The opposite side of the coin, of course, is that the alliance of divine and
human superegos reinforces the mechanisms of superego anxiety. The
anxiety of conscience and the sense of guilt are not simply projections, since
the institutionalization of morality in terms of the divine relationship does
not suspend superego functioning. But conscience and guilt acquire a
further level of significance in terms of the personal aspect of the individual's
relation to the will of Yahweh.

The projection of the superego upon the figure of God cannot be regarded
as simply a sadistic one. If one looks only at the punitive aspects of guilt
feelings, it is relatively easy to regard the effect of religious belief as
reinforcing superego sadism. But the mechanism also serves adaptational
goals. The reinforcement of achieved renunciation results in part in an
increase of self-esteem and thereby serves narcissistic objectives. One
cannot simply divorce ego and superego interests in this regard, for in many
respects they share a common interest. Ego-interest is presumably reality
oriented, and the congruence of superego and ego interests lies in the realm
of reality testing. To be sure, the demands of morality may violate reality
and thus represent neurotic demands of the superego, but this is an
empirical conclusion and cannot be presumed.

Nor can the supposition be supported that all guilt is effectively neurotic guilt or that it represents superego sadism. The superego and ego are allies and reinforce each other across broad areas of normal psychic functioning. Even as depression is often not simply a matter of superego aggression but may involve loss of self-esteem within the ego, so the phenomenon of guilt may reflect not only superego accusations but also a realistic appraisal of moral failure by the ego, acting primarily in terms of its intrinsic reality function.

Consequently, the institutionalization of the divine figure as proposer and guarantor of the moral order can be seen as a creative effort to reinforce and sustain the more highly organized and integrated adaptational concerns. These concerns depend in large measure on the capacity of the ego for adaptive symbolic organization of experience. We must not lose sight, however, of the relation of these adaptive concerns to the fundamental sources of anxiety—instinctive disruption as well as external threat and existential anxiety.

The religious enterprise, then, must be seen in its existential and adaptive context. From the point of view of intrapsychic dynamics, authentic religious inspiration serves a uniquely integrative function. As Heinz Hartmann (1939) observes:

> The continued influence on the human mind and the synthetic achievement of religions rest on their integrative imagery and on their being tradition-saturated, socially unifying wholes which are fed by the contributions of all the three mental institutions [id, ego and superego], and provide a pattern, accessible to many people, for satisfying the demands of all these three institutions. Religions are the most obvious attempt to cope both with these mental institutions and with social adaptation (through forming communities) by means of synthesis. (p. 79)

It is interesting from this point of view that the god of the ancient Hebrews must be seen, as a projection of the maternal as well as the paternal image. He is not only a god of power and majesty, punishing those who disobey his law, but also a loving god, protecting and caring for his people, feeding and guiding them. He is a jealous god, but slow to anger and merciful.

It has recently been argued that Freud's conception of religion was filiocentric rather than patrocentric (Bakan 1966). His image of God was that of the punishing father projected by the infantile fantasy of the son. He made no room for the possibility that the paternity of God may be a projection of man's own paternity—the ideal of human fatherhood raised to an exalted level.

Israelite Monotheism

In the context of the emergence of Israelite monotheism, it seems very likely that the concepts of the fatherhood of God and his uniqueness stand in close psychological relationship. The Hebrew traditions preserve a distinctly familial flavor. And, true to the religious heritage of Mesopotamia, the relation between God and man is the personal relationship between father and son: "Thou art my son, this day I have begotten thee." Thus, Israel is the chosen son, and between Israel and Israelite there obtained a bond of communal participation and identification that strengthened the individual's sense of personal relationship while it enriched his sense of communal identity.

The God of the Israelites, then, responds to the most basic human concerns, needs, and anxieties. But to see this as the sum and substance of Israelite religion is to miss its most significant aspect. Even the remnants of the earliest strata of the tradition preserved in the Genesis redaction of the creation myth place men on center stage. They express the inner striving of the mythic consciousness to search out the meaning of its own existence. Man is the culmination of the divine creative effort and is appointed to rule over the universe. He therefore stands in special relation to God.

It is interesting that Hebrew belief did not include a clearly developed notion of immortality. It was impossible for the Hebrew mind to conceive of the *ruach*, or spirit of man, existing without his body. The distinctions that later Greek thought produced had no place in the Hebrew conception of living man as a concrete totality. The concept of afterlife is simply absent from the earlier books of the Old Testament. References to the restoration of Israel (Ezekiel 37:1–14) or other references to the servant of Yahweh (Isaiah 53:10–12) cannot be taken as expressions of a doctrine of personal return to life. The belief in personal resurrection emerges with startling abruptness in the Maccabean period (2 Maccabees 7:9, 11, 23), and there only in reference to the just.

The Search for Meaning

It would seem reasonable, therefore, to question whether the loss complex can sustain the weight of explaining the evolution of Israelite monotheism. Understanding of religious dynamism must be cast in the more evolved contemporary theory of ego functioning. The conception of religion as a neurotic adaptation to infantile wishes then shifts to that of a more positively adaptive function of the ego. There can be no doubt that the functional complex of loss and restitution is part of the motivational gestalt. The further question, as yet unresolved, is whether the religious disposition also reflects a primary autonomous dynamism of the ego directing itself to a more integral and adaptive condition.

It is not immediately apparent that the primary role of the ego in this context is equivalent to the restitutive phase of the loss complex, which is undoubtedly a creative and adaptive effort that is phenomenologically indistinguishable from a primary effort of the ego. Differentiating them depends on whether a prior experience of loss is an integral part of the process. At the same time, it is undeniable that the religious quest for meaning and its contribution to man's emergent sense of identity serve specific narcissistic objectives.

The picture that emerges from these reflections is of the development of man's religious enterprise as an adaptive effort of the ego in the face of the multiple and fundamental challenges to its integrity and vitality. There is a sense in which the ultimate stake, from a psychic point of view, is the integration and preservation of the individual's sense of integrity and identity. The religious concern may serve as a vital psychological force that supports the individual in his attempts at self-definition and realization. As Erikson (1959) has observed:

All religions have in common the periodical childlike surrender to a Provider or providers who dispense earthly fortune as well as spiritual health; the demonstration of one's smallness and dependence through the medium of reduced posture and humble gesture; the admission in prayer and song of misdeeds, of misthoughts, and of evil intentions; the admission of inner division and the consequent appeal for inner unification by divine guidance; the need for clearer self-delineation and self-restriction; and finally, the insight that individual trust must become a common faith, individual mistrust a commonly formulated evil, while the individual's need for restoration must become part of the ritual practice of many, and must become a sign of the trustworthiness of the community. (pp. 64–65)

From the point of view of theological concerns, the intrapsychic dynamics of the worship of Yahweh with which we have concerned ourselves here are neutral. They neither assert nor depend upon any existential conclusions regarding the divine being. We can say only that the belief of Israel was in Yahweh as the one true God who acts in nature and in history. Nor does the argument anywhere contradict the theological insight that finds within these inner mechanisms of the mind the immanence and the presence of the inspiring god.

The psychological argument, however, carries us forward to the frontier between the adaptive functions of the ego and its interaction with the religious community. There is no area of man's adaptation that is more inextricably social or communal than his religious concern. Understanding of the religious enterprise is incomplete without consideration of the interplay between the individual believer and the community of believers. The interplay of communal forces and mechanisms with intrapsychic dynamics constitutes the matrix out of which the religious phenomenon emerges, so that the sense of religious identity is irrevocably a sense of community in belief. Our consideration, therefore, remains incomplete for the present.

Part 3

RELIGION IN PSYCHOANALYTIC PERSPECTIVE

6. DEVELOPMENTAL ASPECTS OF
RELIGIOUS EXPERIENCE

As recent psychoanalytic research has suggested, partly as a result of unresolved conflictual aspects of his own personality and partly as a result of a relatively limited conceptual frame of reference, Freud left us a limited conceptualization of religious experience. The two primary criticisms that have been leveled against Freud's view of religion are that he based it on the notion of the internalization and reexternalization exclusively of a paternal imago—derived from the vicissitudes of the father-son oedipal relationship, with its inherent conflict and ambivalence—and that he provided an account of religious experience that looks in a rather limited and prejudicial fashion at the more infantile dimensions and derivatives of religious experience.

Besides the determinants already suggested, a very obvious factor contributing to this limitation of Freud's view was the one suggested by Pfister (Meng and Freud 1963), namely, that Freud simply had little experience with the broad spectrum of religious involvement. His own religious experience was highly colored by dynamic inputs from his own childhood, and his attempts to educate himself about religious phenomena tended to emphasize the occult, superstitious, or relatively primitive forms of religious experience.

The argument I will be pursuing here takes its point of departure from the observation that Freud's religious conceptualization was apparently confined to one segment of man's religious experience. Further, I contend that the segment of religious experience which Freud chose to emphasize reflects a particular background of genetic derivatives and a particular set of developmental achievements. In the subsequent history of psychoanalysis, the developmental perspective has become extended and elaborated in ways that now allow us to have a more amplified view of developmental experience and its role in a variety of forms of adult psychological and cultural expression. It is my contention that man's religious experience in its broad variety and many levels of expression bespeaks the derivatives and transformations of the residues of all levels of his developmental experience. At each phase of the developmental progression, issues are generated and resolved that provide the inherent structures and dynamic residues that can then be transformed into forms of religious experience (Faber 1975).

THE DEVELOPMENTAL SCHEMA

My objective is to sketch out a developmental typology or schema based on psychoanalytic parameters within which the full range of religious behavior and experience may be conceptualized. This attempt cannot in any terms be definitive, but I hope to suggest a line of argument and investigation that may in future bear fruit.

Before proposing the schema, it may be useful to specify some of the implications inherent in such an approach. An appeal to a developmental framework makes the assumption that the phases of the process are in some sense related to the normal and general experience of children. Thus the phases of the schema will have to be tested against the emergence of developmental parameters in children, particularly as they are reflected in religious ideation and experience. The phases provide an epigenetic sequence; successive phases of the process create, work through, and resolve certain developmental vicissitudes that provide the basis for maturational potentialities. The developmental achievements of each phase contribute to the potentiality for growth, maturation, differentiation, integration, and stabilization of elements of the adult personality. At the same time, the success of this process depends on the resolutions of previous phases. Thus, when the process is considered as a whole, the developing personality is a composite of its successive developmental achievements and their more or less successful integration, on the one hand, and specific residual deficits and archaic remnants reflecting earlier developmental difficulties and the persistence of unresolved elements from one or more developmental strata, on the other hand.

Certain aspects of the child's developmental experience seem particularly relevant for the shaping of his religious experience and ultimately for his experience of relationship to God. At the most rudimentary level, the child's early experiences of "mirroring" in interaction with the mother provide the basis for important elements in the structuring of his concept of God. In his experiences of the mother as a loving and caring presence, in nursing, and in the mother's participation in the act of mirroring by which the child finds himself narcissistically embraced, admired, recognized, and cherished, he finds a symbiotic union with the mother that can serve as the basis for an evolving sense of trust, acceptance, and security.

As Rizzuto (1979) has observed, the need for this kind of narcissistic mirroring is never entirely lost but rather evolves during the course of life.

The rudiments of the mirroring phase of infantile experience may be distilled into the person's experience of his relationship to God. If the mirroring has been defective, he may enter further stages of life with a basic sense of being cut off or lost, or he will defensively elaborate a sense of his own omnipotence, a feeling of being *like* God that substitutes for the lost sense of being *with* God.

To the extent that the child is able to pass beyond the mirroring phase to a stage of dependence on an idealized maternal imago, his notion of God can be gradually shaped around this idealizing experience and thus further elaborated with fantasy. These aspects of the child's emerging religious experience are both derivative of and intertwined with the child's ongoing experience of the real mother.

> At the moment of their encounter it becomes clear that the child is small and needs the adult and that the adult is powerful and "knows" the child internally. Now the fate of the child and the God representation alike depend on how the two characters—mother and child, God and child—are seen and the real and fantasied nature of their interaction. (Rizzuto 1979, 188)

The parental influence continues to play a role in the development of the child's religious thinking. There seems little doubt that the influence of the family in general plays an important part in the development of religious experience. The close relationship between family and religious structure has been frequently noted (Vergote 1969). The family is ultimately the model for both religious relationships and values. The parents' religious attitudes, behavior, and even language are immediately transmitted to the child. In addition, the patterns of protection, well-being, and authority inherent in family structure find their natural extension and elaboration in religion.

The child's earliest imaginings about God are cast almost exclusively in the image of the parents. However, it should be noted that additional representational components may derive from other significant objects in the immediate family context (grandparents, siblings) or the broader contexts of extrafamilial social and cultural influence (priests, nuns, ministers, rabbis). The confusion between parental and divine images is at first almost total. From about the age of three or four years, the child has no difficulty in imagining a God. But the universe of the divine is filled with fantasy and fascination, not unlike the world of fairy tales. And from the beginning, the child's image of God is colored with ambivalence; while there may be feelings of trust and dependence on a kind, loving, and protecting God, there are also elements of awe and fear. This ambivalence can be colored by the child's emerging experience with the mother. Depending on its quality, the child experiences the mother more or less ambivalently. She is experienced on the one hand as good—that is, as

providing love, protection, and nurturance, the mother with whom the
child feels a sense of security and trustful reliance. But there is also the bad
mother, who withholds, punishes, and is not available to satisfy the child's
infantile wishes and needs; she becomes an object of fear. In the infantile
terms of the child's fantasy, the fear is often of destruction and of being
devoured. The child's fantasies at this level are highly oral in character, in
both their satisfying nurturing components and their fears of being orally
devoured and incorporated. The history of religion provides numerous
examples of this split in the image of the mother, particularly in the form of
benign and loving mother-goddesses as opposed to threatening and de-
vouring goddesses.

To the extent that the child's early experience with the mother has
tipped the balance in the direction of more positive and gratifying experiences, a basic sense of trust is laid down that provides a foundation for the
later development of a sense of trusting faith in the relationship to God.
Where early infantile experience is discolored with insecurity, uncertainty,
or anxiety, the foundation is laid for a basic mistrust that can contaminate
and distort the later experience of God.

The succeeding phase of development, described by Freud in libidinal
terms as the anal phase, particularly its latter, anal-sadistic portion, is a
time for the conjunction of a number of important developmental parameters. Besides the familiar struggles over anal control and the related issues
of autonomy and independence, there are the progressive vicissitudes of
separation and individuation as well as the dawning of Piaget's symbolic
function and the emergence of emotional object constancy. Sometime
during this phase the child discovers that objects in the world are made by
people, thus giving rise to an initial and rudimentary notion of anthropomorphic causality. Soon the endless questions begin about how things are
made or where they came from. The answer that God made the world or
the sky can be envisioned only in anthropomorphic terms—God is a person
who is big enough, powerful enough, to make very large things. Before
long, the child runs afoul of the notion of God as the uncaused cause, the
cause that nobody has made but simply is. The child's mind is abuzz with
theories, imaginings, and fantastic ideas. God becomes a problem in that
he looms as someone powerful and important, to whom adults pay respect
and reverence, yet who cannot be seen, talked to, or touched. Yet he rules
everything and is everywhere. The child has little recourse but to imagine
this God in terms of the most formidable human beings he knows—that is,
his parents. For this purpose he tends at first to use both father and
mother, but increasingly the father as he grows older; this development is
reinforced by the extent to which the father becomes the more powerful,
aggressive or punitive parental figure.

As the child begins to move beyond the age of oedipal concerns and
involvement, he gradually becomes aware of the distinction between God

and his parents. His view of his parents becomes gradually more realistic, more attuned to their limitations and inherent incapacities as human beings. He begins to discover with some disappointment the loss and contamination of his narcissistic ideals. He finds that his parents do not know everything and are not able to do everything; their power to influence the world around them seems to him to be increasingly problematic and constrained. The child becomes more and more aware of the faults and contradictions that characterize his parents, both father and mother. At this stage, in some sense he begins to salvage the narcissistic investment in an omnipotent ideal by resorting to a heavenly Father, who may indeed be all-powerful and perfect, as his earthly parents are not. This is also the period for the emergence of the family romance, with its investment of the imagined parents of the romanticized family with idealistic empowerment and perfectability. Just as with the idealized picture of God, the romantic parents are envisioned as embodying characteristics of strength and virtue that stand in stark contrast to the looming imperfections of the real parents.

The object relations that provide the basis from which the child derives his representation of God can shift their positions in regard to the relation to God in a variety of ways. There may be direct continuity between the parental image and the God image, so that they can be used more or less equivalently or as substitutes in the face of defensive pressures. Or they may be directly opposed, so that they become antagonistic, usually reflecting underlying processes of defensive splitting. God in this scenario may be utterly good and protecting, while the parents are regarded as mean, ungiving, or unloving. The opposite—idealized parents and devalued God—can take shape as well. Or the good and bad qualities of both God and parents may be seen in various combinations (Rizzuto 1979).

But however important are these growing realizations in the child's mind, the transition to a heavenly Father is strongly influenced by the attitudes and behavior of his parents. The extent to which they in their own religious faith and conviction recognize the existence of and their personal relationship with a transcendent God plays an important role in the child's evolving conceptions. To a child of four or five it is a significant revelation, for example, that his own father and mother had fathers and mothers of their own, just as he does. The myth of the absolute or omnipotent parent thus begins to crumble, which can be disillusioning or disconcerting to the child's mind.

As the dissociation of the image of the father from the image of God evolves, the child's notion of God shifts to a more universal one that is often cast in pragmatic terms. God is the maker of everything in the world, or he is the protective power of good, fighting against the evil personified by the devil. As Gesell (1947) has noted, to a child of this age God is envisoned in terms of his relationship to the everyday world and in terms of specific and practical questions. The child asks what God looks like, whether he is a man, what he does, and where he lives. He wants to know if God can be called on the telephone, or whether he makes cars. Some children are at the same time very aware of God's presence and are even afraid that God watches them and sees whatever they do.

To the child of six, God is the creator of the world, of all the animals and the beautiful things in it. He is able to accept these ideas even though he soon becomes more skeptical. He likes to listen to Bible stories over and over. God has become more real for him, and the child is beginning to develop a relationship with him. Consequently, prayers become more important, particularly insofar as he feels a growing sense of confidence that God will listen to and answer them. At the same time, his evil counterpart also takes shape in the child's mind in the form of the devil. In an earlier era, the notion of the devil was more immediate in the minds of Christian believers and became a much more vivid and dramatic focus for the child's nameless anxieties and phobic concerns.

The child's notion of God at this stage of his development is essentially anthropomorphic. He sees God as a human agent and envisions his actions in and on the world as forms of human action. Increasingly, however, his notion of God's activity undergoes a transformation in conjunction with his representation of God. Early on, the anthropomorphism is direct and specific: God lives in a house, he eats, sleeps, and so on. During latency, children still tend to think of God in markedly anthropomorphic terms, but these are qualified to the extent that God is regarded as somehow different from other men in that he lives with the angels in heaven and cannot be seen or touched by ordinary men. However, as the child approaches puberty, more spiritualized notions of God come to predominate. Certainly, by this time children's notions of God seem to lose the fairytale, magical, and fantastical qualities of the notions held by oedipal-age children.

The anthropomorphic characteristics of the child's view of God are also expressed in his fantasy of how God acts in the world. As Piaget has described, children between the ages of six and eleven tend to explain nature and the world by an appeal to animism or to some human form of technology. When the child begins to question the perfection and omnipotence of his parents, some of the qualities formerly attributed to adults can be transposed to the divine being. The child first imagines God along the lines of a specifically human model and thinks of God in human terms. However, from time to time the dissociation between God and all other men breaks this pattern, so that the child's view of God becomes increasingly cast in symbolic terms. This symbolic quality of the child's thinking reaches operative expression only in adolescence.

In general, the child's ambivalence toward the representation of God, expressed particularly in terms of reverence, awe, and fear, increases with age. God is viewed not simply as one who is benevolent and good; his almighty power is to be both revered and feared. The child progresses from a naive trust in God to a fuller understanding of his majesty, transcendence, and power, which are to be approached only with fear and reverence.

Piaget has emphasized the essentially egocentric quality of the young child's thinking. It is only with the emergence of object relationships, the establishment of object constancy, and the working through of oedipal involvements that reality increasingly impinges on the child's awareness and draws him away from this egocentricity to an involvement with objects. Only gradually does the child come to accept the existence of other people as centers of activity and influence. To the child, the concept of God remains for a considerable time more or less immersed in his affective self-centeredness. The persistence of this infantile self-centeredness together with its narcissistic components can have profound effects on the development of his representation of God and can give rise in adult life to severe religious conflicts or even to religious rebellion in the form of atheism. The religious truth of the child appears to adult eyes as mere infantilism, so that the adult who has not been able to grow beyond this level of religious experience has no recourse but to shake off these infantile residues.

The same narcissistic trends that give rise to infantile egocentricity are also at the root of the forms of magic so often seen in infantile religiosity. Piaget, for example, has studied the child's sense of immanent justice. A child of six, for example, believes that a wrong deed will be punished automatically by some catastrophe. This belief in immanent justice is reinforced by his animistic belief in humanlike intentions behind events in the world. This animistic sense of intentionality is often directly translated into religious terms, particularly in children who have received enough religious education to have a sense of the immanence of God. They thus might attribute immanent justice to the will of God and connect this to their belief in God and his providence. The belief in immanent justice diminishes with age, so that by the time of puberty it is practically nonexistent, at least in children raised in Western cultures.

It is worth noting that belief in immanent justice nonetheless persists on an unconscious level in many religious believers. Particularly under certain forms of stress and in the face of great anxiety, there may be a revivification of intense unconscious guilt and a regression in superego functioning that have strong implications for the individual's attitude toward God. In such individuals, this dynamic is recognizably pathological, although the Freudian argument, as we have seen, tended to regard it as typical. In a child's mind, however, these attitudes merely represent a mixture of emerging religious beliefs with magical beliefs.

Similar manifestations of religious attitudes can be found in primitive religions, but in the child they remain open to gradual purification and modification during the rest of the developmental sequence. The persistence of such beliefs can be identified in animistic beliefs in divine protection or divine punitive intentions. They may also find expression in belief in the causal efficacy of prayers, particularly in the expectation that God will hear and answer the petitioner's prayers. Sacramental signs and rituals in particular provide an arena in which such magical expectations may play themselves out. A child often believes that the sacraments have some automatic and magical effect that is produced independently of the recipient's consciousness. The residues of such magical belief can be identified even in adolescence. This trend in religiosity can be reinforced by the natural obsessionality of the latency-age children, as evidenced in their frequent development of obsessional practices, for example, repeating certain numbers, counting groups of objects, avoiding cracks in the pavement, and so forth, that reflect a more or less secular form of magical ritualistic behavior that is easily translated into a magical religious form of ritualism.

Adolescence is one of the most crucial periods in the development not only of personality but of religious attitudes and experience as well. In this regard, Rizzuto (1979) has observed that

adolescence confronts the growing individual with a need to integrate a more cohesive and unified self-representation which will permit him to make major decisions about life, marriage, and profession. That developmental crisis, with its intense self-searching and reshuffling of self-images in the context of trying to find a niche in the world for oneself, brings about new encounters with both old and new God-representations. They may or may not lend themselves to belief. (p. 201)

At about the age of twelve or thirteen there is a shift from thinking about God in more or less attributional terms to increasing personalization of the God image. God is specifically God the Savior, God the Father. The notion of God is increasingly interiorized, and God is regarded in primarily subjective attitudes of love, obedience, trust, doubt, fear. This development follows the natural course of affective adolescent development. Thus, the themes and the corresponding God-representations that enunciate the adolescent's experience of religion are heavily laden with his affective needs. Frequently, this highly personalized and subjective God-representation presents a difficulty for the adolescent in integrating it with the more objective attributes proposed by organized religion.

The personalized adolescent image of God is most often cast in terms of a providential father who watches over and guides the adolescent in making his way along the uncertain path of life. Often adolescents attribute to God the qualities they would seek in special and intimate friends—

that is, emphasizing understanding and some form of affective communication. Moreover, the increased titer of narcissism that characterizes adolescent development and influences the ego-ideal in particular at this time plays itself out in the religious sphere as well. The adolescent idealizes his companions and friends as well as the adult figures whom he seeks to imitate and with whom he ultimately wishes to identify. The components of his inner, idealizing narcissism are thus transferred to the object in whom the adolescent seeks the perfection that he himself wishes to possess. Consequently, he is able to attain it by identification.

This idealization affects the God-representation insofar as God is cast in the role of a pure and perfect being. Adolescent boys tend to emphasize these objectively idealized qualities of the God-representation more than girls, who tend to emphasize qualities of loving relationship in connection with the God-representation. God becomes the ideal confidant, who understands everything and responds to the girl's most intimate wishes and needs. The frequent waning of religious experience toward the end of adolescence reflects the diminishing intensity of the narcissistic idealizing process with the adolescent's gradual assimilation of more adult life patterns and commitments. Among Christian groups, the figure of Christ in particular becomes a target for this form of narcissistic idealization and attachment. Where adolescent idealization is not tempered by a greater maturity of judgment and discretion, the figure of Christ can become a superhuman model and a repository for fanatical tendencies.

Adolescence is also a period of increased sexual conflict and guilt. The degree of superego repression and the intensity of guilt can be reinforced by religious prescriptions and ideals. This inherent moralism then carries a sense of sinfulness, which can become such a burden and a narcissistic impediment that it results in a rebellion against religious standards and values. Frequently adolescents find themselves caught between moral laxity and hyperrigid moralism.

Along with these tendencies to moralism and internalization of religious experience, adolescence is also a time of intensifying religious doubt. Doubt is often an expression of the adolescent's need for autonomy in the face of the regressively reactivated pull to dependency on parental objects. For some adolescents the quest for independence can be pursued only through overthrowing and rejecting parental norms and standards. Religion in such cases may become the symbolic repository for parental authority and the corresponding conflicts of continuing dependence. The adolescent who needs to reject authority may find this need penetrating his religious experience and his relation to God as well.

This doubt may be reinforced by adolescent affective turmoil, particularly by conflicts over sexuality. Plagued by sexual conflicts and feelings of guilt, the adolescent may be overwhelmed by shame and insecurity over his inability to live up to lofty religious standards of conduct. Consistent with the continuing influence of parental figures and family milieu, the adolescent's religious crisis often reflects conflicts and tensions between his parents or between them and their children. The result may be a form of rebellion and alienation that not only impedes the adolescent's growth to maturity but corrupts and subverts his further religious development as well.

The resolution of adolescent issues only leads the young believer to the threshold of a religious struggle that he must carry on for the rest of life. In this regard, Vergote (1969) writes:

> But after adolescence the young believer thinks more freely about the meaning of existence. He must make his mental synthesis of the world. He has come to be less centered on himself and is more deliberately committed to human society. This leads him to query the different theories of life with which he meets; he also reflects on the human necessity of having some religious belief and on the significance of institutionalized religion. This new questioning is more objective than earlier doubts had been, and is part of the effort which the adolescent makes to assume personally the religion he has inherited. Man does not acquire true religious faith, that is, a really personal faith recognized in its transcendent finality, before the age of thirty years. Experience has shown that after adolescence the whole religious formation apparently has to undergo revision—not because the child or the adolescent has not hitherto been authentically religious, but because man does not acquire sufficient maturity to make a real personal choice and to recognize reality, before he has become adult. (p. 300)

In terms of the understanding of religious experience, the experience of the adult may come to represent the more or less satisfactory integration of derivatives of all developmental phases. Primitive experiences from archaic developmental levels may be successfully transformed and integrated with later developmental achievements—and thus take on a different significance and a more differentiated symbolic reference. This transformation of function and significance allows us to identify both the original relevance of the archaic symbol and its more evolved, symbolically differentiated and enriched context without reducing their connection to an identity or resorting to the developmentally obtuse formula of repetition. The essence of development lies in the "overcoming" and differential superseding of origins, not in their simple repetition.

At the same time, an epigenetic schema recognizes that development does not take place in linear or blocklike progression. The individual's emerging religious experience may achieve developmental resolution in varying degrees, so that the result is a heterogeneity of relatively mature and relatively archaic elements, stemming from any of the developmental levels and phases. As Rizzuto (1979) comments:

> For the rest of the life cycle the individual will again find himself in need of critical changes in self-representation to adapt to the inexorable advance of the life cycle as well as to new encounters with peers and parental representatives. God—as a representation—may or may not be called in to undergo his share in the changes. Finally, when death arrives, the question of the existence of God returns. At that point, the God-representation, which may vary from a long-neglected preoedipal figure to a well-known life companion—or to anything in between—will return to the dying person's memory, either to obtain the grace of belief or to be thrown out for the last time. (p. 201)

We may draw the lines of the developmental schema along three major dimensions: narcissism, dependence, and faith. In tracing narcissistic phenomena, we will be following the outline originally provided by Kohut (1966, 1971) and subsequently elaborated into a developmental frame of reference by Gedo and Goldberg (1973). The analysis of dependence as a critical aspect of object relationship derives particularly from the formulations of Winnicott (1965, 1971). And the formulations regarding faith, particularly its cognitive-symbolic dimensions, are based on some preliminary work by Fowler (1974) and my own previous work (Meissner 1969).

Narcissistic development starts from a state of primary narcissism, prior to any investment of love in objects outside the self—more exactly, prior to any differentiation between self and objects. The first alteration in this state of unconditional omnipotence is the differentiation between a grandiose self and an idealized parent imago (Kohut 1971). Although this discrimination implies subjective differentiation between self and objects, the latter are conceived as necessary concomitants of the existence of the self, because without them the self is threatened with dissolution. Consequently, the primary anxiety at this level of development is that of catastrophic annihilation.

Further integration of these nuclear narcissistic elements allows for the organization of a cohesive self, which implies that external objects are no longer so critical for the internal organization and maintenance of the self but that their potentialities for gratification have become relatively focused in the service of maintaining the child's self-esteem. Infantile narcissism and its corresponding illusions of omnipotence become focused in the area of sexuality in the form of phallic narcissism. The corresponding danger and narcissistic risk is castration. Thus the primary anxiety no longer has to do with annihilation or impairment of the sense of self but is focused on castration.

Under the developmental stimulus of the formation of the superego, the idealized parental imago is further modified and internalized as the ego ideal. This sets up a potential conflict between the emerging ego and the superego, with its now internalized ideals, so that the pressing danger at this stage of development is moral anxiety based on ego-superego conflict. Later developmental vicissitudes have to do with the gradual metabolism and integration of remnants of infantile narcissism and their transformation into elements of wisdom, empathy, humor, and creativity.

Winnicott describes the child's gradual emergence from a situation of absolute dependence into relative independence. In the beginning, the child's dependence includes symbiotic union with the mother as a necessary component of his psychological health at that stage. Bit by bit the child's dependence on the mother lessens until he is able to attempt some small degree of independent behavior; this gradually leads in the direction of his increasing separation and individuation, a process that has been exhaustively described in Margaret Mahler and her coworkers (1968, 1975). The behavioral descriptions Mahler provides cannot be adequately understood without positing a parallel modification of inner structures and organization of self-representations in the service of integrating a cohesive self that can then sustain the child's emerging sense of autonomy (Meissner 1978a).

In Freud's presentation of the development of religious thinking and particularly of the individual's attitude toward God, he attempts to trace some of the derivation of the God-representation to early infantile experiences, particularly with the parents. Working out of the argument of *Totem and Taboo* (1913), Freud was inclined to regard religious ideas as originating in the residues of primeval, racially inherited memory traces that shaped the individual's unconscious thinking. The child's developmental experience, particularly with the father, served to activate and modify these innate traces so that the childhood image became merged with inherited memory traces of the primal father to form the individual's image of God (Freud 1923b). Freud relates this set of events specifically to the issues of infantile dependence and its prolongation into adult life:

> He therefore harks back to the mnemic image of the father whom in his childhood he so greatly overvalued. He exalts the image into a deity and makes it into something contemporary and real. The effective strength of this mnemic image and the persistence of his need for protection jointly sustain his belief in God. (1933a, 163)

In Freud's view, the ambivalent struggle with the father forms the matrix out of which the religious orientation to God takes shape. With regard to one of his most famous patients, whose religious preoccupation formed a significant part of his obsessional childhood neurosis, Freud (1924) comments on the Wolf Man's identification with the figure of Christ:

> If he was Christ, then his father was God. But the God which religion

forced upon him was not a true substitute for the father whom he had loved and whom he did not want to have stolen from him. His love for this father of his gave him his critical acuteness. He resisted God in order to be able to cling to his father; and in doing this he was really upholding the old father against the new. He was faced by a trying part of the process of detaching himself from his father.

His old love for his father, which had been manifest in his earliest period, was therefore the source of his energy in struggling against God and of his acuteness in criticizing religion. But on the other hand this hostility to the new God was not an original reaction either; it had its prototype in a hostile impulse against his father. . . . The two opposing currents of feeling, which were to rule the whole of his later life, met here in the ambivalent struggle over the question of religion. (p. 66)

This shaping of the image of God does not become static or closed but rather remains open to continuing influences stemming not only from the parents but also from the child's relationship to significant nonparental figures. The detachment from the parents and the growth from infantile dependence to more mature independence are linked with the transformation and gradual evolution of these critical representations. Freud writes:

The course of childhood development leads to an ever-increasing detachment from parents, and their personal significance for the superego recedes into the background. To the imagoes they leave behind there are then linked the influences of teachers and authorities, self-chosen models and publicly recognized heroes, whose figures need no longer be introjected by an ego which has become more resistant. The last figure in the series that began with the parents is the dark power of Destiny, which only the fewest of us are able to look upon as impersonal . . . but all who transfer the guidance of the world to Providence, to God, or to God and Nature, arouse a suspicion that they still look upon these ultimate and remotest powers as a parental couple, in a mythological sense, and believe themselves linked to them by libidinal ties. (Freud 1924, 168)

The dimensions of the development of faith constitute an area in which our grasp is less than certain (Meissner 1969). This phenomenon is an exceedingly complex entity that will not yield readily to simple analysis. We can identify certain elements that relate to parameters of trust and fidelity, but these parameters suggest that the experience involves a complex integration of instinctual (libidinal) and ego functions. Thus the experience of faith entails to a significant degree a cognitive aspect that plays itself out in various forms and levels of symbolic activity and conceptualization.

The major premise of my approach is that a conceptualization of faith requires a developmental perspective because the inherent elements of faith express themselves in quite different ways with considerably different impact and meaning as derivatives of developmental determinants from various levels of the developmental schema. Thus the element of trust, for example, as an inherent constituent of the experience of faith, cannot be envisioned simply as an infantile, narcissistic investment in and dependence on a need-satisfying object; it should be envisioned as spanning a continuum of developmental states in which the elements of trust are progressively modified to represent increasingly mature levels of integration and expression.

Having said this much about the basic parameters of my concern, I have set myself the task of providing a developmental schema for religious experience, realizing that the attempt is bound to be tentative and incomplete. My suggestion can be validated only by further reflection and exploration. For convenience, I will follow the basic line of the developmental approach provided by Gedo and Goldberg (1973). In identifying a series of modes in the organization of religious experience, I am referring not only to aspects of childhood development as such but also to the residues of those developmental levels in adult religious functioning. With this in mind, let us move on to the descriptive specifics of this religious schema, realizing that we set foot on a dark and mysterious continent.

The first mode of religious experience is a primitive and/or deeply regressive state that is dominated by the conditions of primary narcissism. Developmentally, the individual has not yet reached the level of self- and object-differentiation, so that the conditions of symbiosis obtain. The narcissistic experience is one of unconditional omnipotence and absolute dependence. Faith cognition at this level is entirely undifferentiated, functioning in terms of a preconceptual and prelinguistic disposition to accept the conditions of life. This relates to the conditions of basic trust that characterize the symbiotic union of mother and child. The religious experience at this level would presumably involve merging the boundaries between self-representation and God-representation. The sense of self is without cohesion, in a state of undifferentiated diffusion or severe fragmentation. This represents a state of extreme regression, which may take a psychotic form, issuing in delusions of total omnipotence and Godlike grandiosity. It may also express itself as profound and ecstatic mystical experiences involving loss of boundaries, diffusion of the sense of self, and absorption into the divine. While the mechanisms and the level of organization may be similar, it seems reasonable to maintain a distinction between such mystical experiences and regressive psychosis. The vicissitudes of mystical absorption and its dynamics of self-cohesion remain to be clarified, but we cannot assume that they are equivalent to regressive psychotic states. We are able to indicate here only the direction of an evolving set of concepts, to provide a framework for the analysis of religious experience. However, even if we accept this tentative framework, its viability rests on our capacity to resolve the critical questions regarding such ecstatic states. The problem can be stated in simplified form as follows: in terms of a developmental schema, are we to envision mystical states as embodiments of the highest, most differentiated, articulated, structuralized, and integrated attainments of an evolved religious capacity, or do they, on the contrary, represent regressive phenomena that reflect the most infantile levels of developmental fixation, if not aberration?

Mystical experiences are variously described in different religious traditions. Certainly within the Judeo-Christian tradition they share a note of passivity, ineffability, the sense of submissive immersion in the experience of divine love, and the sense of formless fusion with the object of that love. Following Freud's emphasis on the infantile aspects of religious experience, the general analytic perspective has been to describe ecstatic mystical states in terms of the stark polarity of infantile experience, characterized by the sense of objectlessness or fusion in the earliest stages of infantile involvement with the mother, before any differentiation of self and object has taken place. In these regressive terms, then, such states of fusion represent a reactivation of primitive states of symbiotic fusion with the all-good, all-giving, all-nurturing maternal breast.

One of the central difficulties in this approach has been the inability of the analytic conceptual apparatus to articulate a sustained sense of cohesiveness of self and of mature and developed identity in a context in which such mystical states of fusion seem to take place. Within the analytic framework such states involve feeling a loss of ego boundaries and a fusion with the love object. Nonetheless, it is clear that the sense of fusion with the object in mystical states is not the same as the regressive fusion to primary narcissistic union that might occur in states of psychotic regression. Rather, authentic mystical experience (as distinguished from pseudo-mystical or psychotic experience) not only does not undermine or destroy identity but in fact has a powerful capacity to stabilize, sustain, and enrich identity.

Consequently, we will require a new set of categories that allows us adequately to describe this atypical and highly elevated form of transcendent experience without necessarily citing regression as the predominant characteristic. In fact, it seems that object-relations theorists are moving in just this direction. For example, in a recent discussion of optimal or idealized (and therefore mature) love relationships, Kernberg describes the phenomenon of union with the other in terms of the "crossing of boundaries":

In contrast to regressive merger phenomena, which blur self/nonself differentiation, concurrent with crossing the boundaries of the self is the persistent experience of a discrete self and, as well, a step in the direction of identification with structures beyond the self. In this process, there is a basic creation of meaning, of a subjective ordering of the world outside the self, which actualizes the potential structuring of human experience in terms of biological, interpersonal, and value systems. Crossing of the boundaries of self, thus defined, is the basis for the subjective experience of transcendence. Psychotic identifications with their dissolution of self-object boundaries, interfere with the capacity for passion thus defined; in simple terms, madness is not in continuity with passion. (Kernberg 1977, 95)

If we remember that Kernberg's comments address the optimal expression of sexual passion between humans, we can make an analogy to the mystical state. There expansion of the capacity for object relationship allows for a transcendence of the boundaries of self, a crossing-over within the context of loving submission, so that the self becomes immersed in the object or conversely is subsumed by the loving presence of the object, in this instance the object of a divine love. Consequently, the capacity to reach beyond the boundaries of self, to empty out the self, as it were, in the loving embrace of the object, is a transcendent capacity of the psyche to immerse itself in a loving object relationship. This need not in itself be regarded as regressive.

Nonetheless, an ample case can be made for the translation and transcendental expression of infantile and regressive elements in the mystical experience. The important point, however, is that reaching back to the infantile origins of human experience and revitalizing and translating them in this transcendental experience do not simply constitute a regression. The point is put with poetic intensity and utter clarity by Erik Erikson (1962):

> But must we call it regression if man thus seeks again the earliest encounters of his trustful past in his efforts to reach a hoped-for and eternal future? Or do religions partake of man's ability, even as he regresses, to recover creatively? At their creative best, religions retrace our earliest inner experiences, giving tangible form to vague evils, and reaching back to the earliest individual sources of trust; at the same time, they keep alive the common symbols of integrity distilled by the generations. If this is partial regression, it is a regression which, in retracing firmly established pathways, returns to the present amplified and clarified. (p. 264)

Thus the creative regression represents the power of established identity and the mature capacity for relationship to a significant other to recapture the revitalizing sources of psychic potential buried in infantile experience and to relate them, in Erikson's terms, to the rudiments of trust. A mature identity also builds on such roots the synthetic capacity to reintegrate infantile residues into ongoing loving experience. It is this capacity that not only brings such trustful infantile components into the service of maintaining the internal cohesiveness of self and the stability of one's own identity but also makes them a resource with which to transcend the limits of that identity—to cross the boundaries of self and to embrace the love object or to submerge oneself in the loving embrace of a divine object.

In terms of internal organization, this first mode of religious experience is comprised essentially of the rudimentary qualities of objectless states and the functioning of primary autonomous structures without any secondary elaboration or integration. Developmentally we are speaking of the level at which processes of primary internalization and externalization are at work, contributing to the emergence of an elementary differentiation between internal and external, between self and object. In regressive states, however, the basic mechanism becomes incorporation (Meissner 1971, 1978a), by which the distinguishing qualities of the external object are lost. Incorporation blends what has been internalized into an overriding, global sense of primitive narcissistic grandiosity. In contrast, the *unio mystica* may represent a dissolution of the sense of self and a diffusion of the self-representation so that its elements are absorbed into the transcendent and sublimely loved object. This transcendent absorption of object love stands in opposition to psychotic self-absorption.

The second mode of religious experience follows differentiation of a grandiose self from perception of another as an idealized parental imago. This developmental stage implies a more differentiated operation of the processes of introjection and projection. The interplay of these basic mechanisms shapes the emerging experience of the inner and outer worlds —that is, of the introjected grandiose self and its correlate projected in the idealized parental imago.

At this stage idealization of and dependence on the parental imago are essential for sustaining and maintaining the inner cohesion of the self. Vulnerability to fragmentation of the sense of self can be countered only by intensification of narcissistic defensive measures, specifically, regression to grandiose fantasies of unconditional omnipotence. The God-representation at this stage is built on the omnipotence and omniscience of the perfected and idealized imago. The quality of the faith experience is riddled with a sense of utter dependence, a terror of the omnipotence of the godhead, and a superstitious and magical need to placate by ritual and ceremonial.

The primitive fear of separation can be overcome only by illusions of omnipotence and by magical practices. The anally determined issues of submission, the conflicts between autonomy and relative dependence, and the obsessional quality of magical thought processes permeate the religious experience and color the subject's relationship to the image of God.

Religious experience tends to be strongly shaped by elements of animism, based on the operation of projective mechanisms similar to those Freud describes in his account of a demonological neurosis (Freud 1923b). Projective mechanisms are largely put in the service of defending against intense and unresolved ambivalences and the associated narcissistic peril of separation.

In general, the interplay of projective and introjective elements, together with the lack of cohesion in the self, allows for little distinction between fact and fantasy and causes a blurring of the boundaries between natural and supernatural, although there may be a vague, intuitive sense of the numinous. Cognition and affect tend to be confused or fused, with the affective quality of religious experience generally dominant. God is conceived in animistic and magical terms as an omnipotent and omniscient deity. Thoughts about God may be cast in relatively unspecific, preanthropomorphic imagery (for example, in a relatively pananimistic sense of God as a numinous presence and force in all beings), but they are much more likely to be highly concrete, personalized, and marked by anthropomorphic features. Dependence on this God of omnipotence and idealized power is relatively conflicted and is resolved by masochistic submission and superstitious placation. (Incidentally, we can note that much of the theocosmological construction around which Dr. Schreber's delusional system was organized [Freud 1911] seems to have been of this basically narcissistic and grandiose quality.)

The third mode of religious experience is conditioned by the highly significant developmental achievement of the integration of a cohesive self. As a consequence, narcissistic vulnerabilities are no longer cast in terms of danger to the integrity of the self; rather, they are more extrinsically focused in terms of self-esteem, especially in grandiose illusions in the sphere of sexuality.

The mechanisms of introjection and projection are employed at this level by defensive needs to preserve the residues of infantile narcissism; they no longer serve simply to form self- and object-representations but more consistently work to sustain them against regressive pulls and underlying ambivalences. The greater and more consistent delineation between inner and outer worlds allows for increasing differentiation of verifiable facts and claims from speculation or fantasy.

Matters of belief or valuative judgment are determined primarily by an appeal to trusted authority, although in areas of judgment and action the capacity for using resources of inductive and deductive thought processes increases. Where direct perception is exceeded, as in attempts to explain belief systems or causal origins, recourse is taken to mythic explanations that are embossed predominantly with anthropomorphic accounts. These are accepted and asserted on primarily affective or evaluative bases. There is little capacity to entertain more than one myth or conflicts between myths and the authoritative sources that substantiate them. In the face of such conflicts, an appeal is made to intuitive and affective reliance on an authority in preference to one's own experience or judgment.

In general, the quality of belief systems is less magical, in keeping with the increased capacity to differentiate between internal processes and external reality. The concepts they contain are generally concrete in reference and when symbolic tend to be literal and one-dimensional. The constructs that underlie distinctions between the natural and the supernatural and between the "lawful" and "regular" and the "unlawful" and "irregular" have become operative. The major dimensions of religious experience are cast in terms of fear of punishment for transgressions and preoccupation with rectitude and ritual performance. The emphasis on "law and order" and the ongoing tension between autonomy and dependence in this phase reflect the developmental issues of the anal period of psychic development, with its attendant struggles over autonomy, heightened titer of ambivalence, and aggressivized vicissitudes of separation and individuation.

In contrast to the dominant maternal quality of earlier projections of the image of the Deity, at this stage there is a perceptible shift to a more paternal quality of projection, reflecting the underlying castration anxiety and fear of the punitive oedipal father. It seems likely that the religious behavior Freud divined in the case of the "Rat Man" (1909b) can be traced to this level of organization; so can the ritualized ceremonials of the Wolf Man (1918) at points in the progression of his illness when the obsessive-compulsive neurosis was dominant and the obsessional defenses were functioning relatively adequately. It also seems likely that Freud's theory of religious experience and his approach to understanding it are most pertinent to this phase of religious development, with its accretion of elements from the preceding modality.

A fourth mode of religious experience is articulated around the formation and consolidation of the superego. This central developmental achievement brings about critical internal changes that include the formation of the barrier of repression. The internalization of ideals and values means the organization of conscience. Consequently, danger is henceforth experienced mainly as moral anxiety, or as a sense of failure to attain and satisfy the demands of the ego ideal and the internalized value system—whereas previously the child responded to extrinsic threats and to primitive expectations of retaliation. Reality is no longer seen in unilinear terms but rather in terms of its complex differentiation into a variety of spheres and dimensions. This sense of differentiation is highly influenced by the social structures within which the individual finds himself called upon to function—family, school, work, church, peer groups, friendships, and so on. The capacity to evaluate multiple aspects of experience and in light of the variety of value orientations they require and generate increases.

Thus there is increasing awareness of the multiple dimensions of authority figures and their functions. Conflicts between sources of authority in various spheres of experience are resolved by tactics of hierarchical subordination and/or compartmentalization. Reliance on authority to buttress uncertain judgment persists and is extended during this period, but there is increasing reliance on one's own sense of judgment in selecting and evaluating authoritative positions. On first achieving this mode, the individual is not yet in a position to take responsibility for resolving dissonances between sources of authority.

Cognitively, the constructs that allow for a distinction of forms of valuation and factual knowing begin to emerge and serve as a foundation for clarifying aspects of subjectivity and objectivity. In general, the capacity to evaluate the multiple levels of meaning and connotation in symbols now emerges, although it remains relatively vague. Discrimination is increasingly made between the realms of the spiritual, concerning both the existence of God and the spiritual aspect of human beings, and of the nonspiritual. Awareness of the faith orientation of other individuals or groups remains relatively undifferentiated and tends to be expressed in prejudicial or assimilative terms. The organization of institutional authority and/or sacramental community tends to sustain this level of synthesis and provides a powerful motivation for institutional adherence; the breakdown of institutional structures or sacramental forms may undermine this organization and result in regressive tendencies.

It can probably be safely said that by far the largest portion of adult religious behavior falls into this modality. While the operation of essentially paranoid mechanisms (Meissner 1978a) sustains the form of a coherent belief system and institutional affiliation in this phase, its further evolution depends on the breakdown of the kind of projectively defined and articulated synthesis we have been describing. In this progression, the appeal to authority or consensus and the management of conflict by strategies of hierarchization or compartmentalization prove inadequate. Decisive achievements of internalization and differentiation of reality lead increasingly to acceptance of responsibility for one's view of the world and one's synthesis of beliefs.

One begins to face, in a personal and accountable way, the necessity of resolving ambiguities and tensions inherent in the structure of reality. The breakdown of the synthetic organization of this modality opens the way for either regressive resolution or progressive reorganization. These tensions and the attendant moral anxiety may be resolved by resorting to complete relativism or extreme authoritarian subordination, or to an ideology whose discipline or charism offers readily available and simplified solutions to complex problems, or by regressively reverting to and reaffirming an ideologically consolidated version of an earlier level of synthesis. The variety of avenues for reducing tension and the ways in which institutionalized religions structure and maintain such channels is a fascinating area for further study.

The fifth and last modality of religious experience is characterized developmentally by a number of significant achievements, which include the integration and structuring of drive derivatives with relatively autonomous functions of the ego. Thus anxiety is reduced to a manageable level and is expressed exclusively in terms of more structured signal functions that mobilize rather than overwhelm ego resources. Consequently, dangers no longer arise primarily from the inner world of drive derivatives, although one is never totally absolved of their pressure, but derive rather from realistically based and evaluated extrinsic concerns. It is at this stage that the developmental integration of narcissism reaches the level of wisdom, empathy, humor, and creativity that Kohut (1966) has delineated.

Instead of using the tension reduction strategies and synthesis predominant in the previous modality to deal with unavoidable polar reality conflicts, the fifth modality permits these tensions to be embraced, affirmed, and somehow resolved and integrated into a more balanced faith-orientation and faith-existence. Consequently, the religious belief system and its tradition are seen in increasingly realistic terms that affirm their inherent tensions and ambiguities and accept the relativity, partiality, and particularity of the beliefs, symbols, rituals, and ceremonials of the religious community.

At the same time, this knowing through faith is able to acknowledge the existence and validity of different faith traditions adhered to by other persons and other cultures. It has a capacity for seeing through the particular to the universal values, orientations, and ultimate beliefs. Faith at this level becomes a lived and integrated source of support and strength.

We touch, at the higher reaches of this modality, the realm of integration of the faith experience that bridges over into the spiritual experience often described in terms of special graces, mystical gifts, and spiritual genius. Such individuals reflect an inner life of lucidity, simplicity, and inner harmony that escapes the great majority of humans, yet somehow seems more fully and more profoundly human. The love of God in these souls seems wholly unselfconscious, stripped of the residues of infantile narcissism, and yet capable of integration into a life of activity, responsibility, and generative fulfillment. They often seem capable of profoundly meaningful object relations that are characterized by selfless love and acceptance of others. It is here that the lives of the saints need more careful scrutiny, for it is possible that the model of narcissistic regression is inappropriate to the description of these phenomena and to the evaluation of the higher reaches of spiritual attainment within this modality. A more appropriate model might be found in an enlargement and intensification of the meaning of unremitting object love. It is the quality that Erikson (1964) has hinted at in his descriptions of ego integrity and wisdom.

POSTSCRIPT

The burden of the preceding argument has been that human religious experience, like many other parameters of human involvement and expression, reflects the underlying dynamics of the human personality and derives from critical developmental experiences and achievements. The developmental course, with its attainments, resolutions of crises, deviations, distortions, and developmental defects, sets the frame within which human experience is articulated and evolved. This critical and fundamental understanding I take to be the central import of Freud's argument about man's religious experience. It is, therefore, a historical accident, a cultural confusion, and Freud's dynamically motivated particularization of his own formulations and understanding that have left psychoanalysis with what must be considered a partial and fragmentary account of religious experience. In this light, Freud's account can be seen as presenting critical insight into a narrow range of the dynamics of belief, artificially isolated from the full range and complexity of human religious experience. The broadening of the psychoanalytic account to include the full range of that spectrum is a major task for the future.

Glancing back at the schema I have reconstructed, it is clear that it deals with matters familiar to psychoanalysis. The developmental spectrum is defined in terms of the metamorphoses of infantile narcissism, the changing quality and integration of object relations, the progression and modification of instinctual derivatives, the transition from absolute dependence toward increasing autonomy in function and structure, the progressive internal organization that provides stability and coherence to the psyche, and the gradual emergence, definition, and stabilization of the self as a coherent and integral part of the subjective world. This account also embraces the progressive elaboration and differentiation of specific ego functions, such as cognition, symbolic organization, affective integration, separation and integration of self- and object-representations, reality orientation and testing, the progressive capacity for secondary autonomous functioning, amplification of the range of secondary processing, and inherent subliminatory potential.

These reflections point to broader fields of consideration that may be of significant intrinsic interest and utility in their own right. In particular, I have in mind a problem in the comparative study of religion that may be considerably influenced by the present argument. Although it obviously reaches far beyond our present focus, it may prove to be a profitable avenue of research.

If we can accept and even substantiate a developmental perspective in the understanding of religious experience, that perspective would seem to raise critical questions about the developmental aspects of various religious traditions. I would be persuaded at this point that the developmental parameters described above could be found well distributed in all religious groups and traditions. Within each religious orientation various strata of developmental modalities would be identifiable, since these aspects are reflective of the developmental vicissitudes of individual psyches—they are not essentially group phenomena. Thus the study of contemporary Christian belief and pratice would yield data relevant to all the delimited modalities of developmental religious experience. A further question poses itself: May there not be a primary modality within respective religious traditions? Or may not various religious traditions be characterized by one or more preferred or idealized modalities? One would suspect at least that more primitive polytheisms would tend toward the earlier modalities, as contrasted, let us say, with a more advanced form of Christian theological monotheism.

In offering this suggestion for comparison, I would caution against using an evaluative frame of reference. The developmental modalities are not intended as a qualitative or evaluative scale. Rather, they must be understood in the broader framework of cultural relevance and adaptation. Religious traditions are expressions of human need and potentiality. They arise out of specific cultural and social matrices and cannot be satisfactorily assessed in isolation from those contexts. The respective modalities of religious experience, then, reflect the developmental values and propensities within respective cultures. They answer specific cultural requirements. The larger task, then, is to try to understand the interaction between the levels of cultural influence and of inner developmental exigency and expression. It is only in this sense that the integrative and self-sustaining aspects of religious phenomena can ultimately be understood.

7. RELIGION AS TRANSITIONAL

There is little doubt that throughout his long and productive career Freud saw himself as a destroyer of illusions. Whether he cast himself in the role of the conquistador, conquering unknown lands and untracked wastes of the mind, or in that of the prophet leading his people to the Promised Land, the image carried the connotation of conquering the tribes of illusion. He set himself to shape and establish psychoanalysis as a science by overcoming what he felt to be opposed illusions.

Writing to Romain Rolland in 1923, Freud speaks of himself as a Jew as belonging to the race that had been blamed for the troubles of Europe from the Middle Ages down to the German defeat in World War I. He says, "Such experiences have a sobering effect and are not conducive to make one believe in illusions. A great part of my life's work (I am ten years older than you) has been spent [trying to] destroy illusions of my own and those of mankind" (E. Freud 1960, 341). When Freud sent Rolland a copy of *The Future of an Illusion* (1927), Rolland replied that he agreed with Freud's judgments on religion but regretted that Freud had not properly appreciated the true source of religious sentiment, namely the "oceanic feeling" that Rolland saw as the source of all religious sentiment. Freud (1930) confessed that this illusion caused him no small difficulty. Only a few years later, on his eightieth birthday, Freud dealt with his discomfort again by writing to Rolland of his disturbance of memory on the Acropolis (1936). On this occasion too Freud found the opportunity to lay his psychoanalytic axe to the roots of Rolland's religious illusion (see above, chapter 2).

Even optimistic assumptions or beliefs about human nature had to be laid waste. Speaking about the instinct of aggression, Freud (1933a) addresses the optimistic belief that human nature must be essentially good:

> No, man must be naturally good or at least good-natured. If he occasionally shows himself brutal, violent or cruel, these are only

passing disturbances of his emotional life, for the most part provoked, or perhaps only consequences of the inexpedient social regulations which he has hitherto imposed on himself.

Unfortunately, what history tells us and what we ourselves have experienced does not speak in this sense but rather justifies a judgment that belief in the "goodness" of human nature is one of those evil illusions by which mankind expect their lives to be beautified and made easier while in reality they only cause damage. (p. 104)

That Freud set his face against such dreamers and optimists is clear from his comments to Theodor Herzl's son (see above, chapter 2). He describes Herzl, the father of Zionism, as one of the "very rare and dangerous breed" "who have turned dreams into reality"—a breed he considers "the sharpest opponents of my scientific work" (Falk 1977, 19). Freud viewed such illusions as based on the principle of wish fulfillment, analogous to dreams. In discussing the question of whether psychoanalysis leads to a particular Weltanschauung, Freud (1933a) describes a Weltanschauung as "an intellectual construction which solves all the problems of our existence uniformly on the basis of one overriding hypothesis, which, accordingly, leaves no question unanswered and in which everything that interests us finds its fixed place" (p. 158). Such a Weltanschauung is an ideal wish fulfillment for human beings, who would find it a source of security in life and a norm for dealing with emotions and the problems of life in an expedient way. It is derived from revelation, intuition, or divination and so stands in stark opposition to science, in which these processes have no place. Freud comments that even if they did exist as sources of new knowledge, "they may safely be reckoned as illusions, the fulfillment of wishful impulses" (p. 159).

For Freud, illusions, like dreams, stood in opposition to reality:

We welcome illusions because they spare us unpleasurable feelings, and enable us to enjoy satisfactions instead. We must not complain, then, if now and again they come into collision with some portion of reality and are shattered against it. (Freud 1915a, 280)

It is for this reason that Freud rejected the Marxist illusion of the classless society, which, he says,

hopes in the course of a few generations so to alter human nature that people will live together almost without friction in the new order of society, and that they will undertake the duties of work without any compulsion. Meanwhile it shifts elsewhere the instinctual restrictions which are essential in society; it diverts the aggressive tendencies which threaten all human communities to the outside and finds support in the hostility of the poor against the rich and of the hitherto powerless against the former rulers. But a transformation of human nature such as this is highly improbable. . . . In just the same way as religion, Bolshevism too must compensate its believers for the sufferings and deprivation of their present life by promises of a better future in which there will no longer be any unsatisfied need. (Freud 1933a, 180)

Freud lost no time declaring such idealism—the elimination of human aggression by guarantees of material satisfaction and equality of classes—an illusion.

The sole exception to this sweeping attack on illusion seems to have been art. Artistic productions, in Freud's view, were illusions that stood in contrast with reality but nontheless had a valuable role to play by reason of their connection with fantasy (Freud 1930). The satisfaction of the artist in creating fantasies and giving them expression and embodiment entails a special brand of sublimation. But such satisfactions are available to only a few, and even then they provide no armor against the slings and arrows of outrageous fortune. Artistic creativity and enjoyment form a realm of satisfaction based on internal psychical processes. Of the life of fantasy, Freud (1930) says:

> The connection with reality is still further loosened; satisfaction is obtained from illusions, which are recognized as such without the discrepancy between them and the reality being allowed to interfere with enjoyment. The region from which these illusions arise is the life of the imagination; at the time when the development of the sense of reality took place, this region was expressly exempted from the demands of reality-testing and was set apart for the purpose of fulfilling wishes which were difficult to carry out. At the height of these satisfactions through fantasy stands the enjoyment of works of art—an enjoyment which, by the agency of the artist, is made accessible even to those who are not themselves creative. People who are receptive to the influence of art cannot set too high a value on it as a source of pleasure and consolation in life. (pp. 80–81)

Freud's comments on art are of interest in that they seem to present a break in the otherwise unrelenting attack upon illusion in human affairs. He seems to be saying that the illusion of art, however feeble and transient it may be, is nonetheless to be valued for its capacity to allow men to step aside from the pressures of reality and to receive some imaginative satisfaction. Was Freud suggesting here not that illusion is to be disparaged and discouraged because it is in conflict with reality (after all, art and reality in this sense are opposed) but, rather, that it is to be decried and destroyed where it interferes with the human capacity to deal with the struggles of life? In another place, Freud (1915a) even comments: "To tolerate life remains, after all, the first duty of all living beings. Illusion becomes valueless if it makes this harder for us" (p. 299).

Can we infer, then, that illusion is to be tolerated, even encouraged, if it makes this primary duty more possible? If Freud was able to recognize the function of art as a buffer against reality, and also, at least to some extent, the need for such a buffer, he would tolerate the use of such illusions only within fairly limited constraints. Religious beliefs certainly did not fall within this area. In fact, Freud regarded religion as a dragon to be slain, particularly with the sword of science. He drew a strong line between religious beliefs and reality. In one of his most trenchant statements on the subject, he describes the state of mind that finds it necessary to withdraw from painful reality:

It regards reality as the sole enemy and as the source of all suffering, with which it is impossible to live, so that one must break off all relations with it if one is to be in any way happy. The hermit turns his back on the world and will have no truck with it. But one can do more than that; one can try to re-create the world, to build up in its stead another world in which its most unbearable features are eliminated and replaced by others that are in conformity with one's wishes. But whoever, in desperate defiance, sets out upon this path to happiness will as a rule attain nothing. Reality is too strong for him. He becomes a madman, who for the most part finds no one to help him in carrying through his delusion. It is asserted, however, that each one of us behaves in some one respect like a paranoic, corrects some aspect of the world which is unbearable to him by the construction of a wish and introduces this delusion into reality. A special importance attaches to the case in which this attempt to procure a certainty of happiness and a protection against suffering through a delusional remolding of reality is made by a considerable number of people in common. The religions of mankind must be classed among the mass-delusions of this kind. No one, needless to say, who shares a delusion ever recognizes it as such. (Freud 1930, 81)

Freud's view of religious belief, then, was that it was a delusion, not merely an illusion; nor was he slow to reiterate this view. He saw the religious approach to life as consisting in "depressing the value of life and distorting the picture of the real world in a delusional manner—which presupposes an intimidation of the intelligence. At this price, by forcibly fixing them in a state of psychical infantilism and by drawing them into a mass-delusion, religion succeeds in sparing many people an individual neurosis" (pp. 84–85).

It is well to remind ourselves from time to time that the essence of Freud's view of religion was that it was the equivalent of psychosis. Consequently, where we read "illusion," which is certainly the more benign and less prejudicial term, we must ultimately understand "delusion." Freud consistently emphasized the infantile and wish-fulfilling aspects of religious beliefs. He regarded such beliefs as illusions, fulfilments of the oldest, strongest and most urgent wishes of mankind. The secret of their strength lies in the strength of those wishes. As we already know, the terrifying impression of helplessness in childhood aroused the need for protection—for protection through love—which was provided by the father; and the recognition that his helplessness lasts throughout life made it necessary to cling to the existence of a father, but this time a more powerful one. Thus, the benevolent rule of a divine Providence allays our fear of the dangers of life; the establishment of a moral world-order insures the fulfilment of the demands of justice, which have so often remained unfulfilled in human civilization; and the prolongation of earthly existence in a future life provides the local and temporal framework in which these wish-fulfilments shall take place. (Freud 1927, 30)

Freud in fact vacillated between the terms "illusion" and "delusion." Because of his underlying conviction, he did not resolve the issue. He observes that illusion is not simply error. Illusions may be false, but they characteristically derive from wishes. In this respect, they come close to being delusions, but delusions necessarily contradict reality, while an illusion is not necessarily false or in contradiction to reality. Thus, a middle-class girl might entertain the illusion that a prince will marry her, but this is a more likely event than the coming of a Messiah to establish a glorious kingdom on earth. Freud (1927) then comments, "We call a belief an illusion when a wish-fulfilment is a prominent factor in its motivation, and in doing so we disregard its relation to reality, just as the illusion itself sets no store by verification" (p. 31). However, despite their emphasis on wish fulfillment, it is clear that Freud saw religious beliefs as standing in contradiction to reality at many points; for him, then, they clearly fell into the category of delusions.

TRANSITIONAL PHENOMENA

Despite the intensity and scope of Freud's unremitting onslaught against illusion in many areas of human experience, the intervening years have brought about a shift of attitude within psychoanalysis; the current perspective not only has found a place for illusion but has defined it as a powerful and necessary force in human psychic development and in the continuing nourishment and health of the human spirit as well. This change in perspective regarding illusion has come about as a result of the thinking of Donald Winnicott perhaps more than any other single figure. Winnicott has staked a claim that illusion is an important aspect of man's capacity to involve himself in the world of his experience, a capacity that ultimately finds expression in man's creativity in shaping a human and meaningful environment and in achieving what Piaget describes as accommodation and assimilation.

Winnicott's contribution to our understanding of illusion was his analysis of "transitional objects" and the development of other transitional phenomena derived from the use of such objects. In Winnicott's view (1971), the child's use of transitional objects begins with his early use of his fist, fingers, or thumb to stimulate the oral erotogenic zone and to bring satisfaction to the oral instincts. Within a few months of this, infants become fond of playing with some special object to which they become attached, even addicted, in a peculiarly intense manner.

The dynamics of this progression are intimately connected with the pattern of the very earliest mother-infant interaction. Mother and child in this early stage of their relationship are caught up in a form of undifferentiated unity composed of their dual participation. The participation of the "good-enough" mother in this unity serves to preserve the infant's sense of continuity in his existence. Such a mother's empathic ability to meet the baby's emerging need and to harmonize with his biological rhythms becomes crucial for achieving this function. If the infant's hunger reaches an extreme point, his sense of unity may be disrupted. Good-enough mothering includes a capacity for holding that provides the infant with a sense of unity and security to serve as a foundation for basic trust. Conversely, where the mother's holding fails to meet the infant's needs, the basis may be laid for distrust and a sense of deprivation or, in the extreme, more chaotic rageful discharge reactions that may approach the experience of fragmentation or panic.

The use of the hand for self-pacification is a first step in the direction of separation from this maternal matrix. The sequence of events that draws the newborn from the first fist-in-mouth activities to his later attachment to a teddy bear or doll or blanket may follow a wide variety of patterns. While oral excitement and satiation may play an important role in this process, other aspects must be considered. Important elements in the process are the nature of the object, the infant's capacity to recognize the object as "not-me," the place of the object (that is, whether it is experienced as outside, inside, or at the border of the infant's sense of himself in relation to the outside world, depending on the infant's capacity to create such an object) and, finally, the manner in which the use of the object reflects its connection with significant and affectionate forms of object relationship (Winnicott 1971).

In this sense, the infant's hand becomes a substitute for the mother's breast; gradually the infant's interest turns to some other object, often part of a sheet or blanket that gets included in his mouth along with his fingers. The object that is chosen for this soothing purpose varies considerably, but the important point is that it becomes vitally important to the infant, usually when going to sleep and thus provides a defense against anxiety connected with the loss of the mothering figure. The adopted object becomes of crucial importance and must be available at all times. Moreover, it cannot be altered in any significant way. If it gets dirty and smelly enough, the mother may feel compelled to wash it for hygienic purposes. But she then learns that this introduces a disruption in the continuity of the infant's experience of the object—a disruption, in fact, that may destroy the object's meaning and value to the infant.

Winnicott (1971) summarizes the special qualities of such objects:

1. The infant assumes rights over the object, and we agree to this assumption. Nevertheless, some abrogation of omnipotence is a feature from the start.
2. The object is affectionately cuddled as well as excitedly loved and mutilated.
3. It must never change, unless changed by the infant.
4. It must survive instinctual loving, and also hating, and, if it be a feature, pure aggression.
5. Yet it must seem to the infant to give warmth, or to move, or to have texture, or to do something that seems to show that it has vitality or reality of its own.
6. It comes from without from our point of view, but not so from the point of view of the baby. Neither does it come from within; it is not a hallucination.
7. Its fate is to be gradually allowed to be decathected, so that in the course of years it becomes not so much forgotten as relegated to limbo. By this I mean that in health the transitional object does not "go inside" nor does the feeling about it necessarily undergo repression. It is not forgotten and it is not mourned. It loses meaning, and this is because the transitional phenomena have become diffused, have become spread out over the whole intermediate territory between "inner psychic reality" and "the external world as perceived by two persons in common," that is to say, over the whole cultural field. (p. 5)

Winnicott is thus staking a claim for an important aspect of human life in addition to human involvement in interpersonal relationships and the inner world of psychic functioning. He is defining an intermediate area that he calls "experiencing," to which both the inner psychic reality and the external involvements contribute. He comments, "It is an area that is not challenged, because no claim is made on its behalf except that it shall exist as a resting-place for the individual engaged in the perpetual human task of keeping inner and outer reality separate yet interrelated" (p. 2). It is in these terms, therefore, that he asserts the importance of illusion in human psychological development and functioning.

It is usual to refer to "reality-testing," and to make a clear distinction between apperception and perception. I am staking a claim for an intermediate state between a baby's inability and his growing ability to recognize and accept reality. I am therefore studying the substance of *illusion,* that which is allowed to the infant, and which in adult life is inherent in art and religion, and yet becomes the hallmark of madness when an adult puts too powerful a claim on the credulity of others, forcing them to acknowledge a sharing of illusion that is not their own. We can share a respect for *illusory experience,* and if we wish we may collect together and form a group on the basis of the similarity of our illusory experiences. This is a natural root of grouping among human beings. (p. 3)

The infant's potential for creating illusion is elicited even in the earliest context of breast feeding with the mother. The mother's empathic attunement to and identification with the child allow her to respond to the child's emerging need in such a way that she provides what is needed in the right place, in the right amount, and at the right time. Her responsiveness offers an opportunity for the infant to begin to utilize illusion, without which, in Winnicott's terms, any contact between psyche and environment becomes impossible. Thus, the empathic mother brings the breast to the child's mouth at just the moment when the child creates a corresponding illusion of the breast. The mother's response thereby facilitates the illusion that the child has indeed created the breast. This optimal adaptation between mother and child constitutes an illusion that there is a world that corresponds to the infant's needs and to his capacity to create. The child gains an illusion of magical control over a world of satisfying objects. Winnicott contends that without this "primary illusion" of omnipotence a capacity truly to enjoy reality will never develop. Frustration can teach the child to perceive, adapt to, and test reality, but only out of this sense of unique fulfillment flowing from the conjunction of magical wish and attuned response, can he learn to love reality.

It is important to note that the good-enough mother is an essential participant in the process of the creation and use of such transitional objects. The art of the good-enough mother is that she intuitively knows when and how to introduce a delay between the infant's emerging needs and the kinds of satisfaction she is able to provide. If the infant has had the experience of magical creativity involved in the primary illusion, he can discover how to make up the difference that may be produced by the absence of the gratifying mother. The use of a transitional object allows him to reestablish continuity as a function of his growing capacity to recognize and accept reality. Deri (1978) describes this process in the following terms:

If his hallucinatory wish fulfillment previously coincided with the appearance of the real breast, then in the following stage objects available in outside reality can be perceived and felt as receptive for illusory use. At first it can be the thumb or the fist, later a piece of soft material found near the crib, even later a soft stuffed animal, and finally, any toy which can fulfill the function of a good transitional object. From the baby's point of view, these are neither external objects nor pure wishful hallucinations: *they are both at the same time.* (p. 51)

As Winnicott (1971) observes, there is no way in which an infant can move from the pleasure principle to the reality principle without facilitation by a good-enough mother. The good-enough mother's active adaptation to the infant's needs gradually diminishes in proportion to the infant's increasing ability to tolerate frustration. The mother's initial almost complete responsiveness and adaptation to the infant's needs are gradually titrated as the infant grows able to deal with and adapt to her failure. Winnicott (1971) comments:

> *If all goes well* the infant can actually come to gain from the experience of frustration, since incomplete adaptation to need makes objects real, that is to say hated as well as loved. The consequence of this is that *if all goes well* the infant can be disturbed by a close adaptation to need that is continued too long, not allowed its natural decrease, since exact adaptation resembles magic and the object that behaves perfectly becomes no better than a hallucination. Nevertheless, *at the start* adaptation needs to be almost exact, and unless this is so it is not possible for the infant to begin to develop a capacity to experience a relationship to external reality, or even to form a conception of external reality. (p. 11)

The original fit of need and adaptation provides the opportunity for the child's illusion of magical omnipotence. The mother's task as the child matures is gradually to disillusion the infant. If the primary illusion has been reasonably well established, the way to successful disillusionment then lies open. The gradual disillusionment and the increase of the titer of frustration set the stage for the frustrations of weaning.

An essential part of Winnicott's view is that the dialectic and the tension between illusion and disillusionment plays itself out through the whole of human experience and human life. The task of coming to know and accept reality is never fully completed. No human being is ever free from the tension of relating inner to outer reality. Further, relief from this unending tension is gained only in the intermediate area of illusory experience, which even in the life of the adult remains unchallenged, as in the arts and religion, for example. Winnicott (1971) comments:

> Should an adult make claims on us for our acceptance of the objectivity of his subjective phenomena we discern or diagnose madness. If, however, the adult can manage to enjoy the personal intermediate

area without making claims, then we can acknowledge our own corresponding intermediate areas, and are pleased to find a degree of overlapping, that is to say common experience between members of a group in art or religion or philosophy. (p. 14)

It should also be observed that the vicissitudes of transitional objects can also go awry. The earliest forms of transitional objects—that is, those the child uses prior to making any distinction of "me" as opposed to "not me," just as he does not distinguish between his mouth and the breast, which is merely experienced as a cluster of satisfying sensations—have been described as normal autistic objects—autistic in the sense that no object is recognized as beyond the limits of the self (Tustin 1980). However, the use of such autistic objects may also be pathological, as is often the case in psychotic children. Such pathological objects are used not as playthings or as vehicles for the child's fantasy, but rather in a bizarre, ritualistic fashion with an intense preoccupation that does not share the features of fantasy play. Consequently, such objects, rather than serve as a developmental vehicle for gradual separation from the maternal matrix and involvement with the not-me world of objects, become a way station in which this developmental process is frustrated and subverted.

The potentiality also exists for the transitional object to deteriorate into a fetish object. This process and its developmental implications have been discussed by Greenacre (1971). The fetishistic potential increases in proportion to the unavailability of the mother and her failure to meet the child's needs, which create a situation of traumatic deprivation. Children who are seriously deprived often never reach the stage of forming good transitional objects but cling rigidly to fetish objects without any capacity for play, enjoyment, libidinal investment, or fantasy—as in the case of the autistic objects mentioned above. Such rigidly possessed objects do little more than defend against severely distressful anxiety and infantile terror. The positive developmental potential of the transitional object can be clearly differentiated from the arrested and rigidly frozen quality of an infantile fetish. Greenacre (1971), for example, stresses the role of early body traumata, whether directly experienced or merely witnessed, in establishing an early acute castration fear against which the fetish object serves as a defense. In this sense, she describes the fetish "as a patch for a flaw in the genital area of the body image" (p. 334).

Both the capacity to form good transitional objects and their further evolution, in the direction of either a healthy capacity for symbolization and a creative approach to life or a deterioration into a fetishistic and hostile approach to symbolization, depend on the quality of the mother-child interaction and the extent to which the mother is present to the child. The empathic good-enough mother arrives in sufficient time to prevent the metamorphosis of the good transitional object into a fetish object. The metamorphosis in the direction of the fetish is in a sense a developmental cul-de-sac. But with good-enough mothering the transitional object evolves in the direction of the formation of a broader intermediate transitional space where symbolic activities and creative effort can find their natural living place. This is the area in which the play of human imagination and cultural activity takes place.

The child's involvement with transitional objects consequently undergoes a natural evolution into a capacity for play. Deri (1978) comments in this regard:

> The stage of transitional objects merges into what could be called the stage of playing. If everything proceeds optimally, the child can play, freely and creatively, and with concentrated dedication. The play will have form, with a beginning, a middle, and a natural end. It will be neither unimaginative and repetitive (reminiscent of fetishistic rituals), nor overexcited and disorganized, indicating the presence of raw instinctual forces. (p. 54)

Winnicott (1971) himself emphasizes certain aspects of the playing experience that underscore its illusory character. The playing of the young child is characterized by preoccupation; content is secondary but the state of relative withdrawal plays an important role. This withdrawal is analogous to states of concentration in older children and adults, but through it the child enters an area that neither is easily left nor easily admits intrusion. This area of playful illusion is not part of the child's inner psychic reality; it is at the same time external to the individual and not part of the external world. There the child gathers objects derived from his own inner world. He invests these external objects with meanings and feelings derived from his subjective world. The capacity to play reflects a sense of trust derived from the potential space between the baby and the mother, between the baby's near-absolute dependence and the mother's empathic and adaptive capacities. Play involves the body, not only in terms of the necessary manipulation of objects, but also insofar as certain forms of intense interest are connected with aspects of bodily excitement. Excitement in the erotogenic zones may jeopardize play and thereby threaten the child's sense of existing as a person. But even when it leads to a high degree of excitement or anxiety, play is satisfying. If the anxiety becomes unbearable, it may destroy the capacity to play. But when play is pleasurable, it implies that instinctual arousal is not excessive or disruptive. Play also has an inherent excitement that derives not from instinctual arousal but from the precariousness of the interplay between the child's subjectivity and what is objectively perceived and received. Winnicott notes that there is a direct development from the appearance of transitional phenomena to the capacity for play and from isolated play to shared playing, and hence from shared playing to the capacity for cultural experience.

Thus, the child who can play well demonstrates a capacity for blending illusion and reality that has been established at an earlier point in his development. At that stage gratification and frustration must have been reasonably well balanced, allowing for a relatively smooth integration of both libidinal and aggressive impulses. The capacity to utilize both libidinal and aggressive energy is essential not only in the play of children but in more adult forms of creative activity as well. The creative impulse requires the capacity to invest in the products of one's activity while at the same time retaining the capacity to surrender them, even to destroy them, to make way for new creations. Both the creating and the destroying have their place in the play of children and serve to consolidate the child's capacity to be in, make use of, and at the same time retreat from the area of illusion.

TRANSITION

The vicissitudes of transitional phenomena also lay the basis for the child's emerging capacity for symbolism. In a sense, the piece of blanket can be taken as symbolizing the mother's breast, but, as Winnicott suggests, its actual transitional function is as important as its symbolic value. He observes, "Its not being the breast (or the mother), although real, is as important as the fact that it stands for the breast (or mother)" (Winnicott 1971, 6). The use of transitional objects, then, is more a step toward the symbolic function than it is an actual use of symbolism. When symbolism is achieved, the infant has already gained the capacity to distinguish between fantasy and fact, between internal and external objects, between primary creativity and perception, between illusion and reality.

However, the capacity to use transitional objects points in the direction of later symbolic capacities. In a loose sense, symbols can be regarded as the *unio oppositorum,* in the sense that some extrinsic object or form is adopted as a vehicle for expressing something from the subjective realm. Dream symbols represent such a conjunction of intrinsic and extrinsic elements. Manifest objects, events, or even persons in the dream content become express subjective affects, meanings, and significances and thus add a symbolic dimension to the explicit content of the dream by allowing it to be a channel for the expression of a latent content (Grolnick 1978).

By the same token, real external objects and experiences can become vehicles for the expression of similar subjective intentions and significances and can thereby take on an added, symbolic dimension. The symbolic quality of such experiences and objects participates in the intermediate realm of illusion, which is compounded from elements of external reality intermingled with subjective attributions that express the human capacity to create meaning. Thus, even though the dream takes place entirely within the intrapsychic realm, it can be regarded as a form of transitional experience.

The basic notion of transitional phenomena has been extended in a variety of directions and applied to various aspects of adult experience. Modell (1968) has developed the notion of a transitional object relationship. As is the case with the child's transitional object, the transitional human object stands midway between the inner and outer worlds. As Modell observes:

> The transitional object is not completely created by the individual, it is not a hallucination, it is an object "in" the environment. It is something other than the self, but the separateness from the self is only partially acknowledged, since the object is given life by the subject. It is a created environment—created in the sense that the properties attributed to the object reflect the inner life of the subject. (p. 35)

As the transitional relationship plays itself out in the context of the analytic relationship, the reality of the analyst as a separate person who has his own personality, and personal involvements apart from the patient is completely denied. The image of the analyst is, rather, created in accord with the inner needs of the patient, so that the analyst exists for him alone. Such a relationship tends to be dyadic and exclusive. To such an object magical qualities are often attributed, so that an illusion of connectedness between the self and the transitional object results. The subject feels little or no concern for the needs of the object, in that he is unable to acknowledge the object's separateness and individuality (Modell 1968). Other analytic authors (Greenson 1978; Meissner 1981) have developed the notion that the transference and the transference neurosis are specifically transitional forms of object relationships.

Gilbert Rose (1978) has suggested a further extension of the transitional notion, that human psychological development and functioning can be envisioned as a lifelong "transitional process" that sets up a dynamic oscillation and process of interchange in which the self is viewed as an open system continuously engaged in influencing and being influenced by the outside world. The term "transitional process" suggests that there is a dynamic equilibrium between a more or less fluid self and external reality that is not simply limited to the transitional object phenomenon of childhood but continues into adult life. Moreover, the process of adaptation in the course of everyday life demands an element of creative originality and imagination that reflects a continuing transitional interplay between self and reality. Consequently, adaptation itself can be considered creative in impulse, not just as utilizing creative resources to achieve its purposes. Each human being selects, abstracts, and creates an idiosyncratic and unique *Umwelt* of his own by which he integrates his sense of reality. As we shall see, this exchange between the inner and the outer worlds takes place in unique and important ways in the realm of cultural experience.

THE PLACE OF ILLUSION IN CULTURAL EXPERIENCE

I have already suggested that the realm of cultural experience offers a vehicle for the adult residues of transitional phenomena to express themselves. Following the basic outline provided by the understanding of transitional phenomena, Winnicott (1971) approaches this problem by locating cultural experience specifically in the potential space that arises between the experiencing individual and his environment. Here the analysis of play is especially pertinent, since cultural experience has its origin in the imaginative and creative expression first manifested in the play of children.

The capacity of each individual to create and use this potential space is different and is determined by his very early life experiences, particularly his earliest experience with objects, out of which the capacity for transitional experience evolves. As Winnicott (1971) observes, "From the beginning the baby has maximally intense experiences in the potential space between the subjective object and the object objectively perceived, between me-extensions and the not-me. This potential space is at the interplay between there being nothing but me and there being objects and phenomena outside omnipotent control" (p. 100). The cultural life of any human individual, then, is determined by the fate of the potential space that arises between the baby and the human (that is, fallible) mother.

This third area, the area of cultural experience, takes its place alongside the inner or personal psychic reality and the actual world of activity and interaction that constitutes the individual's environment and can be objectively perceived. This is initially the area of play, which subsequently expands into a capacity for creative living and for cultural experience. As Winnicott (1971) notes, "I have located this important area of experience in the potential space between the individual and the environment, that which initially both joins and separates both the baby and the mother when the mother's love, displayed or made manifest as human reliability, does, in fact, give the baby a sense of trust or of confidence in the environmental factor" (p. 103).

Basic to the cultural experience is the manner in which man transforms or transfigures his environment and the objects it contains by attributing to objects, shapes, and figures in the real world a symbolic value and meaning. Through culture, man introduces the external realm into the inner world of personal significance. In this fashion, all art involves permeating external forms with subjective meaning. This creative transformation can be seen in the earliest human art forms.

The cave art of Cro-Magnon man, for example, provides an important example (Modell 1968). The appearance of these paleolithic relics corresponds with the appearance of Homo sapiens on the European continent.

While this artistic capacity may itself have a history, the evidence surrounding its emergence is lost to us, so that it seems to suggest a discrete
advance over the preceding Neanderthal culture. The paintings are found
in the dark recesses of limestone caves and were created under the sparse
illumination of oil lamps. Undoubtedly, they were incorporated into the
performance of magical and religious rites, so that these caves may be
regarded as sacred places of an archaic religion.

Moreover, the Paleolithic artist utilized the characteristics of the actual
surface of the cave walls in creating his representations. The cavities
produced by the dripping of water upon the stone are sometimes used to
represent animals' wounds. Rounded protuberances of rock are transformed into bison; stalagmites, into bison rearing on their hindquarters. A
hole in the rock becomes the pupil of a bison's eye. As Modell (1968)
points out, the created environment fuses with the real environment. Thus,
the cave art serves as a creative illusion that provides the participant in the
magical religious rite with a sense of mastery over the elemental forces of
life and death. In the logic of the magical sphere, acting on the symbolic
animal representation would influence the real world and what happened
to the real animal, thereby creating a world of illusion in which all
distinction between symbol and object was lost and omnipotent magical
wishes had their play.

Art in contemporary culture no longer carries the primitive magico-
religious expectation and the wish for omnipotence that seem to have been
an essential part of Paleolithic cave art. But the artist still creates an
illusion, still brings together in imaginative fusion the created and the real
environments to produce an area of illusory experience. The potential
space of which Winnicott speaks arises in the process of artistic creation
itself, as a place where the real materials with which the artist works—can-
vas and oils, wood, stone, cloth, clay, and so on—can receive the imaginative vision, the creative impulse by which he transforms material from the
real, external environment into something that has meaning, value, implication.

If the potential space is an essential aspect of the expression of an artistic
vision, that same space must be recreated by those who experience the
product of the artist's efforts. Any work of art, whether a painting, a
sculpture, or a delicate vase, is accepted as a work of art only to the extent
that it enters into the potential space created by the viewer, so that it
becomes an object that can receive the input of his subjective experience.
Consequently, every work of art is experienced differently by each individual who opens himself to it and draws it into the potential space in which he
can experience it as art.

In much the same fashion, in literature, whether poetry or prose, the
language, in its written or spoken form, forms the real, external constituent. In speaking or in putting the poem on paper, the poet must create a

transitional space within which he creates his poetic illusion. The reader must enter this same potential space in order to participate in the illusory experience that the poet creates and tries to communicate. The poem, then, becomes the vehicle for both the creation and the expression of the literary impulse, and the reader who wishes to experience the work must create anew this area of illusion within which he can receive the poet's words and transform them by investing them with his own subjective significances.

The potential space generated by the poet or literary artist is never totally identical with the transitional space created by the reader. Within the confines of the rules governing the use and understanding of language, though, there may be some overlap between these respective intentionalities and their corresponding transitional experiences. To this extent literary forms are capable of communicating a meaning and an intentionality that may be commonly received at least in some degree. But the experience of the poem as it connects with the subjective realm in the experiencing individual is always unique, always idiosyncratic, always caught in the realm of illusion that is conditioned by the quality of each individual's previous illusory experiences.

Another area of illusion is theater. Here the illusory component is evident; while it still reflects the idiosyncratic and differentiated components of individual lives and affective experiences, the members of the audience nonetheless clearly share a common illusion. They sit before a stage with clearly discernible limits and listen to the words and expressions of actors who represent characters clearly different from themselves. The play is a fiction, an imaginative exercise, both for those who play the parts and those who watch and listen. There is a "willing suspension of disbelief," in Coleridge's term, on both sides of the footlights. The players must entertain the illusion that for the space of the drama they are people other than the personalities they enact in real life. And for that space, each member of the audience must enter into the dramatic action with a willingness to entertain and maintain the illusion that what is happening before him is a segment of real life, even though he is quite aware that it is only a play, with no reality other than that of figures and shapes—the physical proportions and contents of the stage, and the actors who play the parts. All this is illusion willingly entertained, maintained in a potential space that is neither wholly real nor entirely the product of imagination.

The element of illusion in the experience of music is somewhat more difficult to grasp because of the nature of the material and of the aspects of psychic experience with which it resonates when it is received. But I would draw an analogy here to literature, particularly poetry. One part of the real substance of the music, its one foot in the real world, as it were, is the black ink in the form of notes and musical annotations on paper that comprises the sheet music. In this it is like a written poem.

When the music is played, however, another modality is introduced into its reality, namely the sound of music with all of its complex and multiple properties. Now it is like the poem being read aloud. But hearing a piece of music played, like hearing a poem read, is not merely experiencing certain sounds in a rhythmic pattern or with varying elements of harmony and pitch. The performing artist creates an aura, an atmosphere, a space within which there is a unique and special form of communication with his listeners. The music is not merely ordered sound; it creates an experience, it carries a message and a meaning, it speaks to man's emotion more than to his intellect—but it speaks nonetheless. The message and meaning of a Chopin mazurka are quite distinct from those of a Beethoven sonata, but the meaning of each is realized only to the extent that the listener comes to meet it, finds it, and even creates it.

This can take place only in the transitional space of which Winnicott speaks. Only there is the illusory experience generated by the playing of the music entered into and creatively absorbed by the listener. The art and the discipline of music lie on the one hand in the capacity of the composer to utilize the resources of musical sound and technique to elicit this response from his hearers and in the capacity of the performing artist to create the music anew in his rendition. At the same time, they rest in the capacity of the listener to discover and create again in terms of his personal experience some portion of the artistic and musical vision. Here again music runs a course parallel to poetry; like great poetry, it is measured by the ability of the composer or poet to generate and express a set of meanings and an emotional impact that will find resonances in the experience of many and will invite them to rediscover that experience through their own creative response.

It is not difficult to see the impact of Winnicott's notions of the transitional object and transitional phenomenon as they extend into the realm of cultural experience. It is also important to recognize the extent to which Winnicott's approach separates itself from Freud's view of illusion. Freud's emphasis on the distortion or contradiction of reality in the service of wish fulfillment is basic to his view of illusion. But what Freud sees as distortion and contradiction of reality Winnicott sees as part of man's creative experience. What Freud sees as wish fulfillment in accordance with the pleasure principle and in resistance to the reality principle Winnicott views as human creativity.

Rizzuto (1979) articulates the tension in these positions:

In ordinary language, the language of everyday life where we all meet publicly, *illusory* and *real* are antithetical, mutually exclusive concepts. This is not so in the private realm of transitional reality where illusory and real dimensions of experience interpenetrate each other to such an extent that they cannot be teased apart without destroying what is essential in the experience. It is impossible to separate the

mother created by the child from the mother he finds. . . . Reality, on
the other hand, can take for the experiencing individual all the shapes
that his psychic defenses need to attribute to it, to make it bearable. . . . The risk in understanding psychic life is to apply to it the
separation of subject and object indispensable in science and philosophy. Freud has shown beyond doubt that man's needs and wishes
color whatever he does and whatever he sees. Man is always playing
with reality, either to create himself through illusory anticipation, to
sustain himself by illusory reshaping of what does not seem bearable,
or simply to fool himself through illusory distortion of what he does
not like. If the illusion, the playing with available reality, goes beyond
immediate need, pathology and delusions ensue. Illusory transmuta-
tion of reality, however, is the indispensable and unavoidable process
all of us *must* go through if we are to grow normally and acquire
psychic meaning and substance. (pp. 227–28)

Illusion, therefore, becomes in Winnicott's view a developmental form of
transition to reality, in the sense that without the capacity to utilize
transitional objects and to generate transitional forms of experience the
child's attempts to gain a foothold in reality will inevitably be frustrated.
Illusion in this view is not an obstruction to experiencing reality but a
vehicle for gaining access to it. If Freud wished to rule out illusion and to
destroy it, Winnicott wishes to foster it and to increase man's capacity for
creatively experiencing it. Winnicott sees that illusion is an important part
of human experience precisely because it is not by bread alone that man
lives. Man needs to create, to shape and transform his environment, find
vehicles for expressing his inner life, or rather the constant commerce
between the ongoing worlds of his external experience and his inner
psychic reality. Winnicott's standard of psychic health is not the separation
of the real and the wishful, as Freud might have had it, but rather their
constant intermingling and exchange. It is through illusion, then, that the
human spirit is nourished. Freud would have man live in the harsh world of
cold facts and realities, ruled by reason. Reason has its place for Winnicott, of course—and its place is not a small one. But the life of the
imagination, the life of creative expression, whether wishful or not, is an
important, even vital, part of human experience. The man without imagination, without the capacity for play or for creative illusion, is condemned
to a sterile world of harsh facts without color or variety, without the
continual enrichment of man's creative capacities. In this respect, Winnicott and Pfister stand together (see above, chapter 4).

Transitional Phenomena in Religion

The thesis we are pursuing here, following the suggestion of Winnicott, is
that religion partakes of the character of transitional phenomena or the

transitional process and as such achieves its psychological reality and its psychic vitality in the potential space of illusory experience. It shares this participation in the illusory with other aspects of human culture but is unique among them because of the extent to which it impinges on what is most immediate and personal in man's psychic life, namely, man's sense of himself—his meaning, purpose, and destiny.

While many aspects of religious experience might lend themselves readily to an analysis of transitional and illusory aspects, I will select for the present discussion the dimension of faith, the God-representation, the use of symbols, and the experience of prayer. My purpose in treating these areas is simply to demonstrate their transitional aspects and some of their impact as such on psychic adjustment. In so doing, I must regrettably ignore many other components of these complex psychic experiences.

The faith experience has a number of attributes that characterize it as a form of transitional experience. The believer does not regard his faith as a matter of wishful hallucination or of purely subjective implications. Rather, his faith speaks to him of the nature of the world in which he lives, of the meaning and purpose of his existence there, and, in most religious traditions, of the relationship of that world and himself to a divine being who creates, loves, guides, and judges. At the same time that faith asserts, however, it cannot demonstrate the independent reality of the spiritual world and to which it lays claim. Consequently, the experience of faith is not totally subjective, nor is it totally objective. Rather, it represents a realm in which the subjective and the objective interpenetrate.

The question we are addressing here is not that of the truth value of the believer's faith. The point, rather, is that to envision his faith solely in subjective terms, as essentially did Freud, is to do a disservice to the believer and actually to distort the substance of his belief. The experience of faith, however, is neither exclusively subjective nor wholly objective by reason of its own intentionality; rather, it is a realm in which both the subjective and objective poles of experience contribute to the substance of belief.

There are also parallels to the infant's experience with the mother in the experience of faith. The believer's faith does not spring from a vacuum but comes to life within a context of belief. The capacity for faith is vitalized in a family environment in which faith plays a more or less significant role, and in the context of a community of believers that presents the individual with a more or less systematically elaborated and coherent set of doctrines to be believed. In this sense, the emergence of faith is much like the infant's creation of the mother. The what and how of belief in any given religious tradition are presented to the child in such a manner that he can respond to them and conjoin them to his own inner need to believe. In this sense, then, the young believer comes to create beliefs in conjunction with the objective reality of a set of beliefs that he finds in his environment.

Obviously, the vicissitudes of this process are complex and extremely variable. The extent to which individuals accept the belief system of an established religious community varies considerably. Ultimately at issue are the establishment and maintenance of the individual's sense of identity in relation to and in the context of a community that he comes to accept as part of his view of himself, his life, and his world, in reciprocation of its acceptance of his individuality as part of the community of believers.

The need and capacity to integrate oneself with such a community must be balanced against the need to rebel and to find and express one's individuality. In some basic sense, the individual, personal faith of the believer is always somewhat removed from, and in tension and dialectical interaction with, the belief or dogma of his religious community. Rarely, if ever, is the sense of faith and commitment complete. At the extremes of differentiation and disparity, one finds expressions of religious rejection, alienation, and rebellion, on the one hand, and complete submission and religious compliance, on the other. Between them lie infinite degrees of variation within which most human beings live out their religious convictions.

The faith of any human being, then, is both received from the religious community of his affiliation and created as a matter of internal and subjective expression. In this sense faith can be regarded as taking shape within the realm of illusory experience, and the faith of religious communities as being realized through the sharing of illusory experience within a given group of believers. Within any religious group, such sharing of illusion is a matter of degree that allows for both individual variation and a community of sharing.

An essential aspect of the faith experience is the individual's representation of the figure of God. The idea of the representation of God as a transitional object has been presented elsewhere (Meissner 1977, 1978). But perhaps the single most important contribution to its understanding has come through the recent work of Rizzuto (1979), who offers extensive documentation of her conclusions, based on the study of a series of patients and on the analysis of in-depth data of a number of them.

She concludes that God is a special kind of object representation that the child creates in the intermediate psychic space where transitional objects achieve their powerful and illusory existence. Like other transitional objects, the experience of God or the God-representation is neither a hallucination nor is it totally beyond the reach of subjectivity; rather, it is located, in Winnicott's terms, "outside, inside, at the border" (Winnicott 1971, 2). Unlike the teddy bear or the blanket, God is created out of representational derivatives that stem particularly from the child's experience of primary objects.

As a transitional object, God is also of a special order in that he does not follow the usual course of such objects—that is, he is not gradually decathected, ultimately to be forgotten or relegated to psychic limbo. Rather, the God-representation is cathected with increasing intensity during the pregenital years and reaches a peak during the high point of oedipal excitement. The representation that endures depends on the manner of the child's oedipal resolution and the resulting psychic compromises. Rather than lose force, the meaning of the God-representation is intensified by the oedipal experience. Even when the outcome is loss of meaning or rejection, God as a transitional object remains available for further processing, for further acceptance or rejection. Even in a state of relative abandonment or repression, the God-representation maintains the potentiality for revivification and further integration. As Rizzuto (1979) puts it, "Often, when the human objects of real life acquire profound psychic meaning, God, like a forlorn teddy bear, is left in a corner of the attic, to all appearances forgotten. A death, a great pain or intense joy may bring him back for an occasional hug or for further mistreatment and rejection, and then he is forgotten again" (p. 179).

The psychic process of creating and finding God—that is, this personalized representation acting as transitional object—continues through the course of the human life cycle. Thus, the characteristics of the God-representation follow the epigenetic and developmental laws that we have attempted to describe (see above, chapter 6). By the same token, the God-representation is the object of other psychic processes having to do with defense, adaptation, and synthesis, as well as with the need for meaningful relationship.

While God shares the transitional space with other cultural representations, the God-representation has a special place in that it is uniquely connected to man's sense of himself, of the meaning and purpose of his existence and his ultimate destiny. Perhaps more important than anything else is the fact that once this transitional object representation is created, whether it is dormant or active, it remains available for continuing psychic integration. The God-representation reflects the ongoing process of exchange that develops in relation to the individual's evolving self-representation. This process is an authentic dialectic insofar as the God-representation transcends the subjective realm. As Rizzuto (1979) notes, "The transitional object representation of God can be used for religious purposes precisely insofar as he is beyond magic" (p. 180). And as Winnicott (1971) notes, "The transitional object is never under magical control like the internal object, nor is it outside control as the real mother is" (p. 10).

One of the striking aspects of religious culture is its use of material objects to signify various aspects of belief. This objective or material aspect of cultural expression has been referred to by anthropologists as "material culture." We are addressing here the concretization of the signs and symbols of religious belief systems. In this category we can include the crucifix, the cross, the symbolic actions and gestures of the Roman Catholic Mass, bread and wine as symbols of the Body and Blood of Christ, the Star of David, the menorah, and the prayers and rituals of liturgical practice, whether in the Catholic church, the Protestant meeting house, or the Jewish synagogue. Each religion provides a rich lore of symbolic gestures and materials that embody and convey the content of its belief system. This applies not only to liturgical practice but to scriptural tradition as well. In this sense, Scripture acquires by reason of its privileged place in the body of religious belief a symbolic value beyond the mere content of the texts.

Such symbols, as they take their place within the religious system, are not to be envisioned merely in terms of their physical attributes. The crucifix is not just a piece of carved wood, nor is the Torah simply a roll of parchment with ancient writing on it. Rather, they are religious symbols and as such become the vehicles for the expression of meanings and values that transcend their physical characteristics. This symbolic dimension is not a product of the objects themselves, however; it can come about only by some attribution to them by the believer. Consequently, the objects as religious symbols are neither exclusively perceived in real and objective terms, nor simply produced by subjective creation. Rather, they evolve from the amalgamation of what is real, material, and objective as it is experienced, penetrated, and creatively reshaped by the subjective belief and patterns of meaning attributed to the object by the believer.

Consequently, the object has its symbolic function only for the believer and his belief system. We are once again in the transitional space in which the transitional experience is played out in the context of religious illusion. Such symbols, even in their most primitive and material sense, serve the articulation and maintenance of belief that are important for the human experience of believing. Human beings are, by and large, incapable of maintaining a commitment to something so abstract as a religious belief system without some means of real—sensory, visual, or auditory—concretization. The individual Catholic's belief in the real presence of Christ in the Eucharist could hardly be maintained, or at least could be maintained only with extreme difficulty, if participation in the Eucharistic liturgy were not surrounded with a panoply of concrete symbolic expressions of what is basically a highly theological and suprasensory understanding.

By the same token, the religious symbols would not be able to serve their function if they were not received into the transitional realm of experience of each participating believer who brings to the reality of the crucifix, for example, his own creative impulse expressed in and through his belief and its attendant faith. Consequently, their meaning and significance are achieved only to the extent to which such symbols become part of the transitional realm of the believer's illusory experience.

As is the case with other forms of transitional experience, this process can be misdirected into infantile or pathological channels. Just as the transitional object of the child can degenerate into a fetish object, transitional religious experience can be distorted in less authentic, relatively fetishistic directions that tend to contaminate and distort the more profoundly meaningful aspects of the religious experience. When this fetishistic course is followed, religious objects or practices begin to take on a magical quality that perverts their authentic religious impulse and meaning. Religious objects, prayers, and rites become magical talismans in the service of magical expectations and infantile needs. At least in some degree, the Catholic devotion to the rosary has been vulnerable to this distortion. In this sense religious objects are reduced to talismans, religious rites become obsessional rituals, and religious faith is corrupted into ideology.

A final place in which the transitional experience comes to fruition in the religious realm is in prayer. In this activity, the believer immerses himself in the religious experience in a more direct, immediate, and personal way than in any other aspect of his religious involvement—whether in common, as a liturgical function, or in private, as a more or less intrapsychic function.

It is here that the qualities of the God-representation and their relationship to the believer's self-representation become immediate. The God he prays to is not ultimately the God of the theologians or of the philosophers, nor is this God likely to be in any sense directly reconcilable with the God of Scripture. Rather, the individual believer prays to a God who is represented by the highly personalized transitional object representation in his inner, private, personally idiosyncratic belief system. Thus, all the unconscious and preconscious as well as conscious and reflective elements of the individual's relationship to God and the characteristics of his God-representation come into play. These may include elements that are more consciously mature and self-reflective but also elements that stem from earlier developmental levels and have a more infantile, dependent, and even narcissistic quality.

One might say that in prayer the individual figuratively enters the transitional space where he meets his God-representation. Prayer thus can become a channel for expressing what is most unique, profound, and personal in individual psychology. All the elements of transference that have become familiar to psychoanalysts can enter into the prayer experience and come to shape the individual's experience both of God and of himself in its context. Indeed, a great deal more can and should be said about the psychology of prayer, but our purpose here is only to indicate the extent to which it shares in the quality of transitional experience and expresses another aspect of the illusory dimension of religious experience.

With these aspects of the transitional elements in religious experience before us, we can return to the basic question that Freud raised. Are religion and God wishful illusions? Was Freud right in admonishing us that men should not allow themselves to remain children forever but should at last take heart and plunge into the harshness of life without the infantile consolation and solace of religion? Rizzuto (1979) states the dissenting case with admirable clarity:

> I must disagree. Reality and illusion are not contradictory terms. Psychic reality—whose depths Freud so brilliantly unveiled—cannot occur without that specifically human transitional space for play and illusion. To ask a man to renounce a God he believes in may be as cruel and as meaningless as wrenching a child from his teddy bear so that he can grow up. We know nowadays that teddy bears are not toys for spoiled children but part of the illusory substance of growing up. Each developmental stage has transitional objects appropriate for the age and level of maturity of the individual. After the oedipal resolution God is a potentially suitable object, and if updated during each crisis of development, may remain so through maturity and the rest of life. Asking a mature, functioning individual to renounce his God would be like asking Freud to renounce his own creation, psychoanalysis, and the "illusory" promise of what scientific knowledge can do. This is, in fact, the point. Men cannot be men without illusions. The type of illusion we select—science, religion, or something else—reveals our personal history and the transitional space each of us has created between his objects and himself to find "a resting place" to live in. (p. 209)

Thus, if it is true, as Ricoeur (1970) claims, that psychoanalysis is inherently iconoclastic, it also seems true in this post-Freudian era that psychoanalysis no longer feels compelled to destroy man's illusions on the ground that they express his inmost desires and wishes. Rather, psychoanalysis has moved to the position of staking a claim for illusion as the repository of human creativity and the realm in which man's potentiality may find its greatest expression.

We need only remind ourselves that for Winnicott the area of illusory experience is a potential space whose foundation is "the baby's trust in the mother *experienced* over a long-enough period at the critical stage of the separation of the not-me from the me, when the establishment of an autonomous self is at the initial stage" (Winnicott 1971, 110). Within this potential space, then, man must revive the roots of his capacity for creative living and for faith experience.

But the assertion of faith carries with it a transcendent element, addressing itself to the most developed form of religious experience. The assertion of faith is not merely a reassertion of basic trust; it is, rather, a creative assertion of something beyond trust and far more significant. Its regression is, if anything, recapitulative: it returns to the rudiments of trust in order to go beyond them. Thus faith ultimately renounces the imperfection and finitude of basic trust in order to reach beyond it and thereby to recapture it more profoundly. This is the creative moment in the illusion of faith. It is this regressive, yet creative, recapitulation that Erikson must have in mind when he writes:

> But must we call it regression if man thus seeks again the earliest encounters of his trustful past in his efforts to reach a hoped-for and eternal future? Or do religions partake of man's ability, even as he regresses, to recover creatively? At their creative best, religions retrace our earliest inner experiences, giving tangible form to vague evils and reaching back to the earliest individual sources of trust; at the same time, they keep alive the common symbols of integrity distilled by the generations. If this is partial regression, it is a regression which, in retracing firmly established pathways, returns to the present amplified and clarified.(Erikson 1962, 264)

Part 4

THE RELATION OF PSYCHOANALYSIS
TO RELIGIOUS EXPERIENCE

8. THE IMAGES OF MAN

From nearly the beginning of its intellectual history, psychoanalysis has taken its position as a basic form of understanding human psychology in the broadest range of its expression. As early as 1895, in a letter to Fliess, Freud writes:

> I am plagued with two ambitions: to see how the theory of mental functioning takes place if quantitative considerations, a sort of economics of nerve-force, are introduced into it; and secondly, to extract from psychopathology what may be of benefit to normal psychology. Actually a satisfactory general theory of neuropsychotic disturbances is impossible if it cannot be brought into association with clear assumptions about normal mental processes.(Freud 1954, 122–23)

Almost from the beginning, then, Freud's psychology carried the implicit intention of embracing the broadest range of human experience and culture.

It has been somewhat enigmatic that the psychoanalytic attempt to bring understanding to one of the farthest reaching areas of human experience, that of religious phenomena, has continued to be relatively inadequate and impoverished. It is not difficult to find reasons for this, particularly for Freud's own religious, or better antireligious, bias. A combination of sociological, ethnic, and historial circumstances has helped to prolong this relative impoverishment. In addition, an atmosphere of mutual suspicion and recrimination has led to frequent psychoanalytic attacks on institutionalized religion and to a reciprocal repudiation of psychoanalysis on the part of religious adherents.

The history and vicissitudes of this relationship are a matter of particular interest, but would carry us beyond our present focus. The time has come, I believe, for a reassessment of the psychoanalytic understanding of religious phenomena and a refocusing of it in terms of the more sophisticated theory that is now within our grasp. The argument I shall advance here is essentially that the original understanding of religious experience

proposed by Freud and persisting within psychoanalysis until compara-
tively recent years is based on a limited concept of religious experience that
reflects only one segment of the range of religious phenomena.

THE PROBLEM

I will be taking as my frame of reference the Judeo-Christian religious
tradition, not because of its inherent qualities but rather because of the
historical accident that it is within the culture produced by this religious
tradition that psychoanalysis has taken root and against it that psychoanalysis has exercised its critique. One of the basic tenets of the Judeo-
Christian tradition is that man is a special object of the Creator's power,
and that his creation was an event of importance over and above that of
God's other creatures. Man was specially chosen by God and stamped with
his image, the *imago dei*. This belief is enunciated in the opening chapter
of Genesis: "God said, 'Let us make man in our own image, in the likeness
of ourselves, and let them be masters of the fish of the sea, the birds of
heaven, the cattle, all the wild beasts and all the reptiles that crawl upon
the earth.' God created man in the image of Himself, in the image of God
He created him, male and female He created them" (Gen. 1:26–27).
Moreover, in the second Yahwistic account (Gen. 2:5–7), God fashions
man out of the dust of the earth and breathes life into him with his own
breath. Thus man becomes a living being by reason of the breath that
comes from the mouth of God. The special quality of man's origins marks
the special quality of his existence, a notion that became a major dimension of Judeo-Christian belief.

Moreover, it is particularly those qualities in man that set him apart from
the rest of creation that are the mark of his special origin and status. By
reason of his mind, and particularly of his intellectual capacities, man
attained this exalted position within the hierarchy of creation. The hege-
mony over all creation is given to him by God as a privileged commission.

Freud saw his psychoanalytic formulations as eroding this narcissistic
posture. As he viewed it, universal human narcissism had suffered three
serious defeats at the hands of scientific research. The first cosmological
blow to the self-love of mankind came from Copernicus, who destroyed
the illusion that man and his dwelling place, the earth, were at the center of
the universe. The second came from Darwin, whose theory of evolution
put an end to the presumption that man was somehow different from and
superior to the rest of the animal kingdom. The final psychological blow
was the most telling and devastating of all. Freud's two discoveries—"that
the life of our sexual instincts cannot be wholly tamed, and that mental
processes are in themselves unconscious and only reach the ego and come
under its control through incomplete and untrustworthy perceptions"—
amounted, as he notes,

to a statement that *the ego is not master in its own house.* Together they represent the third blow to man's self-love, what I may call the *psychological* one. No wonder, then, that the ego does not look favorably upon psychoanalysis and obstinately refuses to believe in it.(Freud 1917, 143)

It is of course little wonder, to paraphase Freud, that a religious belief system in which such generous amounts of human narcissism were embedded should find the inroads of psychoanalysis suspicious and even threatening. Nor was it surprising, conversely, that where Freud saw such a repository of unresolved narcissism, his own analytic acumen and intensity would seek to destroy it. It is hardly surprising, then, that Freud laid his analytic axe to the root of the religious tree.

To carry this argument a step further, the Judeo-Christian tradition emphasizes human intentionality as the peculiar quality by which man is related to divine initiatives and is taken into the economy of salvation. Thus man's is a moral consciousness in which the vicissitudes of intention and choice play themselves out in the drama of spiritual forces. It was by reason of his intellectual capacity, his resources for intentional self-reflectiveness, deliberation, and free choice, that man became the inheritor of the divine right and a participant in the life of grace. By these capacities he was thought able to respond to the divine initiatives and salvational actions that elevated his spiritual level to the position of divine sonship.

This inherent capacity had its deleterious and dangerous aspects as well. If man was chosen by God out of all creation to hold a special place in relation to him and in effect to be the mediator between that creation and its Creator, man was also endowed with the capacity for free choice and thereby with an inherent sinful potentiality. If, because of his special gifts, God had placed Adam, the first man, in the Garden of Eden and had showered him with divine gifts, it was also Adam who committed the first sin, the first violation of God's will, so that through him, as Paul says, sin entered the world. Just as no other creature is capable of responding to the initiatives of divine love through grace, so too no other creature can violate God's law, reject God's loving initiatives, and separate himself from God through sin.

These dimensions of man's existence and his place within the divine economy reverberate through the whole of Judeo-Christian belief. They spell themselves out over and over again in the literature of the Old and New Testaments, in the rabbinical commentaries, in the Midrash, in later Christian theology. The parameters of this dimension of Christian belief came to be expressed in later centuries, particularly in the medieval period and extending even into our own time, in the Aristotelian doctrine that defined man as a union of *anima* (soul) and *corpus* (body) and was given special meaning by the doctrine of Saint Thomas, who taught that the *anima intellectiva* was in effect the *forma corporis.* The impossibility of this formulation in the Aristotelian or later Averroistic metaphysics made it necessary for Saint Thomas to reshape his metaphysics to make room for this fundamental Christian belief. The status of that teaching tells us how central and powerful was the image of man and concomitantly how significant his relationship to God's creative and sustaining power, grace, and divine providence had to be. Bringing this theological image into perspective enables us to envision more vividly the inherent tensions between the image of man that dominated the Judeo-Christian tradition and that advanced by psychoanalysis.

One problem in attempting to compare the images of man advanced by theological anthropology and psychoanalysis is that certainly in psychoanalysis and possibly in theology, they are not unitary or simple concepts. We are appealing to a basic philosophical concept that lies at the root of psychoanalytic theory. But the diversity of its images in psychoanalysis and the ambiguity in Freud's own thinking have had a great effect on that theory (Holt 1972). The contributions of Chein (1962, 1972) have made clear the significant role such an often unarticulated image plays in the formulation of psychological theories—and this insight applies perhaps even more to psychoanalysis than to other psychologies. More recently, reexamination of classical psychoanalytic theories in the context of an overarching developmental schema has brought into focus the extent to which psychoanalytic thinking is based on models of limited explanatory power which apply to restricted ranges of clinical phenomena and behavior, yet which taken together span significant dimensions of human experience and functioning (Gedo and Goldberg 1973). Thus, we will essentially be comparing overly simplified versions of both the theological and psychoanalytic images of man. Yet, as we shall see, the role of these caricatures in illuminating points of difference may help to structure a framework of dialectic.

THE IMAGES OF MAN IN PSYCHOANALYSIS

When we turn to a consideration of the image of man expressed in psychoanalysis, we are confronted not with a unified concept but rather with diverse perspectives that are loosely organized into a general analytic frame of reference. Consequently, we find ourselves dealing with a multiplicity of models rather than with a single organic unity: an instinctually derived model of drive and defense, an ego psychological model, an object relations model, and an emerging model of the self and its psychic organization and functioning.

The multiplicity of the images of man not only bedevils psychoanalysis but has been a thorn in the side of psychology from the beginning. Perhaps the most dramatic tension within psychoanalysis is between the characterizations of man in terms of activity, intentionality, and responsibility, on the one hand, and in terms of reactivity, passivity in response to external stimuli, and a mechanistic psychic life, on the other. Chein (1962) describes the more active image:

> Man, in this image, is a being who actively does something with regard to some of the things that happen to him; a being who, for instance, tries to increase the likelihood that some things will happen and to decrease the likelihood that others will happen; a being who tries to generate circumstances that are compatible with the execution of his intentions; a being who will try to inject harmony where he finds disharmony or who will sometimes seek to generate disharmony; a being who seeks to shape his environment rather than passively permit himself to be shaped by the latter; —a being, in short, who insists on injecting himself into the causal process of the world around him. (pp. 2–3)

However, within psychoanalysis and within psychology generally, the opposite view of man has taken root and has had a powerful sway over scientific attempts to understand human behavior. Such a view sees man as essentially passive and reactive, responding in terms of his biological constitution and of the external forces impinging on and stimulating him. Response in this context is viewed as an automatic outcome of the interaction of constitution and environment, in which the human being plays no significant contributing or determining role. Man in this view is essentially mechanical and robot-like.

The view of man adopted by Freud in his early attempts to conceptualize a model of human behavior was essentially this mechanistic one. His earliest model of the mental apparatus was dominated by the more or less mechanistic requirements of the Helmholtzian physics and physiology of his day. His attempt to articulate this model in his now famous *Project for a Scientific Psychology* (1950b) faltered, but the basic orientation and ideas he develops there continued to influence his thinking through most of his life. The principles on which the *Project* is constructed are both neuronal and thermodynamic. Freud postulates a basic energy in the nervous system that undergoes systematic modifications and transformations in accordance with the laws of thermodynamics (as they were then understood). One of the principles in this model is that of constancy, which relates essentially to the notion of inertia. According to this principle, the nervous system tends to maintain itself in a state of constant tension or excitation. Any heightening of the normal level of excitation, as the result of a stimulus input, for example, results in a tendency to immediate discharge along the path of least resistance, which results in a return to a level of constant excitation.

Freud saw excitation in the nervous system not as arising spontaneously but rather as deriving either from external reality, which served to excite the sensory organs, or from the interior of the body, where endogenous stimuli increased the level of excitation in the mental apparatus and called for discharge. These endogenous stimuli were related to the major needs of the body, including nourishment, respiration, and sexual release. Freud's thinking about the nervous system had at its root a view of neural activity as passively responsive to external stimuli and an understanding of motivation specifically in terms of drive or tension reduction.

This view of the nervous system and of the related perceptual processes was strongly influenced by the views of Helmholtz, namely, that reality consisted of nothing but material masses in motion, and that the basis of the perceptual processes lay in the physical excitation of neural elements by external physical stimuli. There seems little reason to doubt that Freud maintained this highly reductionistic and mechanistic view of man's mental life because of his primary commitment to a natural-science methodology and its underlying thermodynamic principles. But it also seems quite clear that this extremely reductionistic view offers little ground for integration with a theologically derived anthropology.

The argument which has been made with considerable force on the other side of the dialectical fence is that there is a place, indeed a need, for a view of man as an active participant in determining behavioral outcomes.

The early Freudian view of man was based essentially on an economic-energic concept of a closed system, that is, a system that admits no matter from outside itself and is therefore subject to entropy according to the second law of thermodynamics. Some outside energy may play on such a system but has no restorative effect on it and involves no transactions with its environment.

One of the earliest theorists to speak of the personality as an "open system" was Gordon Allport (1960). Allport defined four major criteria for open systems: (1) intake and output of both matter and energy; (2) achievement and maintenance of homeostatic steady states so that any intrusion of external energy does not disrupt the stability and internal order of the system; (3) over time, an increase of order corresponding to the increase in complexity and differentiation of parts of the system; and (4) extensive transactional exchange with the environment.

The mere exchange of material and energy is characteristic of stimulus-response theories in general, but in the more rigorous of these theories other criteria are virtually excluded. Such views of the organism hold that there is a stimulus input and a response output, and whatever machinery operates between them is both unknown and unimportant. The extreme behaviorist points of view would endorse this position, and it seems that it also formed an important part of Freud's early theories. The processes of homeostasis or steady-state equilibrium account for the interchange of matter and energy in most systemic organizations and for the tendency of organisms to maintain inner structural integrity. However, the emphasis in this view falls on stability rather than growth, on the maintenance of equilibrium rather than creativity. In Allport's terms, the emphasis is on being rather than becoming. In Freud's early, relatively closed view of the mental apparatus, it seems clear that the basic principles of inertia and constancy were calculated specifically to maintain such homeostatic balance.

Open systems, however, enjoy an increase of differentiation and complexity over time. In the human personality there is a tendency to go beyond the maintenance of steady states and to elaborate internal differentiation even at the cost of disequilibrium. Theories of homeostatic equilibrium are totally inadequate to account for increasingly complex motivational hierarchies and goal orientations. In fact, only with the emergence of a more developed ego psychology, with its emphasis on autonomous growth, conflict-free motivation, and increasing levels of adaptation, did these aspects of the open-system economy begin to play a meaningful role in psychoanalytic understanding. In addition to these three attributes, the personality as an open system was seen as in constant transactional exchange with its environment. The three previous criteria which Allport discusses are characteristic of the personality as a self-contained system. But the human personality is in fact open to the world and shapes itself in continuing interaction with aspects of that world, including other human beings as well as the complex physical, social, cultural, and other kinds of influences that impinge on it. This aspect of the functioning of the human psyche has been brought into much more explicit focus by the object-relations perspective within psychoanalysis.

The distribution of energy is dynamic and autonomous, and at the same time transactional. Action and transaction are always knit together in an integrally functioning system. One or the other dominates an individual's pattern of behavior, but it is usually difficult to determine to what degree. Modern studies of human behavior have established the principle that behavior is situational. Action and reaction are conditioned by the complex interaction of influences that come to bear in a concrete situation. This insight has opened new avenues to understanding behavior. We have learned that the structure of family relationships is significantly related to the development of the child's personality and functioning. We have become increasingly sensitive to factors of socialization and acculturation that mold the child's responsiveness to the demands and expectations of the community. We have learned that human adaptation and adjustment cannot be explained by intrapsychic variables alone; currents of interpersonal and sociological influence also strongly affect their organization and functioning.

The transactional view of behavior makes the psychologist's work considerably more complex, since it embraces broad areas of interaction in which cause-and-effect relations are easily obscured. But this very openness of man as a functioning system within a transactional network mirrors the complexity of life itself and makes the understanding of man's psychic life all the more accurate. Full understanding demands that the reality of transactional influences be taken into account. It has been a traditional teaching of Christian theology that grace is a reality intimately related to the functioning of the human psyche. The Christian psychologist cannot ignore this, but he has had difficulty making this realization psychologically relevant.

Conceiving of personality as an open system is an essential first step in conceptualizing the psychological relevance of grace, for the closed system banishes grace. But the open system permits us to think of man as functioning on multiple levels in relation to a multiplicity of extrinsic influences. Once ontological grounds for the possibility of an intrinsic action of grace have been established, there is no reason to reject the notion of grace as a transcendental influence that works in a fashion similar to the other elements of a heterogeneous transactional system.

The open system is characterized by an increase of internal order over time. Personality, then, is an integral system with an intrinsic principle of unity. This system is constantly in a state of dynamic flux regarding its capacity for maximizing internal order. The integrity of its organization is neither static nor complete. Moreover, progress toward increasing order over time is derived neither from an extrinsic ordering agency nor from the transactional involvement of the personality. On the contrary, the organizing principle is intrinsic to the evolving structure.

Much of the debate over the passive and mechanical, as opposed to the more active and dynamic, views of man rests upon a supposition about scientific methodology—namely, that the scientific investigation of man takes place without philosophical presuppositions or implications. This would represent a claim that the scientific method is a neutral instrument of investigation that can be applied impartially to any object. But certainly in terms of the human sciences of man, this philosophical neutrality is a myth. Scientific conclusions about the object of investigation are determined by the method of investigation, and the method itself derives from a prescientific and implicitly philosophical view of the object which influences what observation will accept as fact and dictates how it will be interpreted.

Freud's case is particularly germane in this regard. By training and inclination, Freud was deeply imbued with the Helmholtzian views that flourished in the middle and late nineteenth century. His teachers, Brücke and Meinert, whom he admired and took as ideals of scientific work, were heavily committed to a reductionistic and mechanistic view. Freud tried desperately to extend this view in his writing of the *Project,* with the purpose of providing "a psychology which shall be a natural science: its aim, that is, is to represent psychical processes as quantitatively determined states of specifiable material particles and so to make them plain and void of contradiction" (Freud 1950b, 295).

But hardly had Freud finished writing the *Project* than he set himself on an entirely different course. His abandonment of the seduction hypothesis (Zetzel and Meissner 1973) and the results of his self-analysis had brought him increasingly to realize that the important dimensions of human psychology had to do with the understanding of meaning and the relationship of meanings to psychic processes. This transformation in emphasis is admirably documented in his monumental *Interpretation of Dreams* (1900)—where the tenacious hold that the more economic and mechanistic view had on his mind is also displayed, for the model that is the source of so much enthusiasm and disappointment in the *Project* reappears in the famous seventh chapter of *The Interpretation of Dreams.*

As Husserl insisted, the *Lebenswelt*—the immediate lived experience of oneself, other human beings, and the world around oneself—forms a common matrix out of which both philosophy and science derive and thus constitutes their common ground and common point of origin. But a persistent tendency of the natural-science attitude has been to divorce itself from this vital origin in order to construct a view of the world which could substitute for immediate lived experience. This relatively abstract and objective construction is then taken as a representation of the real world, as the standard of objectivity in comparison to which the subjective world of lived experience is given considerably less value and validity. The effect on psychology and particularly on psychoanalysis has been that instead of clarifying the concrete basis of human behavior, this view tends to render the scientific enterprise devoid of meaning by pretending that the psychologist owes nothing of his grasp of the psychological facts to his own immediate, natural, subjective experience.

One of the interesting aspects of this whole matter is the extent to which the various approaches to understanding psychological reality within psychoanalysis have undergone and continue to undergo modifications and progressive elaborations. The diversity of approaches to the understanding of mental functioning is of immediate relevance for the question of the image of man and its place in psychoanalysis and in a more general theological anthropology. The conflict of viewpoints within psychoanalysis has focused on three primary areas in the ongoing debate about psychoanalytic metapsychology: the biological assumptions underlying Freudian psychoanalytic thinking, the methodology of psychoanalytic theorizing, and the nature of psychoanalytic theory itself.

RECENT CONTRIBUTIONS TO THE DEBATE

Exploration of the biological underpinnings of Freud's thinking was given considerable stimulus by the discovery and publication of his early letters to Fliess and of the now famous *Project* (Freud 1950b). Earlier work, particularly by Bernfeld (1944) and Nuttin (1956), had brought into clearer focus Freud's dependence on the physiology of his day and on the concepts of the Helmholtz school in both physics and physiology. The full impact of Freud's scientific roots in late nineteenth-century physiology came to be fully appreciated and articulated only later, in a monograph by Amacher (1965). In any case, these contributions set the stage for a more direct attack on the role of such assumptions in psychoanalytic theorizing.

The attack was launched by Robert Holt (1965), who argued that the suppositions behind the physiological model on which Freud based his theory were fundamentally inconsistent with contemporary knowledge of the functioning of the nervous system. The nature of the nervous system as conceived by Freud's mentors, Brücke, Meynert, and Exner—essentially passive and geared to processing energy inputs from the external environment—is countered by the modern view that the nervous system is essentially and continually active, not merely reactive, to external inputs. The contemporary perspective says that the effect of external stimulation is only to modify the ongoing activity of the nervous system; that the nervous system itself does not transmit energy but rather propagates neural impulses; that the energies involved in the functioning of the nervous system are different in kind from the physical energies impinging on sensory organs in the forms of external stimuli; that these energies of the nervous system are not specific in nature; and, finally, that the energy components of neural activity are quantitatively negligible and that the levels of energic processing bear no essential relation to motivational states. Rather, what is important in the functioning of the neural net is the modification of activity related to the encoding and transmitting of information within the nervous system.

Contemporary thinking about neural functioning has shifted the basis of understanding from the interplay of forces and energies to the transmission of information, that is, the complex processing of encoding and decoding carried out through modifications in neural activity. In short, the theory of neuronal inertia and the principle of constancy which Freud made the cornerstone of his physiologized conception of the psychic apparatus were entirely without foundation, so that any aspects of the theory that derive from these underlying postulates must be held to be not only invalid but completely fallacious. Holt concludes that "many—perhaps most—of the obscurities, fallacies and internal contradictions of psychoanalytic theory are rather direct derivates of its neurological inheritance" (p. 109). Particularly vulnerable to this charge was the economic point of view, because it treated the energies it quantified as having specific qualitative characters. By extension and by implication, therefore, the structural hypothesis had also to be placed in question.

The second major thrust in the attack on metapsychology was a critique of psychoanalytic methodology. The attack was based on the philosophy of linguistic analysis, particularly the work of Ayer and Gilbert Ryle, as well as the work of English object-relations theorists, particularly Bowlby, Fairbairn, and Guntrip. The argument, focused in a seminal paper by Home (1966), took the form of an attack on the underpinnings of psychoanalysis as a natural science. Freud's unique contribution, the basis for all psychoanalytic understanding, was the discovery that symptoms have meaning. With this discovery and the method of treatment he developed from it, Freud essentially took psychoanalysis out of the realm of science and planted it firmly in the humanities.

The differences between these two disciplines are fundamental. The humanities are concerned with "interpretation," while science seeks "explanations." Scientific method demands a clear distinction between observation and inference; the humanities require no such distinction. Science seeks answers in terms of causes; the humanities, in terms of reasons.

Scientific methodology is suited to the study of inanimate objects or of objects that may once have been living but are now dead. Insofar as such objects are not alive, their behavior can be explained in causal terms. Insofar as they have a capacity for movement or animation, however, the methodological resources they demand shift to the more subtle grounds of empathy and identification. In this regard, Home (1966) writes:

> With that which moves we are able to make an act of identification and even with that which is still, provided it is felt to be in a state of dynamic tension. When we identify with an object, we feel what it would be like to be that object. This gives us an understanding of the object and particularly of how it is feeling and therefore of how it will behave. The accuracy of the information we derive from an act of identification will depend on the accuracy of our perception, on our capacity to criticize our transference and on our ability to identify only within the limits of what is actually identical. Within those limits, cognition through identification gives us accurate information and information which can be obtained in no other way. Clearly, however, it will be most full and accurate in relation to the movements of other human beings and of those most like ourselves. It will be least accurate in relation to living things most remote from us in the evolutionary scale and totally inaccurate in relation to the movements of inorganic matter, where the limit of the anthropomorphic fallacy is reached. (p. 44)

The upshot of this view is that science is able to observe dead or inanimate objects and involves no identification. Consequently, there is no room in the scientific account for a principle of living, spontaneous subjectivity. The scientific explanation is made in terms of causes and effects. In contrast, the humanistic mode concerns itself with living objects, expresses questions about these living objects in terms of why things happen, and answers them in terms of motivation.

Obviously, misapplication of the scientific modality of understanding has been a source of untold confusion. By the same token, misapplication of the humanistic mode of understanding has tended to produce empty and misleading theories. It is just as fallacious to apply the humanistic mode, which requires explanations in terms of motivation, to the world of naturalistic observation as to apply the scientific mode to matters of human motivation and personal, as well as interpersonal, events. One such unfortunate application of science has been the Marxian analysis of historical process. A second was Freud's attempt to base a theory of mind on scientific principles.

The third point of attack was essentially an extension of this basic epistemology to a consideration of metapsychology specifically as theory. A major thrust was provided by George Klein (1976), who draws a distinction between the clinical theory and the metapsychology of psychoanalysis. He feels that psychoanalysts tend to view clinical concepts as phenomena of observation rather than treat them specifically as theory, on the assumption that clinical concepts are closer to the psychoanalytic situation and for this reason are somehow less than theoretical, although at the same time they seem to be more than descriptive. But in Klein's view, clinical concepts are no less abstract and theoretical than the concepts of metapsychology. The advantage of clinical concepts, in his opinion, is that they are closer to the activity of clinical observation and to the focus of the analyst's intention. To this extent, they are potentially more responsive to modifications imposed by empirical data and consequently are intrinsically more capable of systematic modification. The difference between the two forms of theory is exemplified in Freud's *Interpretation of Dreams* (1900). In the first six chapters, Freud develops his observations of dream phenomena and elaborates a set of clinical formulations as part of a general clinical theory. However, in the famous seventh chapter Freud recasts his observations and the general concepts he bases on them in the entirely different frame of reference provided by the energic and cathexis reduction models he had already developed in the then unpublished and unknown *Project*. As Klein sees it, it was not the scientific model, the metapsychology, that was so significant and revolutionary in Freud's thinking. Rather, it was the clinical aspect that brought new meaning to the account of behavior which was so compelling and ultimately influential. Klein comments:

A relatively few simple principles enabled us to see *meanings* in the most varied and heretofore senseless behaviors, such as dreams, mistakes, jokes, and symptoms. Yet, as psychoanalysts came to formulate their ideas systematically, they abandoned this level and assumed the aims and mannerisms of natural scientists talking about energies, forces, cathexes, systems, layers, mechanisms, and physical analogies, rather than meanings. Thus, today psychoanalysis presents itself in two guises—the psychology in terms of which Freud interpreted dreams and symptoms and slips of the tongue, etc.—the distinctive meanings that behaviors and experiences acquire when interpreted in terms of sexual and aggressive wishes, conscious and unconscious events, displacement of aims, transference, unconscious fantasy, and related principles, and, on the other hand, a theory which *explains* the theory—the only theory I know of with such a pretension. (Klein 1976, 3)

The last phrase strikes an important note. Klein feels that there is no need of an additional theory to explain the already viable clinical theory. As far as he is concerned, it makes little difference what kind of model one chooses for this metapsychological account, whether it is a thermodynamic model or the more contemporary models of cybernetics and information exchange. The point is that such models are irrelevant to the clinical psychoanalytic enterprise. Consequently, any attempt to elaborate a scientific model to account for clinical data is, to his mind, simply beside the point.

The concepts proper to the clinical theory have to do primarily with motivations and meanings, personal relationships with significant objects, and interpersonal interactions. With regard to the understanding of motivation, Klein writes:

The essential *clinical* propositions concerning motivation have nothing to do with reducing a hypothetical tension; they are inferences of *directional* gradients in behavior, and of the *object-relations* involved in these directions; they describe relationships needed and sought after, consciously and unconsciously, how they are lived out and how they are fulfilled through perceptual encounters, conception, symbol and action. The key factors in the psychoanalytic clinical view of motivation are relational requirements, encounters, crises, dilemmas, resolutions, and achievements—not a hypothetical "tension" reduction. (p. 10)

Klein suggests that a distinction between experiential (intraphenomenological) and functional (extraphenomenological) concepts would be more useful rather than one between clinical and metapsychological theory. Intraphenomenological concepts generally include experiences attributed to the subject, even when he is not aware of them. The analyst might assume that an unconscious fantasy is a basic way in which the patient experiences himself or others; on the basis of this assumption, the analyst gains access to the meaning of the patient's actions and behavior. In this light, the analyst's inferences about the analysand's experiences, even unconscious experiences, can be regarded as the basic data of the psychoanalytic hour. These would include inferences about the analysand's views of himself, of the analyst, and of the situation which he shares with the analyst, and about the analyst's own self-perceptions.

In addition to these intraphenomenological concepts, functional or extraphenomenological concepts also play an important role in clinical theory. These include the concepts of projection, introjection, and repression, and other technical concepts that refer to functions of the subject's mind that he does not properly experience, but that nonetheless form part of his psychic reality. These functional concepts provide some account of the analyst's own experiences and those of the subject that may not be directly accessible to consciousness. As Klein puts it:

> An analyst plunges into phenomenology, but goes beyond it to generalizations that connect accessible and inaccessible levels of experience. These generalizations have almost invariably to do with purpose, function, accomplishment. The analyst's extraphenomenological concepts are meant to illuminate in these terms the *significance* of the experience he infers and the action he observes—not simply the existential ones which are based on conscious experience, but also the meanings or significance of inferred, unconscious fantasies. (p. 14)

This line of argument has been taken up and extended in the recent work of Roy Schafer (1976). Schafer not only develops a more systematic and detailed critique of metapsychology but carries the argument further in an attempt to provide a substitute for it in his "action language." An exploration of the action-language approach is beyond our present concern (Meissner 1979a, 1979b), but the critique of metapsychology is very much to the point.

Schafer centers his attack on the use of the natural-science model in psychoanalysis. This scientific model approaches the problem of explanation by inferring entities, structures, processes, and other properties and qualities of the object of investigation in order to give an account of the regularities observable in the object of investigation. The result of this approach in psychoanalysis is an elaborate system of concepts which infers a complex set of properties, qualities, structures, functions, energies, capacities, and mechanisms to explain a wide variety of behavior patterns. Schafer (1976) puts the argument quite clearly:

> The terms of Freudian metapsychology are those of natural science. Freud, Hartmann, and others deliberately used the language of forces, energies, functions, structure, apparatus, and principles to establish and develop psychoanalysis along the lines of a physicalistic psychobiology.
>
> It is inconsistent with this type of scientific language to speak of intentions, meanings, reasons, or subjective experience. Even though

in the first instance, which is the psychoanalytic situation, psychoanalysts deal essentially with reasons, emphases, choices, and the like,
as metapsychologists they have traditionally made it their objective to
translate these subjective contents and these actions into the language
of functions, energies, and so forth. . . . They have suppressed the
intentionalistic, active mode. In line with this strategy, reasons become forces, emphases become energies, activity becomes function,
thoughts become representations, affects become discharges or
signals, deeds become resultants, and particular ways of struggling
with the inevitable diversity of intentions, feelings, and situations
become structures, mechanisms, and adaptations. And, in keeping
with the assumption of thoroughgoing determinism, the word *choice*
has been effectively excluded from the metapsychological vocabulary. (p. 103)

A particular problem with this natural science approach in psychoanalysis—a problem that Schafer sees, incidentally, as a byproduct of the
natural science mode of thinking—involves the use of metaphor, particularly anthropomorphic metaphor in psychoanalytic theorizing. Freud himself was constantly anthropomorphizing his theoretical constructs. He
often spoke in dramatic terms of the various psychic structures and
topographic systems and even of the instinctual drives, as though they were
purposeful, meaning-creating, choice-making, and action-oriented entities. As Schafer points out, it is as though these entities were minds within
the mind or minute homunculi working within the psychic apparatus—the
"ghosts in the machine" of Gilbert Ryle ([1949] 1965). Such anthropo-
morphisms not only do not belong within the natural science frame of
reference; to Schafer's way of thinking, they serve as dramatic metaphors
that reflect a primitive form of primary-process thinking and substantializa-
tion or reification which hardly merits the name of theory. In creating this
multiplicity of anthropomorphized agencies, these multiple centers of
psychic agency and activity, the natural science model necessarily violates
the role of the personal purposive agent, the experiencing human being
behind the personal "I." It is as though Freud were unable to exclude
something that is essential to the account of human behavior but is
logically excluded by the demands of a natural science approach. He
maintained the two different modes of thinking and languages in his
theory: one a language of natural science processes and functions, and the
other a language of purposes and intentions.

Schafer argues, in fact, that psychoanalysis cannot do without the person
as agent and that precisely this fact of psychic life is central to the
psychoanalytic view of man. The interpreting analyst does not address a
mechanism, but rather a human being. Similarly, it is not ego as structure
or organization of functions that enters into a therapeutic alliance but

rather an integral person. These concepts and the psychoanalytic practice related to them seem to imply an agency standing outside the play of psychic forces and the elaboration of functions and mechanisms. Thus there is an unavoidable gap between the personal agent on one side and the natural science psychic apparatus on the other. The echoes of earlier criticisms by Fairbairn (1952) and Guntrip (1969, 1971) concerning the lack of a personal ego in psychoanalytic ego psychology and the problems inherent in the notion of a systematic or functional ego are easy to identify in Schafer's argument.

In general, these criticisms of the metapsychology move toward a frank rejection of any emphasis on mechanisms, processes, hypothetical forces and their transformations, or the organization of structures that might be seen as mechanical or as involving hypothesized entities irrelevant to and unproductive in the work of psychoanalysis. The approach generated from such criticisms tends to center psychoanalytic concern on issues of meaning, symbolic reference, motivation, purpose, reasons, and intentions (Schafer 1976), and on the goals and values inherent in human behavior (Gedo 1979). The resulting dichotomy in psychoanalytic viewpoints can be posed in terms of the contrast between the notion of psychoanalytic theory as a result of inference and hypothesis formation based primarily on observation and the notion of psychoanalytic theory as the result of analysis of meanings and the relationships between levels of meaning based primarily on immediate experience and symbolic understanding.

Between these dialectically polarized approaches, psychoanalysts struggle to find a clinically relevant and significant path, at the same time endeavoring to avoid theoretical oversimplification that might ultimately do disservice to the clinical enterprise. Many analysts try to weave a difficult middle course between the Scylla of a view of psychoanalysis as merely a natural science and the Charybdis of an emphasis on meaning and symbol that essentially abandons a metapsychological approach altogether. Perhaps one of the major contemporary thinkers who has given his imprimatur to this more complex and nuanced middle course of psychoanalytic thinking is the French philosopher Paul Ricoeur (1970). Ricoeur refuses to abandon an economic-energic frame of reference for psychoanalysis, together with its metapsychological elaborations, in the interest of embracing exclusively and unequivocally his own version of a psychoanalytic hermeneutic, which emphasizes meanings, their connections, and their symbolic references. At the same time, he rejects the idea of psychoanalysis as simply reducible to the terms of natural science. The nuance of his position is best heard in his own words:

Within a topographic-economic explanation, the status of interpretation, or *Deutung,* presents itself at first as an aporia. If we emphasize the deliberately anti-phenomenological bent of the topography, we appear to remove any basis for a reading of psychoanalysis as hermeneutics; the substitution of economic notions of cathexis—i.e., placement and displacement of energy—for the notion of intentional consciousness and intended object apparently calls for a naturalistic explanation and excludes an understanding of meaning through meaning. In short, it would seem that the topographic-economic point of view can uphold an energetics but not a hermeneutics. And yet there is no doubt that psychoanalysis is a hermeneutics: it is not by accident but by intention that it aims at giving an interpretation of culture in its entirety. . . . And if we move from the periphery to the center, from the theory of culture to the theory of dreams and the neuroses, which forms the hard core of psychoanalysis, we are constantly led back to interpretation, to the act of interpreting, to the work of interpretation. . . . But the problem of interpretation is exactly coextensive with the problems of meaning or representation. Hence, psychoanalysis is interpretation from beginning to end.

This is where the aporia arises: What is the status of representation or ideas in relation to the notions of instinct, aim of instinct, and affect? How can an interpretation of meaning through meaning be integrated with an economics of cathexis, withdrawal of cathexis, anti-cathexis? At first glance, there seems to be an antinomy between an explanation governed by the principles of the metapsychology and an interpretation that necessarily moves among meanings and not among forces, among representations or ideas and not among instincts. As I see it, the whole problem of the Freudian epistemology may be centralized in a single question: How can the economic explanation be *involved* in an interpretation dealing with meanings; and conversely, how can interpretation be an *aspect* of the economic explanation? It is easier to fall back on a disjunction: either an explanation in terms of energy, or an understanding in terms of phenomenology. It must be recognized, however, that Freudianism exists only on the basis of its refusal of that disjunction. (pp. 65–66)

The dialectic of these various positions within psychoanalysis leaves us in something of a quandary. We must conclude either that there is no consistent image of man that psychoanalysis embraces and expresses or that the images of man are so multiple, diverse, and complex that they embrace a spectrum of perspectives and approaches, all of which have relevance to our understanding of human psychological functioning, but none of which can stake an exclusive claim to predominance or priority within psychoanalysis. Clearly, we are operating in a conceptual and cultural context decidedly different from the context within which Freud carried on his psychoanalytic thinking. The psychoanalytic perspectives are considerably more open to a variety of influences and determinants that cannot be expressed in terms of intrapsychic dynamics alone. Contemporary psychoanalysis has by no means left the original Freudian insight behind, but it has learned that indeed there are more things in the heaven and earth of psychic functioning than can be accounted for simply by the reductionistic and primitive energic formulations from which Freud began his odyssey.

It seems obvious that the implications of this discussion are profound, not only within psychoanalysis itself, both as a theory and as a clinical enterprise, but also within the immediate discussion of the relationship between psychoanalysis and religion. Insofar as psychoanalytic thinking in general has shifted its ground, the approach within psychoanalysis to religious experience must be made to correspond in focus. The argument that Freud approached within the context of his own scientific and cultural milieu must be reapproached, reevaluated, and reformulated in terms of broader and more developed contemporary perspectives. Clearly, the final word of psychoanalysis on religious experience and its impact on the human condition was not spoken in the closing lines of *The Future of an Illusion*. In fact, the question has in our own time become even more difficult, challenging, and profound.

9. THE RELIGIOUS VERSUS THE PSYCHOANALYTIC PERSPECTIVE

In considering the relationship between psychoanalysis and the understanding of religious experience, we clearly encounter a tension between points of view that may not be entirely resolvable. In the initial approach to the understanding of religious phenomena offered by Freud, the opposition seems diametric and offers little possibility for reconciliation or meaningful dialogue. However, as I have suggested above, the analytic understanding of psychic functioning has undergone considerable development and modification of the earlier Freudian views. Moreover, the contemporary theological perspective has become considerably more nuanced under the influence of a succession of important developments in theological understanding, and particularly as a result of the emergence and development of a more articulated and sophisticated theological anthropology. Such developments on both sides of the psychoanalytic-religious impasse have opened up the possibility for more meaningful dialogue and for a significant and possibly productive dialectic of positions.

A useful way of advancing this understanding is by exploring various tensions and polarities in the interaction of psychoanalytic and religious thinking, so as to grasp the extent to which psychoanalytic thinking and religious thinking have moved toward a possible softening of their respective positions that might allow these tensions and conceptual polarities to be modified. The dialectic between the psychoanalytic perspective and the religious perspective can be spelled out in terms of a number of points, of which I shall focus on the following: (1) the relative emphasis on consciousness versus unconsciousness; (2) the relative emphasis on freedom versus determinism; (3) the view of behavior as truly teleological rather than as causal; (4) the understanding of man's experience in epigenetic as opposed to reductionistic terms; (5) the view of human behavior as moral as opposed to instinctually motivated, and (6) the view of man's experience as supernatural as opposed to merely natural.

Consciousness versus Unconsciousness

The principal emphasis in the Judeo-Christian tradition is on the conscious aspects of human experience. The psychology implicit in a theological anthropology is essentially a psychology of the ego and the superego, with their functions. The introduction of a psychology of the unconscious conflicted with this overarching perspective of conscious man at some of its most sensitive points. This was particularly the case insofar as the understanding of the unconscious as especially dependent on and powered by instinctual drives, both libidinal and aggressive, posed a considerable threat to the more rationalistic, controlled, and idealistic view of human psychology embedded in the religious tradition. As has often been noted, the misapprehension of the Freudian model of the unconscious as containing nothing but libidinal drives and the popular misconception of Freud's thinking about the unconscious as an endorsement of sexual license undoubtedly contributed much of the early and persisting hostility to psychoanalytic formulations, the reverberations of which are not limited to religious circles but can even be heard from the mouths of some psychiatrists.

We have no difficulty at this point in recognizing such a view as a distortion of Freud's thinking. Even so, the emergence of a psychoanalytic psychology of the ego has changed the overall picture considerably. Psychoanalysis can no longer be described as a psychology of the unconscious alone; its theory now includes an elaborate and highly complex psychology of ego and superego functions which has significantly expanded the range of its explanatory subtlety and power. In particular, the elaboration of concepts of conflict-free areas of ego-functioning and of the autonomy of the ego, both primary and secondary, has brought the psychoanalytic theoretical perspective much closer to the traditional philosophic concerns that characterize the Judeo-Christian tradition.

The existence of unconscious mental processes forms the fundamental postulate of and the basic source of data for psychoanalytic thinking. It has come to be an absolutely essential working hypothesis of psychoanalysis, with solid and continuing confirmation in clinical experience. There has been a widely accepted view that unconscious processes go on outside of and without any attendant conscious functioning in such a way that consciousness could be seen as only a secondary expression of mental operations, while the primary modality of psychic functioning was unconscious. More recently, however, conscious and unconscious levels of mental operation have been seen as more intensely interacting in a variety of modalities.

In general, the emphasis on unconscious meanings and on the interplay between levels of conscious and unconscious significance has tended to narrow the extreme gap that had been placed between unconscious phenomena and their conscious derivatives. Ricoeur's (1970) attempt to address levels of psychic meanings in terms of a hermeneutic methodology that would decipher the latent level of significance behind the more conscious and available semantic text exemplifies this recent tendency to read the unconscious and the conscious in interrelated terms. Much of the evidence of the unconscious provided by Freud was based on his analysis of dreams, a phenomenon in which layers of meaning and their interlocking significances are particularly available for such a semantically based account. Freud also provided countless examples of the role of unconscious factors in common experience, particularly in regard to the psychopathology of everyday life (1901) and in his discussion of humor (1905).

The discovery of the unconscious should not have caused much surprise, at least on a descriptive level, since as Freud himself pointed out, poets and dramatists have always known that human beings are capable of living out meanings without being aware of them, or that an individual's action may carry an intrinsic significance of which he remains not at all or possibly only dimly aware. Only later may he discover that the result of his action was in fact what he intended, despite his conscious intentions to the contrary.

But for the philosophic mind, the notion of the unconscious or of unconscious actions poses difficulties, raising the question of what it means to say that there are mental processes that operate outside of conscious awareness, that the mind in its psychic functioning is at least at times deprived of the very quality that seems most essentially to define it, namely, consciousness.

For example, one of the central themes of modern phenomenology is the doctrine of intentionality, which proposes, to simplify a bit, that every act of the mind is essentially directed toward, aimed at, or oriented to an "other." Intentionality is thus a characteristic of all mental acts, including not only cognitive acts such as perceiving, imagining, and judging but affective acts as well. In a phenomenological perspective, then, every act of the mind intends an object, and it is by virtue of this act of intending that objects are rendered present and take on meaning for the subject. The act of intending is simultaneously an act of conferring meaning on the object. In these terms, as, for example, in the philosophy of Husserl, reflection on the structure of the mind and reflection on the structure of its intentional acts become synonymous, in that the mind is defined essentially in relation to intentionality. The reflection on intentionality is usually carried out in reference to conscious acts as an absolutely necessary point of departure. But the theory of intentional analysis also presupposes a crucial distinction between explicit or thematic intentionality and a nonthematic but exercised intentionality. The latter is lived and experienced but not reflectively expressed. Phenomenology sets itself the task of making explicit and thematic what was previously only implicit and lived. This parallel between phenomenology and psychoanalysis has been observed and commented on (Waelhens 1959a).*

Phenomenology has developed in the direction of formulating a view that considers man as a being the meaning of whose existence is determined by and expressive of the significant relationships he establishes between himself and others, both in the immediate world of his experience and beyond (including God). Addressing the problem of the unconscious, Waelhens (1959b) writes:

> It is clear that if the unconscious must be [considered] as made up of an agglomeration of contents—dynamic or not—shot through and manipulated by biological forces radically heterogeneous to consciousness, we end up with the exact contrary of what psychoanalytic experience—obstinately and for more than half a century—proves with an evidence as blinding as the light of the sun: that is, that our actions, beneath their manifest meaning, have a meaning, and one which it is possible to elucidate, *even at the level of the unconsciousness of the one who poses them*. But it is precisely this which becomes absurd if the unconscious is defined as that which is radically other than the conscious and meaningful or—it comes to the same thing—if one holds consciousness and life to be "realities" of simply different kinds. (p. 222)

Thus, the philosophical, phenomenological approach radically reverses the psychoanalytic dichotomy between conscious and unconscious mental processes. It sets itself against the proposition that the unconscious is the true reality and that conscious acts can only be explained or understood when reduced to parallel unconscious processes. Rather, both the conscious and the unconscious are seen as participating in the same order of reality and significance. Intentionality rather than consciousness becomes the defining characteristic of psychic life. Further, the distinction between intentionality as lived and as explicitly thematized gives rise to a view of consciousness and its absence as existing on a continuum in which human mental processes may be conscious and/or unconscious without necessarily being exclusively either.

Such a view is consonant both with actual clinical experience and with Freud's many statements concerning the nature of neurotic symptoms as expressing meaning, as well as with his view of dream processes and other unconscious psychic manifestations. Even the general theory of instinctual drives offers reinforcement to this view—even where Freud seems to be thinking in extremely biological and reductionistic terms. Freud (1915b) defined "instinct" as "a concept on the frontier between the mental and the

---

*For a more extensive consideration of the differences in orientation between phenomenology and psychoanalysis and their potential dialectical integration, see Hougaard (1981).

somatic, as the psychical representative of the stimuli originating from within the organism and reaching the mind, as a measure of the demand made upon the mind for work in consequence of its connection with the body" (pp. 121–22). It is clear that in this context Freud was not drawing a hard and fast line between instinct as biological derivative and as psychical representation.

In Freud's view, then, instinctual drives originate in the body but become translated into a psychological order in the form of felt impulses or needs directed toward specifiable goals. The linking of instinctual drives to the notions of purposive direction and goal orientation introduces an element of finality and purposive meaning into the very concept of drive itself. Thus, the Freudian concept of instinctual drives expresses a fundamental fact about the human condition; namely, that man is driven even as he is self-directing, that he is subject to powerful psychic forces which he also has the capacity to use for his own ends. The basic instinctual drives in their psychoanalytic sense are characterized by an inherent psychic intentionality as well as by an economic-quantitative aspect. In this sense, the energic is dynamically transformed into a significance.

In phenomenological terms, what was once lived and experienced is now past and has ceased to be. But this does not mean that it has lost its character of intentionality or its capacity to influence behavior. In a psychoanalytic view, the lived past results in a concretization, a distillation of meaning, that is located within man's animated body. Moreover, it is through man's body that he exists in the world, and this fact provides the basis for the profound historicity of human experience. The psychoanalytic methodology is nothing less than an approach to the discovery of such concrete structuralizations and derivatives of man's individual history as a means of gaining insight into his lived and experienced intentionality.

The essential discovery of both phenomenology and psychoanalysis, then, is that the basic intentionality of psychic life and its penetration with meaning are a fundamental characteristic of human mental life, and that such intentionality is defined in terms of meanings that are at the same time dynamic and historic. Within this general frame of reference, the existence of unconscious mental activity plays a central role.

In our present inquiry, too, the role of the unconscious occupies a central position. The distinction between conscious and unconscious cuts across the distinction between ego and nonego as components of psychic structure. The parallel distinction between explicit or thematic intentionality and nonthematic or lived intentionality has a descriptive validity that establishes the relevance of meaning at all levels of psychic life. Whether such meaning is experienced or not becomes a secondary issue. The determination of such meaning is a question of central importance to the understanding of human mental life.

Awareness at a given moment is determined by conscious and unconscious elements. Cognitive functions belong to the ego, but their operation is subject to determination by other parts of the psychic structure. Such determination is by and large unconscious, although not exclusively so. It serves to distort or color the reality-oriented intentionality of the ego. The degree to which the ego is able to function on the basis of its inherent reality orientation is a measure of the extent to which its functioning is autonomous. We can add here that the religious perspective embraces the entire spectrum of reality, internal as well as external, supernatural as well as natural.

As long as the reality of a supernatural order of existence is included in the schema, adequate ego functioning must be measured to some degree against the demands imposed by that dimension of reality. Here we are dependent on theology, since it makes explicit what revelation tells us about the character of the supernatural. From a psychological perspective, there is no reason to think that unconscious determinants need stand in opposition to the basic reality orientation of the ego. It is customary to regard unconscious determinants stemming from the id as introducing a certain element of fantasy into the ego's relation to objects, but even this is by no means a necessary condition. In addition, psychoanalysis has come to recognize in recent years that the role of unconscious and primary-process factors is not limited merely to distortion or pathological expression. There is, in fact, a broad spectrum of important adaptive functions carried out by the psychic apparatus that require an interplay with unconscious and even primary-process forms of psychic activity (Wallerstein 1973).

Ultimately, then, in both a philosophical and a psychoanalytic perspective, intentionality is fundamental to the whole of psychic life. This intentionality extends, as we have seen, to the unconscious as well as to the conscious aspects of psychic functioning. But intentionality cannot be considered in merely cognitive terms. Rather, it must be regarded as extending to all aspects of human relatedness. It represents an openness or directedness toward objects and persons—in other words, toward reality. It is operative in the context of action by which the person relates himself to objects. The meaning that corresponds to such intentionality cannot be spelled out in simple logical categories but must carry within itself at least some of the determinants of action.

FREEDOM VERSUS DETERMINISM

The second basic point of confrontation that has set psychoanalytic thinking apart from more religious orientations has been the issue of psychic determinism. As I have already indicated, the capacity for intentionality, along with its correlative, freedom of self-determination and choice, is a core concept in the theologically derived image of man. The notion of freedom in particular is integral to the very concept of man's participation in divine revelation and in a salvific economy. It is easy to see that a doctrine of total psychic determinism poses a serious threat to this orientation. This subject is of considerable importance and is central to the progression of the dialectic between psychoanalysis and theology. We will consider it in detail in chapter 10; here our focus is a more general attempt to locate the dichotomy between freedom and determinism in the context of the shifting currents that shape the contemporary discussion.

The concept of determinism with which Freud approached his work was radical indeed and derived primarily from his background in Helmholtzian physics. But such rigid determinism could not effectively be maintained and in fact makes little sense in the scientific purview of our own day. The essential notion was that psychic products and behaviors cannot be considered to occur randomly but rather must have determining causes that can be specified and understood. But Freud inevitably found himself dealing with the sequences of meanings and the chains of meaning that lay behind certain psychic experiences, rather than with determinative causal sequences. His work on dreams and on the production of psychic symptoms was largely of this order. Moreover, in therapy he found himself dealing with the meanings and connections of meanings that lie behind and seem intimately related to symptomatic events.

Not only did the focus of psychoanalysis shift from an understanding of determinism in rigidly causal terms to a determination of meanings, but its views on determinism have followed apace the shifts in the thinking about determinism in science in general. In his early approach to psychological problems, Freud intended determinism to be absolute and particular, in that every mental event had to have meaning and had to be determined immediately and in itself. Today analysts rarely apply the principle in this mechanical sense; in fact, they would have serious doubts whether mental life could be adequately viewed in such a rigidly deterministic fashion. Rather, the notion of determinism in contemporary psychoanalysis is conceived in considerably broader and more flexible terms.

In his original approach Freud would have found every instance of the psychopathology of everyday life interpretable, much like a dream, and its relation to a specific unconscious wish capable of being established. Thus some wish and its related motive would have been seen as determining the slip or the forgetting. More recently, however, Anna Freud (1967) has made the point that one might not be able to explain every individual act in terms of such specific determinants. With regard to the misplacing or losing of objects, for example, we may have to recognize that in the child's early development a general tendency to misplace or lose things may be established which then may become a part of the individual's character structure. It is the general trait, the tendency to lose things, that becomes operative rather than one particular motive in the present for every specific loss.

This implies that determinism operates at the level of character formation and development rather than as a form of rigid, absolute causality having to do with the immediate behavior. Thus Robert Holt (1972), writing on the tension between the mechanistic and humanistic images of man in Freud's thinking, is able to say:

> What then about free will vs. determinism? Briefly, the two concepts are *not* antithetical: both are necessary and the two can coexist. To maintain that the subjective experience of being able to make a deliberate choice among alternatives is a delusion on the grounds that freedom means a capricious act unrelated to anything else is to miss the point entirely. Truly free behavior is not acting on an unpredictable whim, but acting in *self-consistent* ways, in harmony with one's ego-values. The person who is able to exert will power against temptation and to act with a sense of autonomy is just as much a part of the lawful natural world as one who feels utterly compelled by influences beyond his control, whether these are unconscious needs or external compulsions. Freedom of the will (or, more generally, ego autonomy) is not a philosophical absolute, it is a quantitative psychological variable, which can be diminished or enhanced in ways that are lawful and predictable. (p. 14)

From a religious perspective, the image of man must include self-determination as an essential element. To say that freedom is self-determination is not the same thing as to say that the individual's motivation plays a role in the determination of behavior. Self-determination and motivation are quite different things. One can, however, make a very good case for the influence of motivation, conscious or unconscious, on self-determination. In this sense, self-determination is subject to determination from many sources and is, therefore, overdetermined.

From the point of view of causality, self-determination is equivalent to the insertion of the ego as a causal agent in determining behavior. The essential point underlined by the phrase "self-determination" is that such self-mobilization on the part of the ego is proper to itself—in other words, that the ego is the independent source of its own operation. The ego's activity is thus determined within a context of motivating factors that contribute to its overdetermination, but within the context of its own operation, it is undetermined by anything outside of itself. Much of the argument over determinism and freedom is caught up in the confusion of these differentiable contexts.

TELEOLOGY VERSUS CAUSALITY

Another aspect of the theological view of man is that his functioning is essentially teleological—that is, governed by purposes, goals, and intentions rather than by mechanistic forces that drive his behavior willy-nilly in one direction or another. This problem is obviously related to the issues of determinism already discussed but is not peculiar to the psychoanalytic perspective. Rather, it reflects the inherent conflict between the scientific view of man, broadly conceived, and the religious one. The tension between the religious perspective and psychoanalysis is not as problematic as that between this perspective and certain radical and positivistic forms of behaviorism, but it remains a problem nonetheless.

In psychoanalysis, however, adherence to a radically causal view of behavior has become increasingly difficult. With the emergence of an ego psychology and the growing dissatisfaction with the more deterministic aspects of Freud's economic-energic concerns, there has been a drift in psychoanalytic theory toward more specifically dynamic viewpoints which tend to see behavior in terms of purposive action (Schafer 1973). Although the notion of teleology with its sense of inherent purposes directed toward preordained goals is scientifically repugnant, the psychoanalytic notion of function as process directed toward specific goals is not very far removed from this. In other words, tension is growing between psychoanalytic theorists who place increasing emphasis on the intentionality and purposive nature of man's behavior, whether conscious or unconscious, and those who adhere to a more strictly causal and nonteleological scientific model.

We have already noted the drift in psychoanalytic thinking away from causal models altogether. The proponents of a noncausal, intentional, semantic, and hermeneutically based understanding of psychoanalytic concepts have taken a radical stand against causal, mechanistic, and even substantive explanatory concepts in psychoanalysis (Schafer 1976). Such theorists view psychoanalysis not as a form of natural science but as a humanistic discipline that concerns itself exclusively with the search for meaning and the relationships of meaning that play themselves out in the realm of human intentionality. This noncausal, meaning-oriented perspective must be regarded as considerably more attuned to and congruent with the concerns and objectives of a theological anthropology.

However, the issue for psychoanalysis in determining its proper approach and methodology does not rest on its potential utility to other culture- and meaning-related disciplines. Psychoanalysis must first put its own house in order. Consequently, the questions regarding the appropriate perspective for and within psychoanalysis remain open to exploration and discussion. The point of view that I have expressed here and elsewhere is that psychoanalysis is ultimately a natural science and cannot escape the demands of a natural science methodology. However, it is unique among natural sciences in that it deals with the total complexity of the human organism, including a psychic life that is permeated with meaning and purpose. The constant challenge to psychoanalysis, as well as its continually renewed source of vitality and significance, is the possibility of bridging the chasm that the contemporary mind has constructed between the scientific and the humanistic realms.

EPIGENESIS VERSUS REDUCTIONISM

It must be said that one of the major causes of tension between a theological view of man and a psychoanalytic one has been the historical tendency of psychoanalysts to explain behavior and experience in reductionistic terms. By this I mean particularly the tendency for analysts to make explanations in terms of instinctual derivatives. This style of theoretical discourse prevailed during the early phase of analytic exploration when considerable interest and enthusiasm were invested in the understanding of the nature of the drives and their influence on human functioning.

This period has passed, however; analytic theory has been modified considerably by the addition of an elaborate understanding of ego functioning and its relevance to human behavior. Since the articulation of a more mature ego psychology and the still more recent efforts to articulate a psychoanalytic psychology of the self in superordinate terms, it has been increasingly apparent and consciously realized by analytic theorists as well as clinicians that reductive explanations cannot give a complete account of behavior, even though they may have considerable power and value in specific clinical contexts.

If the tendency to reductionistic explanation has been strong in the analytic tradition, it must also be said that the religious tradition has been excessively antireductionistic. Religious thinkers often tend to accept explanatory concepts that pertain only to the highest level of psychic organization and in terms of a more or less idealized schema. Just as it has historically been difficult for psychoanalysts to accept and integrate higher-order explanations into the analytic frame of reference because they fear that the more characteristically analytic insights, based on derivation from specific drives, will be diluted or contaminated, it has similarly been difficult for religious thinkers to integrate the influence of unconscious drive derivatives into their explanatory frame of reference because they have a corresponding fear that the explanation "from below" might undermine the inherent value of a higher-level and more religiously attuned understanding.

Our grasp of theoretical concepts and our sophistication in applying them have sufficiently advanced, I think, for us to realize that neither form of explanation taken exclusively can be adequate and that both approaches can be placed in conjunction and integrated within a broader frame of reference. In fact, this is what has been taking place—the broadening of psychoanalytic understanding has led to the incorporation of higher-order constructs and concepts dealing with man's organization and mental functioning, while the broadening of the theological image of man has opened the way to a gradual integration of those aspects of human motivation and emotional life that have been the stock in trade of psychoanalysis. Theology has become increasingly sensitive to the implications of man's sentient existence—to the import of man's humanity for his spirituality.

MORALITY VERSUS INSTINCT

There are, however, certain corollaries of these differential perspectives that have created fairly significant difficulties in integrating theological and psychoanalytic perspectives; perhaps the most prominent and telling of these concerns is morality. There is a tendency within the religious perspective to see human behavior primarily in moral terms; that is, it is relatively difficult for the religiously oriented thinker to acknowledge thoughts, feelings, actions, or behavior outside of accepted moral categories. The underlying religious concerns tend to raise the question of the moral relevance and value of each action, often in somewhat obsessional terms.

Thus the religious mentality tends toward hyperresponsibility, whether in the positive sense of seeking merit and grace or in the negative sense of accepting blame and guilt for sinful behavior. This general tendency to stress superego dynamics is a corollary of the stress on intentionality and inherent capacity for self-determination which is central to the religious perspective and which demands moralizing about behavior of all kinds. The trend in psychoanalysis has been diametrically opposed in that the appeal to unconscious determinants and specifically instinctual derivatives, seen as biologically based forces operating on a mental apparatus, tends to make significant inroads on this moralizing tendency.

The parameter of morality may cause great difficulties in attempts to talk across disciplinary lines: the religiously oriented person often sees moral implications and consequences where the psychoanalytically oriented observer sees none, or at least none of any consequence. Thus, for example, it is very difficult for religious persons to tolerate or even to acknowledge libidinal or aggressive impulses without immediately mobilizing superego condemnation. But it is also curious, from the opposite perspective, that one of the important dimensions of the therapeutic task within psychoanalysis is to bring the patient to accept his impulses and gradually to integrate and take responsibility for them. In neither case can the issue be said to be the unrestrained gratification of instinctual impulses; rather, it is the integration of such impulses within the broader framework of the reasonable, realistic, and responsible exercise of ego functions. There is a substantial paradox in this. Psychoanalysis, which takes psychic determinism as its starting point, finds its therapeutic objective to be the expansion and consolidation of human freedom and responsibility.

The Supernatural versus the Natural

The last point of divergence between the theological and the psychoanalytic views of man is perhaps the most significant and the least resolvable. It is the difference that still matters, that radically separates the religious perspective from all others, including the scientific. The religious view of man is specifically supernatural: it envisions man as related to a divine Creator and as specifically ordained by that Creator with an idealized and supernaturalized existence. This aspect of the religious perspective has no corollary in the psychoanalytic approach. It has no relevance for any natural science, psychoanalysis included. Moreover, it is an irresolvable point of difference in that the analytic perspective inherently has nothing to say about it. One either accepts the religious perspective through faith and embraces the religious belief system, or one does not. There are no grounds within psychoanalysis for either accepting or rejecting. Ricoeur (1970) comments in this connection:

> It is difficult to pinpoint what is properly psychoanalytic in Freud's interpretation of religion. However, it is essential to put into sharp focus those elements of his interpretation that merit the consideration of both believers and unbelievers. There is a danger that believers may sidestep his radical questioning of religion, under the pretext that Freud is merely expressing the unbelief of scientism and his own agnosticism; but there is also the danger that unbelievers may confuse psychoanalysis with this unbelief and agnosticism. . . . Psychoanalysis is necessarily iconoclastic, regardless of the faith or nonfaith of the psychoanalyst, and this "destruction" of religion can be the counterpart of a faith purified of all idolatry. Psychoanalysis as such cannot go beyond the necessity of iconoclasm. This necessity is open to a double possibility, that of faith and that of nonfaith, but the decision about these two possibilities does not rest with psychoanalysis. (p. 230)

Conclusions

It is clear from the foregoing considerations that the tensions that polarize the psychoanalytic and the religious perspectives cannot be completely resolved. Nonetheless, the degree of disagreement seems to have been significantly reduced by the evolution of attitudes and concepts that has taken place since the hardened opposition and relatively unbending scientism and dogmatism of an earlier time.

In some of the dimensions we have discussed, the degree of rapprochement and integration seems considerable. Certainly, in relationship to the dichotomy between consciousness and unconsciousness, there is no longer ground for a serious disparity between points of view. The philosophical and religious orientation has come to accept as a basic and essential part of human nature man's unconscious life and its implications. Similarly, psychoanalysis has developed resources for conceptualizing and utilizing a meaningful account of conscious behavior, not just as a derivative of unconscious determinants, but as inherently intelligible and relatively autonomous in its own right.

Similarly, the debate over the issue of freedom and determinism seems to have lost some of its intensity. Our current ability to understand the implications of freedom and to provide a more sophisticated and nuanced understanding of determinism has allowed for significant integration on this front. Nor does the issue of teleology versus causality press with the urgent insistence of earlier days. The contemporary approach to causality in a framework of a more developed scientific epistemology is considerably less rigid and leaves ample room for the play of intentions, purposes, goals, and directed action in general. We now understand that nothing of significance is lost to a scientific purview by an admission of such teleology. In former times, including Freud's, insistence on rigid causality was thought to be a necessary bulwark of scientific method.

Similarly, the old emphasis and reliance on reductive explanation, in terms of either unconscious derivatives or historical antecedents, has given way to a more nuanced understanding of the epigenetic transformations that dynamic configurations undergo in the course of an individual's development and life history. Thus, while a patient's frigidity may be described in terms of oedipal conflicts, this reduction does not provide a total explanation of the phenomenon. In fact, oedipal attachments have a history and development of their own that interact with the ongoing current of the patient's life. Frigidity is not merely an expression or a repetition of childhood infantile conflicts but is in addition an expression of ongoing problems occurring in a variety of forms throughout the patient's history and manifesting themselves in a context of meanings, relationships, interactions, purposes, and intentions that play themselves out in the immediate context of that patient's lived experience.

To whatever degree these currents have found their way into a common channel, there remain important differences whose reconciliation is problematic and whose divergences are the subject of the continuing dialogue. Common ground is more difficult to find around the issues of morality and supernaturality. Perhaps these tensions in the dialogue are irreducible. After all, it is the business of psychoanalysis to be amoral—and I emphasize that this does not in any sense mean *immoral*—as well as to assume that the substance it deals with is essentially natural. By the same token, it is the business of religion to concern itself with what is moral and supernatural.

From one point of view, these two disciplines serve each other's interests best by occupying themselves primarily with their proper concerns. Confusion arises when they try to play in each other's backyards and is acutely compounded when psychoanalysts try to decide moral issues on psycho-analytic bases, or when religious thinkers try to fuse spiritual concepts with psychoanalytic understandings. But it is important, nonetheless, for the continuation of the dialogue that all parties have an informed understanding of the real issues of debate, as well as an idea of the spurious issues. Undoubtedly, for example, moralists have a great deal to learn from psychoanalysts in the area of moral thinking, about the dynamics, implications, and expressions of the basic forces of mental life. By the same token, psychoanalysts may not be above profiting from some of the correctives of moral theory, particularly in the areas of ethics and values as they play themselves out in the psychoanalytic situation. While psychoanalysts have been assiduous in trying to maintain that the psychoanalytic situation is value-free or at least value-neutral (H. Hartmann 1960), the question still remains whether certain important values are inherent in the structure of the psychoanalytic situation, beyond the mere commitment to health that Hartmann is willing to allow (Meissner n.d.).

While progress can be anticipated in the area of moral and ethical considerations, the same may not be true of the divergence between the natural and the supernatural perspectives. I think the most we can expect in this area is a proper respect for the limits of human understanding and of the explanatory power of a given discipline. For example, the fact that psychoanalysis has no grounds on which it can decide the issue of super-natural influence does not reflect a failure of psychoanalytic method, although some analysts take umbrage at such an idea. What is at issue is simply a limitation of scientific methodology, neither more nor less. Even if, for example, we elucidate the unconscious roots of certain mystical experiences by tracing them back to infantile determinants and gain some understanding of their psychic function by identifying certain forms of interaction between the components of psychic functioning, we may have an understanding of no more than the psychological components of the mystical experience. There is nothing in such an account that could prove that the experience was therefore completely explained as a purely natural phenomenon. Nothing in psychoanalytic methodology either excludes or argues for the possibility of some form of supernatural activity. Considerations of this kind lie completely beyond the scope of psychoanalysis and must rest upon an other than scientific basis.

Consequently, I would argue that in these complex areas of human understanding progress is possible only when we keep acutely and accurately in mind both the grounds of compatibility and the discrete areas of incompatibility. If we understand our capacity to know and acknowledge the limits of our knowing in certain areas of human experience, possibilities for deepening our understanding and for avoiding the pitfalls of misunderstanding obtain.

10. FREEDOM IN PSYCHOANALYSIS
AND IN THEOLOGY

Among the tensions that separate the psychoanalytic image of man from the theological one, the concept of freedom is central. In the previous section, I discussed some of the modifications in the understanding of both freedom and determinism that allow for greater rapprochement and dialogue between the respective positions. However, there is more to be said about the notion of freedom in both its theological and its psychoanalytic significance. I would like to explore in greater depth the implications of freedom in both realms, in the hope of emerging with a clearer view of their congruence and divergence.

Freedom in Theology

The concept of freedom has always held a central position in Christian theology, because so much depends on it, and because the very notion carries a residue of mystery that defies definition. One might say that the concept of human freedom is the most significant element in the image of man provided by a theological anthropology.

There is probably no concept more necessary to the reconstruction of a psychology of grace either. Yet it is the concept that is most easily misunderstood and abused. Christian theology from the time of Paul has been preoccupied with the problem of freedom, because, it seems to me, human freedom is the one element without which religious existence becomes an impossibility. In some fundamental sense, the very acceptance of revelation depends on man's free decision. The participation in a supernatural order, as Rahner (1961) has suggested, demands a free response, such that participation on any other grounds would constitute a violation of the structure and dynamism not only of man's nature but of the supernatural.

Theologians in the Christian tradition without exception have taken human freedom as an established fact. The capacity to choose between limited alternatives has been felt to be a given of human nature. But the unique capacity of the human agent is to determine lines of future activity when different possibilities of reaction and contingency remained open. In this sense, human beings are capable of deliberate choice, and freedom reaches beyond the bounds of mere contingency. The result of such free action is in itself contingent, but this contingency is the result of deliberation, decision, and responsible choice. For the greater part of the theological tradition, there has been little need to prove that human beings acted in this way. Theologians considered freedom to be an existential given of the human condition, however problematic.

In so doing, the theological mind refused to confuse issues of contingency and liberty. Liberty was a derivative of rational action, an affirmation that man comprehends the limits of possibility and exercises choice in controlling its actualization. The consequences of this affirmation are considerable. Any suppression or limitation of man's liberty, by coercion, external force, or moral pressure, is equivalent to treating man lower than accords with his natural dignity. Insofar as a man allows himself to be so treated, he opts for a condition of diminished worth.

The very existence of choice expresses the fact that freedom implies self-affirmation. Beyond this lies the question of the nature of the self that affirms itself. Embedded in the essence of Christianity is the notion that man deals with reality in terms of giving meaning, and consequently the self that gives such meaning is definable, intelligible and has an inherent structure. Any affirmation that is ultimately inconsistent with the structure of the self is thus not a self-affirmation but a self-denial or a self-negation. Such self-negation, further, is not a manifestation of freedom but an abuse of it. The basic notion of freedom does not imply absolute indifference to either of two alternatives, although in the case of finite agents one must suppose that either alternative is a possible object of choice. But in the normal course of events, only one of the alternatives can be regarded as in better accord with the structure of the human self. Thus, the Christian and theological notion of freedom is not that of an expression of unconditional autonomy. Theological freedom is more an acceptance of responsibility than an absence of law. In the divine order of things, freedom is not given to man so that he can do good or evil; it is given to him so that he can do good in a meaningful and rational way.

A Christian theological perspective in this sense takes a stand on freedom opposed to any other. The theological concept of freedom implies certain qualities of the self. Theologians would insist that the human being as a free agent is rooted in the ground of being that transcends any particular human agent, but without which an agent is nothing and has no meaning. Human existence derives from a source beyond itself, and human activity reveals ultimately the effects not only of a finite agent but of an infinite agent as well. Second, the human self cannot be realistically and meaningfully conceived only in terms of an atemporal idea of man abstracted from either personal or human history. And finally, human history cannot be adequately embraced by the understanding of man alone. Man's history takes on a fuller meaning only when it is contemplated within a vision of man as possessed by an author of history. This particular vision is achieved only through the exercise of divine graciousness in the form of a personal self-revelation that invites man to faith.

The consequences of this radical stand on the notion of freedom are significant and far-reaching. In the Christian theological view, historical man is flawed. Original sin introduces into the heart of human nature a limitation, a defect, that cannot be overcome by natural means. At best, humankind can reduce its effects, but the defect itself cannot be eliminated. In consequence, human actions carry within them this inherent deficiency by which they are at one and the same time self-realizing and self-defeating. Man cannot reach a level of perfect self-affirmation, since insofar as he affirms himself he affirms a self torn between the polarities of being and nonbeing. In this regard, theology sets itself against all forms of optimistic naturalism that suppose that man can achieve totally satisfactory self-expression through education, welfare, training, guidance, or even asceticism. A self-destructive impulse vitiates all purely human effort. This issue was taken up in the struggle between Augustine and his Pelagian and semi-Pelagian opponents. Augustine's victory has put its stamp on the subsequent centuries of Christian theology.

The Augustinian view of freedom, with its implicit assertion that man's self-affirmation must ultimately be an affirmation of God in the self, is anathema to most naturalists. There is no room in their view for a concept in which man transcends the order of nature, or in which he can truly realize himself and his existence only beyond nature. But the theological view of Western Christianity has always denied that a purely secularist or naturalist orientation can have ultimate meaning for mankind. This same divergence in point of view reverberates throughout the debate between Freud as naturalist scientist and his theological opponent Pfister (see above, chapter 4). From the theological point of view, secularism and naturalism are self-defeating and therefore limit more than liberate human action. Beyond this, however, is a further divergence between the theologian and the secularist. The theologian asserts that God has made a revelation concerning the nature and the destiny of man. The secularist in turn denies that there is any such revelation and claims that the destiny and the meaning of man can be envisioned only within the limits of the natural world. This divergence of opinion cannot be resolved on the ground of freedom, for one is as free to believe as not to believe. To assert that there is a revelation is as much a manifestation of freedom as to deny it.

Christian freedom, then, cannot be absolute. The unconditioned freedom of the Creator is not and cannot be the freedom of man. History, and indeed psychoanalysis, helps us to understand the extent to which man is capable of abusing his freedom and the ways in which such abuse brings suffering both to individuals and to the community. But within the Christian perspective, there is belief and trust in the omnipotence, benevolence, and ultimate efficacy of divine will. The designs of God's providence cannot be thwarted by human willfullness or rebellion. In the face of the inherent defectiveness of human nature and the abuse and willfullness of human freedom, God exercises his divine beneficence by giving rise to an inspiration within the souls of men to bring them to a more meaningful and authentic use of their freedom.

This divine action goes by the name of grace, the gracious intervention of God in a limited and imperfect world that prompts men toward the fulfillment of divine purposes, the enrichment of God's kingdom in this world, and the achievement of the Christian vision of man. Thus, there is a constant tension in the Christian dialogue between the weakness and limits of human freedom, on the one hand, and the power and majesty of God at work in human beings and human history to bring about God's purposes in this world, on the other. Such doctrine is not delusion, nor does it leave open only the path of passivity and resignation. If it accepts suffering, disappointment, and loss, it does not pretend that they can be transformed into satisfactions or pleasures. It does not deny the role of the human agent in forming his own destiny or the course of history. It is, in fact, an affirmation that history is more a divine comedy than a Greek tragedy.

Such a view of freedom as proposed by Christian theology is ultimately a challenge and a program to achieve the maximum degree of freedom of which man is capable. It calls for the elimination of obstacles to human choice, whether they derive from external forces, from the human condition, or from the limitations and inhibitions imposed by defects of character and by neurosis. True freedom cannot be achieved by retiring from the struggle with the world and with oneself. Christian man is always open to the world and its action. His faith challenges him to meet the world on its own terms and to struggle with the problems of individual psychology, of society and culture, and of nations and history, to allow for the growth of freedom. He is called to activity, to struggle, to creativity—to the effort to do his best despite the limitations of knowledge and energy.

Despite the risks and uncertainties, the failures and frustrations, the man who so uses his freedom, however defective and limited it may be, buttressed by faith and the power of grace—that man is free in the fullest sense. More than the mere capacity for choice, here there is the potentiality for action, creativity, and the liberation of human potential. In the theological perspective, then, the issue is not merely freedom *from* but rather freedom *for*. The theological view of freedom, in other words, does not seek merely to liberate man from the chains of his inhibitions, compulsions, doubts, and neurotic self-involvement. Rather, it seeks to liberate man for the purpose of becoming something greater—more dynamic, more creative, more a force in the world—in order to realize not only his own potential but the betterment of all mankind.

Freedom, then, is a complex notion which cannot be defined by any simple set of formulas. We are forced to view it from many perspectives. That is why the theological reflection on freedom is open-ended and must be renewed continually.

Fundamental to the notion of freedom is a second notion, that of self-affirmation. Freedom is an act of self-affirmation. The description of freedom as a choice between certain limited and nonessential goods is the most superficial and meaningless level of analysis. Much more profoundly, freedom involves an affirmation of the self that is essential to integral human existence. The self needs affirmation, or else it withers, withdraws, becomes less and less self. Affirmation is necessary to the growth and maintenance of spiritual life.

One can carry this notion a step further. The self is a structured reality, no matter how the terms of its structure are defined. We have been attempting to indicate some of the psychological aspects of that structure, but that is only one dimension. The essential point is that self-affirmation is in and of itself self-construction. The structure of the self is evolving, is always in the process of attainment. The affirmation of self in and through freedom may also be defined in terms of structural organization. Freedom is thereby the *via regia* for self-organization, self-structuralization, and self-perfection. We can crystallize the psychological dimension of this aspect of freedom in the term "self-synthesis." The free act, therefore, is an act of self-definition by which the ego shapes and elaborates the reality of the structure of the self. It involves a transition from potency to actuality, from imperfection to perfection, from indetermination to determination.

It is important, of course, to realize that human freedom from another point of view is a limping, fragile affair. The affirmation or structuralization of self is always incomplete and tenuous. It achieves its objectives, if at all, in a painfully partial and piecemeal fashion. Perhaps man's hardest task is to become a fully autonomous and total self. Psychoanalysts know this bitter truth all too well.

Yet, this is precisely the task man is called to by the dynamisms inherent in his own nature. In fact, the goal of liberty—perfect self-affirmation—is beyond his capability. Herein lies the most perplexing and mysterious, yet the most essential facet of human existence: man, who is compelled by the most profound dynamisms of his nature to seek the perfection of his own self-affirmation, carries within himself obstacles to that achievement. His very affirmation is an affirmation of a torn and divided reality. His situation is not desperate, however, as we well know. The self-affirming and creative aspects of human freedom are an integral and highly significant part of the divine plan. The dynamisms inherent in man's freedom are contiguous with the dynamisms of the salvific intervention of God. The completion of man's self-affirmation is made possible only through the action of grace. But one cannot say that man's self-affirmation is completed by grace. That is an impossible statement because it destroys the reality of man's self-affirmation and distorts the nature of grace. Affirmation of self must remain an active process carried out through the agency of man himself, or else it is no longer self-affirmation. Further, it is essential to the nature of grace that it exercise no effect independent of the agency of man himself. Rather, we must say that man's self-affirmation becomes more perfectly affirmation of self through the action of grace.

In a theological perspective, then, freedom is not so much a property as an enterprise demanding intense activity and setting objectives as severe as any man proposes to himself. The enterprise is to become fully oneself. But the vision of what he is to become is itself beyond man's capacity. The goal of man's self-affirmation must be seen in the light of revelation: there the complete vision of man and his nature is embedded. It is the work of theological reflection to bring that vision into focus. It is interesting, therefore, that Christian theology stresses the profound reality of freedom and emphasizes its significance in the Christian life. In so doing, it gives to human freedom a most important role in the image of man consonant with a theological anthropology.

Freedom in Psychoanalysis

The primacy of freedom is a fundamental given of the theological image of man. For the psychoanalyst, however, freedom is neither a given nor fundamental to his image of man. Rather, it is a hard-won inference whose existence is always precarious and dependent on proof. If theology presumes freedom, psychoanalysis always questions it—and, in fact, most often presumes a lack of freedom in human actions.

This tension inherent in the dialogue expressed itself in Freud's time in terms of the opposition between determinism and freedom. I have already argued that the discussion has moved beyond that particular polarity. Our scientific understanding no longer demands absolute separation and opposition of these concepts. We can see that science does not demand immediate and absolute determinism. We can also understand that freedom does not imply an absence of determination but rather is relative and must coincide with various forms of causal determination. Moreover, freedom implies a form of determination proper to itself. It is not, therefore, beyond nature; it is an essential part of man's nature.

Although the distance between these concepts has been reduced, the tension between them has not thereby been completely eliminated. Theology presumes freedom as the given consensual basis of its reflection.

Psychoanalysis, however, makes no such presumption. It deals with freedom in concrete, historical, and existential terms. In its view, freedom is always fragile, uncertain, limited, and demanding demonstration. It is a goal to be achieved, if only partially, through the therapeutic work of the psychoanalytic process. This sense of freedom is different, then, from the assumed and idealized, as well as normative, sense of freedom that pervades theological reflection. While the substance may be identical, the approach and the manner of conceptualization differ radically. The question, then, has to be whether theology and psychoanalysis can speak to each other across this chasm.

It is advisable in approaching a subject as complex and difficult as that of human freedom and its implications that we be as explicit as possible about the intent and extent of what we have to say. This is particularly necessary in view of the fact that what we have to contribute from the vantage point of modern psychoanalysis is only one aspect of a problem whose multiple facets are not exhausted by the analyses of many disciplines. The concern of psychoanalysis reaches into the inner being of man, into the depths of his conscious and unconscious mind. It grapples hand to hand with the complexities of human freedom in its existential realization in the human psyche. It confronts the human mind struggling to achieve or to avoid its own freedom. This vantage point is very special; above all else it is therapeutic. The analyst's basic concern about human freedom is the intensely personal question why a particular living human being has not achieved the full freedom of mind and spirit that is his human heritage, why he has not realized it in the ongoing current of his life and experience.

I would like to subdivide my remarks on this aspect of the problem of freedom by addressing first the question of the nature of psychoanalytic understanding. I put this first on the agenda because I feel it is important to be clear about what we can expect from a given discipline and how much weight we can give to its contributions. Second, I would like to consider some of the clinical phenomenology that relates to the problem of freedom. Then I will explore the complex question of psychic determinism and its relation to the problem of freedom, since this is a basic and necessary postulate of psychoanalysis. Next, I will attempt to formulate a theoretical understanding of freedom in psychoanalytic terms. And last, but certainly not least, I will consider the question of responsibility, which in a sense is the repository of freedom.

The Nature of Psychoanalytic Explanation

The problem of human freedom has traditionally been the province of philosophy and theology. Psychoanalysis, however, comes to the problem by way of psychic experience, which is associated with the diminution or absence of freedom as well as with its presence and exercise. Psychoanalysis is fundamentally a science, and its approach to any problem is generated from the available evidence. It attempts to formulate theory in such a way as to clarify, organize, and integrate in some intelligible fashion the mass of data that its practitioners are continually collecting. It is essentially an empirical enterprise.

The vantage point of the psychoanalyst is a very special one. It is primarily from the inner experience of the patient, insofar as it can be communicated and shared in an intense personal relationship,, that the psychoanalyst works. If he can claim any distinctive methodology, it is the personal interaction by which he reaches the inner core of the patient's feeling and experience. Psychoanalysis is, therefore, a science of interpersonal interaction and inner experience. But it is also necessarily an art— the two aspects cannot be divorced since they depend so intimately on each other. The analyst is the unique instrument of his science. It is through his interaction with the patient that he gathers the data on which he bases his attempts at theoretical understanding. Psychoanalytic understanding, therefore, always contains a subjective element that contaminates even as it contributes the basic evidence of the science. The fundamentally introspective and intersubjective aspects of psychoanalytic evidence impose certain unavoidable limitations on the validity of inference and make it necessary that the criteria for acceptance of evidence, formation of theories, and validation of constructs function in unique ways that do not fit the hypothetico-deductive and constructural models of the physical or even of the rigidly behavioral sciences (Meissner 1966b).

The psychoanalytic approach to freedom is consequently governed by the inner experience of freedom. Writing in 1936, Robert Waelder sets down the problem of freedom in these terms:

> The problem to be investigated is the purely psychological one of freedom *from* something, for example, from affects or anxiety, or freedom *for* something, say freedom for coping with a task set before one. Anyone afflicted with an obsessional neurosis and acting under a compulsion is psychologically not free; if he is "freed" from his compulsion, he will have acquired a measure of freedom. (p. 89)

Freedom to Waelder means that man is not tied to his biological or social environment, to what he calls "the *hic et nunc*" of his actual existence. By virtue of his freedom, man is able to make himself an object of his own reflections and to abstract himself from his immediate situation. This form of transcendence, the capacity to rise above oneself and one's environment, distinguishes man from all other creatures. It is this transcending experience that Knight (1946) later terms "the sense of inner freedom."

It is important to remember that the psychiatric approach to freedom is generated out of a context of experience and is governed by that experience. Analytic interest is focused on experience: the expression "a *sense* of inner freedom" underlines its experiential quality and limits the inquiry to that aspect. The further question, whether man is indeed free, is left unanswered. Psychoanalysis limits itself to a theoretical understanding of the experience. The further question lies beyond its phenomenology and its understanding; it belongs to the realm of metaphysics. Curiously, the metaphysical argument rests in part on the experience of self-imposition and self-determination as a self-originative act—the so-called experimental proof of freedom. Psychoanalysis and philosophy share a common datum, and it would seem that their respective conclusions should not violate each other.

Phenomenology

Psychoanalysis concerns itself with the presence or absence of the sense of inner freedom. Psychoanalysts work primarily with people who have experienced some disorganization or impairment of their intellectual and emotional functioning. To clarify what we mean by the sense of inner freedom, we might ask what kinds of clinical states are associated with the diminution or intensification of this psychic experience.

States in which all experience is missing—for example, death, coma involving loss of consciousness, and phases of sleep in which there is no conscious dreaming activity—obviously fall into this category. Other states—mental confusion, disorientation, delirium from various causes, and clouding of consciousness—are associated with conscious experience but are deprived of any sense of freedom. In them, the subject feels incapable of self-directed and integrated activity.

States in which there is a breakthrough of instinctual, drive-dependent forces are also associated with a diminution of the sense of freedom. In acute schizophrenic episodes the patient feels as though he has lost control, as though his behavior is driven by forces which he has no power to direct. The loss of control over feelings and thought processes is often an intermittent feature of chronic schizophrenic states as well. These conditions are strongly marked by a diminution of secondary-process mental organization and by a predominance of primary-process organization. Along with this relative disorganization, there is a loss of the sense of mastery, and the ego feels inundated by unconscious forces. Similar phenomena are observable in other psychotic states. A manic-depressive in a manic phase feels as driven and incapable of control as an acute schizophrenic.

It might be useful to say a word here about so-called borderline personalities. Such states of personality organization, at least in their more primitive or lower-order presentations (Meissner 1983), are characterized by symptoms of the neuroses or of character disorders but also display transient psychotic decompensations under the influence of stress or drugs. They have a chronic, diffuse, free-floating anxiety and usually present a variety of neurotic symptoms, including obsessions, phobias, conversions, dissociative states, and hypochondriacal and paranoid trends. Their sexuality is often what Freud described as "polymorphous perverse." The borderline syndrome is characterized by a developmental inadequacy of the ego, which lacks the capacity for impulse control and has never evolved appropriate channels of sublimation. The basic defensive mechanism is splitting, by which good and bad aspects of the self and of objects are actively separated. The use of splitting in conjunction with primitive introjection and projection leads the subject to shift between clinging to an idealized, "magical," all-powerful and -providing object and elaborating fantasies and behavior of primitive omnipotence. The fantasy of omnipotence is an infantile one, but it serves a restitutive function in that it protects the individual from the threat involved in his primitive need for and fear of others. The borderline is threatened constantly by loss of control and by the inner struggle of conflicting emotions. The sense of self-possession and inner trust essential to a sense of inner freedom is quite impaired.

Depressive states are also characterized by a diminution of the sense of freedom. Psychotic depressions are associated with a complete loss of control in a kind of paroxysmal sense of impending destruction. But even in less acute depressive states a patient often describes feelings of lethargy, of being burdened, and of guilt. The simplest decision or initiatives require more energy than he can muster. He has a sense of worthlessness and impoverishment. The patient feels unable to assert control, weak and deprived rather than out of control. The sense of inner capacity and control associated with freedom are lacking.

In other drive-dominated states, such as extreme hunger and thirst as well as extreme fatigue, the sense of inner freedom is impaired. Similarly, in states of sexual or aggressive arousal the individual feels himself in the grip of forces that prevent him from deliberately choosing a course of action. Certain neurotic states are associated with a diminution of freedom. One thinks particularly of compulsions and phobias, but in fact all neurotic manifestations are to some extent characterized by the struggle between repressed unconscious forces and the repressing and defensive functions of the ego. The diversion of ego energies into countercathexis deprives the ego of energies that might be available to reinforce the ego's sense of mastery and control.

There are certainly artificial states as well that seem to display a lessening of the sense of freedom. Hypnosis and other states of increased suggestibility seem to be associated with a transient diminution in the sense of free will. It also seems that certain drug-induced states are associated with such a diminution. The hallucinogenic drugs often produce an experience of forced thinking or of passive modification of thoughts and feelings. Experiences with LSD are often of this quality, and even marihuana often produces a kind of dream-like euphoria. Amphetamines can produce a driven quality in thought processes associated with loss of control and its concomitant anxieties. Ellinwood (1969) has described the amphetamine psychosis, which presents an extreme form of this state, with aspects of loss of control and ego disorganization found in other psychotic states.

Organic syndromes should also be mentioned, since a variety of central nervous system pathologies can produce similar phenomena. Brain tumors, cerebro-vascular accidents, trauma, and other organic afflictions can produce ego disorganization and impairment of the sense of inner freedom. Particularly noteworthy are temporal lobe syndromes of any etiology. Temporal lobe seizures, more accurately denominated as limbic seizures, are associated with impaired impulse control, amnesias, complex psychic experiences that are often illusory or hallucinatory in quality, bizarre experiences of derealization, depersonalization, or déjà vu, and forms of automatic behavior that are often quite complex and are carried out in a kind of fugue state. Often the differential diagnosis between such seizure states and psychiatric disorders is quite difficult to make.

It has also been pointed out by Ernest Hartmann (1966) that the activity of dreaming in normal persons is one in which the sense of freedom and control is also diminished. The dreamer has a sense of the dream "happening," as though he were caught up in a process over which he had little direct control. There is a similar quality to daydreams. When they steal upon us we lapse into a revery in which our thoughts seem to run their own course for a time and then we "snap out of it" to assert once again our conscious control.

When we survey these various states of diminished freedom (and I have not attempted to present a complete catalogue), two aspects stand out. First, these states represent forms of permanent or transient weakening of the ego. The ego loses control and becomes dominated by other intrapsychic forces that steer it without its being able to direct the process—or at least with diminished capacity to do so. And second, these states represent a shift from a predominance of secondary-process thinking to a predominance of primary-process thinking. The predominance of primary process and the weakening of ego will give us a handle with which to further consider these states later on.

If there are states involving a diminished sense of freedom, there are also, evidently, states involving a sense of increased or intensified freedom. It is difficult to denominate such states, and I suppose that it is best for each individual to consult his own experience. There are times when each of us feels more in control, more secure, more adequate, more confident. At such times the doubts and anxieties of our individual neuroses seem to fade into the background. It seems to me that such experiences are associated with an increase in basic self-esteem and trust. There is an inner feeling of worth, trustworthiness, autonomy, and capability. I think this feeling is linked to what Robert White (1959) means by the term "competence" and to what other ego theorists have been calling "ego strength." It is apparent that the sense of inner freedom presents itself phenomenologically across a broad spectrum, ranging from total disruption to a high degree of intensity. The experience of every individual, moreover, varies along this spectrum—moving back and forth between states of relatively diminished freedom to states of relatively increased freedom. It is my feeling that in some rudimentary fashion the inner sense of freedom, however diminished and compromised by pathological states, is never totally absent in a conscious person. Even in the most regressive and psychotic states, as Freud observed, there is always a hidden psychic corner in which the ego preserves its nonpsychotic and observant capacity —and it is in this segment of preserved ego that the sense of freedom lies hidden.

Psychic Determinism

Before attempting a more theoretical approach to the sense of inner freedom, it is important that we deal with a basic issue in psychoanalytic thinking: How can psychoanalysts talk about freedom and its correlative responsibility when psychoanalysis as a science is postulated on psychic determinism?

The conflict is well displayed in Freud himself. Freud was an uncompromising determinist and relentlessly applied the principle to his analyses of behavior and experience. He made room, however, for the conception of free will as a conscious experience, although he maintained that strict determinism prevailed at the unconscious level:

> According to our analyses it is not necessary to dispute the right to the feeling of conviction of having a free will. If the distinction between conscious and unconscious motivation is taken into account, our feeling of conviction informs us that conscious motivation does not extend to all our motor decisions. *De minimis non curat lex.* But what is thus left free by the one side receives its motivation from the other side, from the unconscious; and in this way determination in the physical sphere is still carried out without any gap. (Freud 1901, 254)

He calls "psychical freedom" an illusion that he categorically denied (Freud 1916–17) and goes on to say, "I ventured to tell you that you nourish a deeply rooted faith in undetermined psychical events and in free will, but that this is quite unscientific and must yield to the demand of a determinism whose rule extends over mental life" (p. 106).

Yet in *The Ego and the Id* (1923a) he writes: "analysis does not set out to make pathological reactions impossible, but to give the patient's ego *freedom* to decide one way or the other" (p. 50). Freud was able to speak comfortably on both sides of the issue of free will. He conceded the experience of freedom at a conscious level but insisted on strict determinism at the unconscious level.

This view has dominated the post-Freudian era in psychiatry. But in most considerations of the matter, as in Freud's work, there is a presumption that free will and psychic determinism are mutually exclusive. The late Robert Knight was one of the first to see that this was not necessarily the case:

> In the psychological and philosophical realm there is also no real alternative to psychic determinism. To defend "free will" as an alternative is to be guilty of semantic confusion. Determinism refers to the complex of causal factors, heredity and environment, internal and external, past and present, conscious and unconscious, which combine to produce a certain resultant in a given individual. Determinism is thus a theoretical construct which fits the observed data, as demonstrated by predictions which were fulfilled, and which is essential to any psychology which claims to be scientific. The antithesis to this construct is the construct, indeterminism—pure chance, chaos. "Free will," on the other hand, is not on the same conceptual level as are these constructs. It refers to a subjective psychological experience, and to compare it to determinism is like comparing the enjoyment of flying to the law of gravity. (Knight 1946, 371)

Knight is perfectly accurate in seeing that free will and determinism are not strict opposites, but he sidesteps the basic problem by recourse to the Freudian solution—freedom is reduced to a conscious experience while determinism is regarded as a matter of real causal influences.

It is not clear that either presumption is entirely valid. Even granting substantial influence to the prior unconscious event, it alone cannot satisfy the causal conditions required for the act itself. Action requires the activation of multiple integrated systems—imaginative, emotional, motor, and so on. Thus, unconscious influence must be counted as part of a complex process that results in a particular segment of behavior. Moreover, a given behaviorial segment can be overdetermined—that is, subject to the influence of more than one unconscious determining influence. Consequently, this kind of determination is not exclusive but is exercised jointly with other determinants as well as with other efficient or motor causes.

It is on the level of efficient causality that free will enters the picture. Some clarifications are necessary here. No one would hold that all human activity involving the use of the will is free. The will is free only where it is not forced, where it has the opportunity to choose among alternatives. When a man appraises a certain object as unreservedly good and desirable, the activity of the will is not free but necessary. The conditions of such necessity, however, are seldom realized, since the objects and activities to which men are drawn in this life are seldom unmixed goods. When a man is confronted with a nonessential but attractive object, he is capable of either pursuing it or not. Under such conditions, the doctrine of free will maintains that nothing outside or inside a man forces him to choose between available alternatives. His decision is therefore said to be free.

But what about psychic determinism? Let us suppose that I choose at this moment to stop writing and enjoy a cup of coffee. My decision is not forced; I could just as easily have gone on writing. The decision is undoubtedly determined by certain unconscious influences. With extensive free association, it would be possible to explain why I posed the question at this time and not at another, why I decided to drink coffee and not tea, and so on. The explanation would describe why I chose one set of alternatives over another, why I had these alternatives available and not others, and why I chose at all; but it would not deal with the fact *that* I chose and committed myself to a particular course of action. It would explain the *what* but not the *that,* the determination of action but not its efficiency, the content of my deliberation but not the fact of decision. There is nothing in the given alternatives that forces my decision. Unconscious determinants can explain why I made a particular decision, but they do not account for the decision itself. I myself am the cause of my own free activity.

Other approaches to the problem of determinism have focused on the meaning of "causality" in psychological science. It has been argued that the role of the causality principle has been undermined in contemporary physics so that its application to mental events is no longer justifiable. Causality and determinism are therefore not coextensive (Angel 1959). If determinism does not imply causal influence, what does it mean?

Some clarification of this matter has been provided by Ernest Hartmann's (1966) analysis in terms of horizontal and vertical relationships. If we propose a stratified model of mental organization, at the lowest level there are the basic physiological and biological events that constitute the ongoing life of the organism. Stimulus input sets off a series of complex causal interactions that result in behavioral output. The analysis at this level is causal; events are strictly determined by causal relations. At the highest level of organization of mental functioning, conscious psychological experiences take place with a certain sequence and organization. Relations between states at this level are not causal, nor are those between events of different strata. Rather, their relationships are those of concomitance or what Hartmann calls "indicator" relations. Every psychic state indicates a correlative physiological state, but a given physiological state need not have a correlative psychic state. To understand the relationships between strata, psychological theorists interpose a system of mediating concepts. In psychoanalysis these intermediate concepts include a description of unconscious processes. The question involved in psychic determinism can be resolved into what kinds of relations obtain between psychic states at each level of the model—between conscious psychic states on one level and between intermediate states on another. It is clear that the relations are not simply causal, on the physiological level.

One of the contributions of the phenomenological movement has been to point out the role of meaning in such relationships. Psychic determinism is not that of external forces operating on and in the psyche but has to do with connections of meaning—with the necessities of meaning. Freedom is not associated with a lack of determinism—rather, that act is most fully free which is most fully determined. But this is a determination that the ego imposes on itself in deliberate consciousness of the necessities imposed by the inner and the outer worlds. Thus free association establishes a chain of meaningful necessities, but the necessity is retrospective and reconstructive. The best formulation of this aspect of analytic explanation is provided by Freud himself:

> So long as we trace the development from its final outcome backwards, the chain of events appears continuous, and we feel we have gained an *insight* which is completely satisfactory or even exhaustive. But if we proceed the reverse way, if we start from the premises inferred from analysis and try to follow these up to the final result, then we no longer get the impression of an inevitable sequence of events which could not have been otherwise determined. We notice at once that there might have been another result, and that we might have been just as well able to understand and explain the latter. The synthesis is thus not so satisfactory as the analysis; in other words, from a knowledge of the premises we could not have foretold the nature of the result. (Freud 1920b, 167)

Thus what may be "freely" established at any point in the chain of events becomes in retrospect one of the "necessities of meaning" (Fisher 1966).

It is my position that real freedom can coexist with such necessities of meaning. But it must be added that such necessities do not in themselves totally determine current behavior and experience. The experiences they represent are embedded in the personality and have not only a past existence but also a present reality. In the transference, for example, infantile love and hate for the parent are directed at the analyst—as immediate, vital, and active forces. As Freud has remarked, the ego is a precipitate of object relations. Thus, relations to other persons are internalized and become more or less permanent structural acquisitions of the personality. The past lives on, transformed and unconscious, as a functional and dynamic aspect of the present life of the human organism. Thus the necessities of meaning, while they serve a vital explanatory function, are at the same time caught up in the complex interaction of causal systems and psychic influences out of which the ongoing current of behavior issues. The determinants of action are complex, partial, and multiple—the explanation is therefore never complete, and the personality must be regarded as a truly open system. In such an open system there is room for the exercise of freedom, not instead of determination, but as an additional determinant interacting with other determinants of the course of action.

The Metapsychology of Freedom

In the light of what has been said above, and in the face of a psychoanalytic tradition that clings to a narrow conception of psychic determinism—a conception based on a more or less mechanical notion of causality which leaves no room for free choice and allows only for a subjective sense of freedom—I would like to pull together the elements of a theory of ego functioning that does leave room for the exercise of free choice.

The emergence of a psychoanalytic ego psychology has brought with it the realization that the earlier emphasis on the ego's dependence on—and, we might also say, determination by—drive forces did not present a complete picture. Beginning with Heinz Hartmann's ([1939] 1958) revolutionary introduction of concepts of autonomy and adaptation, appreciation for the independence of the ego has grown. Rapaport ([1957] 1967) speaks of independence from drive forces as "autonomy of the ego from the id" and of independence of behavior from external stimulation as "autonomy of the ego from external reality." The ego is not merely a passive agent driven by outside influences; rather, it maintains a relative autonomy, and it is the implications of that autonomy that I wish to explore.

The autonomy of the ego is of more than one kind. Hartmann ([1939] 1958) introduced the concepts of primary and secondary autonomy. The ego has certain apparatuses of primary autonomy—memory, motor and perceptual systems—which are biologically derived and given by evolution. These provide the basis for the organism's capacity to fit in with or adapt to its environment. The apparatuses of secondary autonomy, however, are not given but must be developed out of instinctual modes and vicissitudes. Thus, structures derived from instinctual sources or defenses are elaborated through conflict and thus acquire an adaptive function. Such structures undergo a "change of function" —from defense to adaptation—in the course of which they acquire autonomy from the instinctual or drive-dependent context in which they arose. The ego is then capable of applying them in the interest of other, independent ends. Rapaport ([1957] 1967) sees these forms of autonomy as related:

> Man's constitutionally given drive equipment appears to be the *ultimate* (primary) *guarantee* of the ego's autonomy from the environment, that is, its safeguard against stimulus-response slavery. But this autonomy too has *proximal* (secondary) *guarantees*: namely, higher order superego and ego structures as well as the motivations pertaining to them. Like the ego's autonomy from the id, its autonomy from the environment also is only relative. (p. 727)

The maintenance of such relatively autonomous structures requires a measure of stimulus-nutriment. If stimulus-nutriment is decreased, as in sensory deprivation, the ego's maximized autonomy from the environment produces a correlative minimizing of its autonomy from the id. Similarly, the maximizing of the ego's autonomy from the id as a result of obsessive-compulsive defenses leads to maximal dependence on environment. Only a relative autonomy of the ego from the id—within an optimal range—is compatible with its optimal autonomy from the environment. Relations with reality therefore guarantee autonomy from the id, and, paradoxically, instinctual drives guarantee autonomy from the environment.

The maintenance and effectiveness of relative autonomy depend in part on the elaboration of the structures of secondary autonomy. The structural organization of ego and superego provides the basis on which independence from external and internal forces is attained. Freud long ago defined identification as the mechanism of structural formation. Through identification the organism acquires an increasing internalization of control so that what was originally required as external control becomes part of its inner resources for control and mastery. The process of structuralization provides a measure of independence from drive-derivatives and opens the way for the adaptive use of structural derivatives in the service of other needs of the organism. Thus, what originated in the resolution of conflict can undergo a change of function and become part of the conflict-free sphere of the ego. But while relatively autonomous structures may derive from drive vicissitudes, they never become absolutely autonomous. Under the influence of regression, these structures can once more fall under the influence of the instinctual drives.

Correlative to the development of secondary autonomy and psychic structure is Hartmann's notion of neutralization. Freud originally described neutralization in relation to identification and structure formation. Through identification, the object-libido originally directed at the object was turned toward the self and thereby desexualized. Libidinal energy was in this manner neutralized. Hartmann ([1955] 1964) extends this notion to aggressive energies as well. The evolution of structure is accompanied by an increasing availability of neutralized energies and an increasing capacity to neutralize. The development of structure makes increasing amounts of energy available for the conflict-free interests of the ego. Other theorists have argued that one need not appeal to neutralization for the origin of such drive-independent energies; there are independent ego energies which in no sense derive from instinctual drives (White 1963).

The development of structure, secondary autonomy, and the capacity for free choice is correlative. The first analyst to formulate this principle is Waelder (1936). He regards freedom as the capacity to transcend the conditions of human existence. What enables man to do this is his super-ego. Waelder sees the formal function of the superego as the observation or objectification of oneself, and the attainment of a position above one's own ego:

> Freedom then in its most general sense is found in the existence of the superego, in that formal function of the superego in virtue of which man rises above himself and apprehends the world from without and beyond his immediate perceptions and his biological needs. (p. 92)

Man's capacity to transcend his instincts, to achieve some degree of autonomy from inner drives and outer environment, is not due simply to his superego. The optimal degree of functional autonomy and the balance of the forms of secondary autonomy rest on the integral functioning of ego and superego. The capacity for freedom involves a degree of inner regulation which preserves an optimal degree of autonomy, as described by Rapaport. For this to be achieved, the integration of ego and superego functions is essential. The truth of Waelder's statement is that an optimal degree of superego development is essential for the internalization of the drive-independent controls which are the basis of ego autonomy and freedom.

The issues of autonomy have been enriched and extended by the more recent emergence of a psychology of the self in psychoanalysis. A distinction can be drawn between ego autonomy and self-autonomy. The concepts occupy different levels of conceptualization. While the philosophical and theological levels are concerned with free will, freedom of choice, responsibility, and so on, on the psychoanalytic level, ego autonomy is defined by Hartmann ([1955] 1964) as "stability . . . of ego function, or more precisely its resistivity to regression and instinctualization." Moreover, the concept of autonomy applies to specific and separate ego functions, not to the ego as a whole. The ego is an abstraction which is not observed clinically. Rather, we observe manifestations of specific functions in action, in thought, in affect. Clinically some functions may be regressed, while others are at the same time highly developed and autonomous.

The autonomy of the self is of a different order.

> When we observe what appears to be conscious freedom of choice, we may in a descriptive and empirical way speak of a kind of "autonomy of man." We may say that unconscious factors bring the individual to a point where he has to choose between conscious alternative possibilities. He must exercise judgment and thought. Here we can say the person (or self) has "freedom of choice"—in fact, we think of the goal of psychotherapy and psychoanalysis as the patient's becoming capable of choosing his own way of life when he has insight into his unconscious conflicts. But we may also say that the person's choice, even at this moment of conscious choice, is nevertheless also determined by deeper unconscious factors as well as by external forces. (D. Beres, in Meissner 1976).

It is possible now to return to phenomenology, with which we started this consideration. The states of diminished freedom I have described reveal a common set of characteristics. All are states of diminished ego capacity and weakness. Moreover, where consciousness is maintained they reveal a predominance of primary-process thought organization. Primary-process thinking is dependent on and derived from the influence of instinctual drives. It implies an increase in drive-dependent organization of thought processes and represents a diminution of the degree of secondary autonomy required for the maintenance of secondary-process thought organization. It implies, therefore, a minimization of autonomy from the id and a correlative maximization of autonomy from reality.

The concept of real freedom of choice is a viable one in terms of psychoanalytic ego theory. It need not be restricted to a mere subjective sense of freedom. It requires a degree of maturity of integral ego and superego functioning to ensure some degree of autonomy from other determining forces impinging on and influencing the course of action. The act of free choice can thus be seen as derived from an executive function of the ego responding to a determining context of meaning and autonomously directing the course of action into one meaningful channel rather than another.

Responsibility

The correlative of real freedom in the subjective world of intrapsychic realities is responsibility. The problem of responsibility arises in relation to the determination of legal responsibility as well as in the context of moral responsibility. These are complex areas, and I will leave them for those who are more competent to discuss. Responsibility remains, however, a central concern in psychoanalysis. It is one of the major goals of therapy and one of the cornerstones of mature and adult adjustment. I would like to explore briefly the meaning of responsibility, its relation to inner freedom, and its importance in the psychotherapeutic process.

To have a sense of responsibility is to have a sense of inner reality and identity. To be responsible is to assert one's sense of vitality and mastery. The responsibility we are concerned with is what Weisman (1965) calls subjective responsibility:

> *Subjective responsibility* . . . accords primacy to man as the initiator of acts instead of to man as an object acted upon. It recognizes the reality of choice, freedom, consciousness, motivation, and the capacity to control the consequences of purposeful action. These realities are a man's private property, and he cannot barter, share, or surrender them. Subjective responsibility corresponds closely with the sense of reality for what we are and what we do. Existentialists call this *authenticity*; psychoanalysts call it *identity*. (pp. 167–68)

In this psychoanalytic view of freedom and responsibility, man lives with his unconscious, not by it. He is capable of recognizing his own uniqueness and value even in the face of obligation and conformity. The sense of inner harmony and self-esteem which is linked with the sense of responsibility derives from a sense of trust and trustworthiness and implies an approximation of ego functions to the implicit values of the ego ideal. Thus superego-derived values serve as a system of internal regulation that stabilizes and reinforces the ego's capacity to choose freely and act responsibly. Superego functions support responsible actions only insofar as they are harmoniously integrated with ego operations. Without such integration they can evoke guilt, remorse, and depression and in fact undermine the individual's capacity for freedom and responsibility.

To catch up the threads of the previous argument, the idea of a capricious or undetermined free will, on the one hand, and of rigid psychic determinism, on the other, leave little room for responsibility. Responsibility is the power to respond, to choose and carry out one path of conduct rather than another. Causal necessity without choice destroys responsibility. An indeterminism that makes choice a random selection from an unlimited range of possible courses also evacuates responsibility. An individual's reality is not limited to an organization of processes. The unconscious belongs to the person, not the person to the unconscious. Man uses his psychic equipment, it does not use him. "There are unique dimensions of existence in which each person exists alone, not only influenced by his unconscious processes but committed to responsible activity and able to exercise a measure of control" (Weisman 1865, 175).

The relationship between relative autonomy and responsibility has been noted by Lewy (1961). He recognizes that autonomy and adaptability of the ego are the foundation on which individual responsibility is built. Man cannot be held accountable for his actions unless those actions are attributable to him in some authentic sense. They must be *his* acts, directed, governed, and controlled by virtue of his inner sense of direction and intention. Yet they are not completely autonomous and undetermined. They are a response born of the individual's capacity for responsiveness to a complex interplay of determinants that supply a constantly developing framework of interaction and process within which the ego responds. The response that enables the ego to insert itself in relevant and realistic ways into this shifting framework is adaptive in that it achieves a "good fit" with the forces of reality, but it is at the same time responsible in that it is a response and not merely a reaction. It is an operation of the ego that is at the same time determined and determining; it responds to a complex of inner and outer determinants and in the same act asserts its autonomy and self-direction. This delicate balance is well expressed by Mendel:

The healthy individual can assert his individuality and responsibility. He can choose his behavior to some extent; he can even choose the problems on which he intends to focus. Free will is limited in each of us by capacity, history, and biology. Yet when we are healthy we have the experience of choosing and we function as though we can choose. As we disorganize and become "ill" our choices become more limited. We are less able to take responsibility for the conduct of our lives and we become more helpless. Finally, the individual who suffers from an illness we call psychosis becomes a helpless victim of his inner world. He has abdicated all responsibility for his thoughts, his conduct, and his stand to reality and to himself. (Mendel 1968, 701)

Thus the capacity for free choice and responsible self-determination is a primary objective of the therapeutic process. To call psychoanalysis a treatment is a distortion. It is a collaboration, a cooperative venture, an alliance between patient and therapist. The therapeutic relation *presumes* in even the sickest patients a core of responsible ego which permits the patient to enter into the therapeutic process. Whatever builds that core of responsibility is therapeutic; whatever diminishes and undercuts it is antitherapeutic.

Therapy is a process of coming to grips in terms of stark existential reality and human concreteness with the forces of psychic determinism and personal responsibility. The analytic process is in part a matter of bringing the determinants into focus and exploring their functioning. The patient often emerges a captive of the past, a slave to his unconscious and to the forces of his inner world. But therapy is more than a process of filling in the picture of determination. The determinants have an immediate reality and force, which are recreated within the transference. But the analytic relation is not restricted to transference. There is also a therapeutic alliance based on mutual trust and respect between therapist and patient and elaborated in and through the mechanism of an evolving identification of patient with therapist. The patient introjects the calm, objective, respectful, trusting, and trustworthy aspects of the therapist and by this identification begins to build within his own ego the resources for increasing self-esteem, self-trust, and inner autonomy. Internalization and identification are the mechanisms of intrapsychic structuralization, and as inner psychic structure is built through the therapeutic interaction, it lays the basis for autonomy and responsibility.

CONCLUSION

The general picture of human freedom that emerges from this juxtaposition of the theological and the psychoanalytic perspectives is complex and ambiguous. The psychoanalytic view of man's limited freedom in a sense sets a realistic constraint on the extent to which the theological vision of the meaning of freedom can be realized in the actual human condition. The theological presumption that freedom is a necessary condition for a life of grace and indeed for any meaningful religious life is not absolute or itself unconditioned. The theological perspective, however, does not assert more than a defect in man's nature—a *vulnus naturae*. The theological concern, therefore, centers on the struggle to overcome the defect and thereby to achieve a full expression of humanity and human existence. Christian theology asserts as a basic postulate that man's nature does not in itself possess the potentiality to overcome its intrinsic limitation and defect. The power of God through grace is required.

The psychoanalytic perspective, on the other hand, has no interest in theological suppositions or implications. It is concerned with the actual conditions and constraints of the exercise of human freedom. Moreover, it makes its business the discovery of the nature of intrinsic impediments to the individual's realization of a sense of autonomy. In a sense, then, theology takes up where psychoanalysis leaves off. There is no room in the psychoanalytic account for a positive impulse toward freedom. Growth toward autonomy and freedom from the constraints and limitations of inner conflicts and inhibitions are cast only in negative terms; that is, the growth to autonomy and maturity is presumed to be a by-product of the release and mobilization of impeded psychic forces. The emphasis falls on analysis rather than synthesis. At this point the theological perspective adds its emphasis on the restorative power of grace. This divergence of emphasis and orientation makes the area of irreconcilability as clear as possible. The two perspectives are in this regard simply different and distinct from each other.

While the divergence and differences must be respected, the important and enlarged areas of mutual reinforcement and dialogue should not be ignored. If psychoanalysis sets limits on the realization of the theological ideal, it nonetheless addresses the terms on which the theological dimension defines itself. By the same token, the theological endeavor can no longer make an unquestioned presumption of the presence or exercise of freedom without taking into account the actual extent of realized freedom in individual humans. Insight into the human conditions of freedom is the preserve of psychoanalysis and its related disciplines. In essence, then, theological reflection cannot take place in a vacuum, as it too often has done in the past. It necessarily involves a theological anthropology that cannot sustain itself without psychoanalytic input.

EPILOGUE

We have come to the end of our ascent and have completed much of our journey. But having overcome the difficulties of the climb, we find that what once appeared to be a summit now seems to have the character of a mere plateau, a resting place where we may pitch our tents only for a while, as we look forward to further heights to be scaled and conquered.

As we look back on the path we have traveled to reach this plateau, several points seem to emerge with considerable clarity. The first is that the operating assumption that psychoanalysis and religion have common interests and goals and at least reconcilable conceptions of man's nature and psychic life provides a meaningful and fruitful starting point from which the project of mutual understanding and exploration can be advanced. Earlier positions, which tended to polarize and dichotomize these two points of view, led only to acrimony and sterility.

It is in the middle ground between such extremes that the dialectic takes on life and flourishes. This middle ground is characterized by a tolerance for ambiguity, by a capacity to reduce the tension between the subjective and the objective, logic and meaning, objective science and inner psychic life. The success of our effort so far is a measure of the degree to which we have found a path through this dense undergrowth. The future potentialities of the continuing dialectic lie in the hands of those who can find and hold this middle ground and thus fashion intellectual tools adequate for the exploration and understanding of the transitional realm of man's psychic experience.

This intermediate ground lies between the polarities of dichotomous categorization. There the oppositions between science and humanism, objectivity and subjectivity, meaning and causality, freedom and determinism, faith and reason, and even the natural and the supernatural grow less radical and enter into a gradual transformation that allows them to converge upon a common ground of understanding with no loss or dilution of their unique and proper conceptualizations. The dialectical process becomes in this middle ground a reasonable and realistic undertaking for

241

those who can hold to it and not be drawn off course by the Scylla of a rigid logic of objectivity or by the Charybdis of undisciplined subjectivity. Freud's commitment to the logic of natural science drew him away from this delicate ground. By the same token, reliance on intuition and subjectivity undisciplined by the requirements of objective observation and analysis of data impede the efforts of many religious thinkers to approach this same area.

It is worth noting that psychoanalysis is no stranger to this middle ground. Despite Freud's demurs, the instrument he fashioned lives and thrives there. In its unique manner, it tries to integrate science and humanism. Its methodology is based not only on causal analysis, but also in important ways on the hermeneutic interpretation of meanings—neither without the other. In concrete terms, it has learned to reconcile the tension in the human condition between freedom and determinism. The central concept and clinical fact by which analysts earn their livings is the transference, a particular blend of fantasy and reality, subjectivity and objectivity, that marks it as a uniquely transitional phenomenon.

One could argue, therefore, that the richest and potentially the most productive contribution to this difficult and fragile area of investigation and discourse will come from psychoanalysis that remains true to its course and adheres to the best in its hard-won approach to the understanding of human phenomena. We can hope that *homo religiosus* will increasingly find his way to the analytic couch, for it is there that psychoanalysis does its best. But close adherence to analytic principles in the applied analytic investigation of religious phenomena as well is both required and eminently valuable.

As we stand on the present plateau and enjoy an earned respite before renewing our climb, I would feel remiss if I did not offer my readers some sense of where this exploration may lead us. Undoubtedly, the reader who has come this far will have his own ideas about where and how the inquiry might proceed. But I would like to sketch out here my own perception of the fruitful areas for continuing exploration that lie ahead.

The question we are posing to ourselves in general terms has to do with the manner in which aspects of man's religious understanding are based on, reflect, and express the structure and form of his inner psychological being. A primary area of interest is the manner in which man conceptualizes and relates to his God. The name and the face of God take shape presumably on the basis of important projections that express and reflect man's inner psychic life. But the matter is complex and leaves much yet to be understood. The name and the face of God have many variants, both personal and communal. The manner in which one's personal image or object representation of God (Rizzuto 1979) is formed, through both intrapsychic determination and communal and cultural influences, is a rich area for future exploration. Clearly, the variants carry residues that reflect

not only individual developmental vicissitudes but also, as I have previously suggested (above, chapter 6), dynamic elements within the culture
that reinforce different crises and resolutions on the developmental continuum as part of its broader character.

Perhaps closely related to the question of the personal image of God is
that of the place of prayer in man's religious life. Prayer has actually been
little studied as an expression of man's religious experience, particularly in
psychoanalytic terms. Obviously, the range of prayerful experience extends from the more or less mundane and somewhat formalized prayer of
the average believer all the way to the deepest and most profound forms of
mystical experience which are restricted to those who reach the highest
degrees of spiritual perfection.

In between lie the many forms of meditation found in all religious
traditions, Eastern and Western. Prayer has a personal as well as communal dimension. Much communal prayer is an expression of liturgy or
ritual. Consequently, the prayer life of the individual believer is in a
variety of ways conditioned by the attitudes and modalities of communal
prayer that permeate his religious group.

But the prayer experience is conditioned not only by the image of the
God to whom the believer prays, but also by important aspects of his own
psychic life. When the believer prays, what he prays for, and why—and
whether he prays at all—are dimensions of this realm of experience that
help focus the issues of inner dynamic forces. The tensions between wish
fulfillment, narcissistic desire, realistic adaptation and resignation, guilt,
and the sense of sinfulness or pride, all play themselves out in personal
prayer.

The interplay between the natural and the theological levels of psychic
experience is also found in the area of virtue. I have in mind here the broad
range of human virtues, but particularly as they are emphasized and
analyzed within various theological traditions. They are generally regarded
as a by-product not only of man's natural endeavor but of some helpful,
restorative, or enhancing intervention on the part of God. Heading the list
are the so-called theological virtues of faith, hope, and charity. There is
ample scope for the introduction of a basic psychoanalytic understanding
of these concepts, since each of them has important developmental components that enter into its shape and formation. Whatever the theological
component of such virtues, there is little doubt that they are essentially
human virtues and therefore partake of the nature and structure of man's
psychic organization. In addition, understanding of how virtues arise and
are formed has undergone considerable modification in theological terms,
moving them from the level of abstract theological analysis to one more
proximate to their human origins.

If one were to select an area of contemporary religious experience that
has considerable ramifications and reverberations for contemporary reli-

gious life, one could hardly do better than to focus on religious values. These core elements shape the individual believer's religious life and give a sense of direction and purpose to religious institutions. Most of the effort of religious persons and institutions is directed at forming, preserving, and extending basic religious values in the body of the religious community. But value formation is in itself an intrapsychic process which undergoes dynamic, genetic, structural, and adaptive vicissitudes. Consequently, it is a prime area for psychoanalytic consideration and remains an open and relatively unexplored area for future dialogue and understanding.

The last area I wish to mention is one that is more specifically a concern of the Western theological tradition, particularly the Judeo-Christian tradition. It is based on the theological supposition that when the divine Creator brought man into the world, man's presence there was not isolated from continuing divine influence. In the Western Christian tradition specifically, man is called to a supernatural level of existence which transcends his own merely natural existence. Man's capacity to achieve the level of existence to which he is called by divine commission is frustrated without some additional capacity provided by a loving God, that enables man to achieve his salvific purpose. Such assistance, prompted by the loving care of a provident Creator, goes by the name of grace. If it is to have any significance or meaning relevant to the human condition, grace must affect man's psychic functioning in some fashion. We can speak meaningfully, therefore, of a "psychology of grace," which has been an area of active theological consideration for some time but in which psychoanalytic thinking has not made much impact or any significant contribution. That challenge still lies ahead.

I have made no attempt here to be exhaustive or even to select those topics of exploration that seem most fruitful. Looking ahead, I have merely picked options that seem to me, from my present perspective, not only to be useful and interesting but to yield some promise for immediate efforts to approach them on the basis of the conceptualizations and understandings we have already achieved. Having said this much, it occurs to me somewhat ruefully that perhaps the easiest part of our ascent lies behind and the most difficult and challenging parts ahead. *Per aspera ad astra!*

REFERENCES

Albright, W. F. 1949. The biblical period. In *The jews: Their history, culture, and religion*, ed. L. Finkelstein. New York: Harper and Bros.

————. 1957. *From the stone age to Christianity*. 2d ed. Garden City, N.Y.: Doubleday.

Allport, G. W. 1960. *Personality and social encounter*. Boston: Beacon Press.

Alt, A. [1929] 1953. *Der Gott der Väter*. In *Kleine Schriften zur Geschichte des Volkes Israel* 1:1–78. Reprint. Munich: Beck. Translation by R. A. Wilson, in *Old testament history and religion*, 1–100. New York: Anchor Books, 1966.

————. 1934. *Die Ursprünge des Israelitischen Rechts*. Report on the proceedings of the Saxon Academy of Scientists, departments of philosophy and history, Leipzig, Germany, vol. 86, pt. 1.

Amacher, P. 1965. *Freud's neurological education and its influence on psychoanalytic theory*. Psychological Issues Monograph Series, no. 16. New York: International Universities Press.

Angel, R. W. 1959. The concept of psychic determinism. *American Journal of Psychiatry* 116:405–08.

Bakan, D. 1966. *The duality of human existence: An essay on psychology and religion*. Chicago: Rand McNally.

Bergmann, M. S. 1976. Moses and the evolution of Freud's Jewish identity. *Israel Annals of Psychiatry and Related Disciplines* 14:3–26.

Bernfeld, S. 1944. Freud's earliest theories and the School of Helmholtz. *Psychoanalytic Quarterly* 13:341–62.

Blum, H. P. 1977. The prototype of preoedipal reconstruction. *Journal of the American Psychoanalytic Association* 25:757–85. Reprinted in Kanzer and Glenn (1979), 143–63.

Bozzo, E. G. 1970. Theology and religious experience. *Theological Studies* 31:415–36.

Brome, V. 1978. *Jung*. New York: Atheneum.

Chein, I. 1962. The image of man. *Journal of Social Issues* 18:1–35.

————. 1972. *The image of man and the science of behavior*. New York: Basic.

Cross, F. M. 1962. Yahweh and the god of the patriarchs. *Harvard Theological Review* 55:225–59.

————. 1973. *Caananite myth and Hebrew epic: Essays in the history of the religion of Israel*. Cambridge: Harvard University Press.

Deri, S. 1978. Transitional phenomena: Vicissitudes of symbolization and creativity. In *Between fantasy and reality: The transitional object*, ed. S. A. Grolnick and L. Barkin, 45–60. New York: Aronson.

Ellinwood, E. H. 1969. Amphetamine psychosis: A multidimensional process. *Seminars in Psychiatry* 1:208–26.

Erikson, E. H. 1959. *Identity and the life cycle.* Psychological Issues Monograph Series, no. 1. New York: International Universities Press.

——. 1962. *Young man Luther.* New York: Norton.

——. 1964. *Insight and responsibility.* New York: Norton.

Faber, H. 1975. *Psychology of religion.* Philadelphia: Westminster.

Fairbairn, W. R. D. 1952. *An object-relations theory of the personality.* New York: Basic.

Falk, A. 1977. Freud and Herzl. *Midstream* 3:24.

Fisher, A. 1966. Freud and the image of man. In W. W. Meissner, *Foundations for a psychology of grace.* Glen Rock, N.J.: Paulist Press.

Fodor N. 1971. *Freud, Jung, and occultism.* Secaucus, N.J.: University Books.

Fowler, J. W. 1974. Toward a developmental perspective on faith. *Religious Education* 69:207–19.

——. 1981. *Stages of faith: The psychology of human development and the quest for meaning.* San Francisco: Harper and Row.

Freud, A. [1937] 1973. *The ego and the mechanisms of defense.* Reprint. New York: International Universities Press.

——. 1967. About losing and being lost. *Psychoanalytic Study of the Child* 22:9–19. New York: International Universities Press.

Freud, E., ed. 1960. *The letters of Sigmund Freud.* New York: McGraw-Hill.

Freud, S. 1953–74. *Standard edition of the complete psychological works.* London: Hogarth.

   1900. *The interpretation of dreams,* vols. 4 and 5.

   1901. *The psychopathology of everyday life,* vol. 6.

   1905. *Jokes and their relation to the unconscious,* vol. 8.

   1907. Obsessive actions and religious practices, vol. 9.

   1909a. Analysis of a phobia in a five-year-old boy, vol. 10.

   1909b. Notes upon a case of obsessional neurosis, vol. 10.

   1911. Psycho-analytic notes on an autobiographical account of a case of paranoia (dementia paranoides), vol. 12.

   1912–13. *Totem and taboo,* vol. 13.

   1914. The Moses of Michelangelo, vol. 13.

   1915a. Thoughts for the times on war and death, vol. 14.

   1915b. Instincts and their vicissitudes, vol. 14.

   1916–17. *Introductory lectures on psycho-analysis,* vol. 15.

   1917. A difficulty in the path of psycho-analysis, vol. 17.

   1918. From the history of an infantile neurosis, vol. 17.

   1920a. The psychogenesis of a case of homosexuality in a woman, vol. 18.

   1920b. *Beyond the pleasure principle,* vol. 18.

   1922. Dreams and telepathy, vol. 18.

   1923a. *The ego and the id,* vol. 19.

   1923b. A seventeenth-century demonological neurosis, vol. 19.

   1924. The economic problem of masochism, vol. 19.

   1925a. *An autobiographical study,* vol. 20.

   1925b. The resistances to psycho-analysis, vol. 19.

   1927. *The future of an illusion,* vol. 21.

   1928. A religious experience, vol. 21.

   1930. *Civilization and its discontents,* vol. 21.

   1933a. *New introductory lectures on psycho-analysis,* vol. 22.

   1933b. Why war?, vol. 22.

   1936. A disturbance of memory on the Acropolis, vol. 22.

1939. *Moses and monotheism,* vol. 23.

1941a. Psycho-analysis and telepathy, vol. 18.

1941b. Address to the Society of B'nai B'rith, vol. 20.

1950a. Extracts from the Fliess papers, vol. 1.

1950b. *Project for a scientific psychology,* vol. 1.

————. 1954. *The origins of psychoanalysis: Letters to Wilhelm Fliess, drafts and notes: 1887–1902.* Trans. E. Mosbacher and J. Strachey. New York: Basic.

Gedo, J. E. 1979. *Beyond interpretation: Toward a revised theory for psychoanalysis.* New York: International Universities Press.

Gedo, J. E., and A. Goldberg. 1973. *Models of the mind.* Chicago: University of Chicago Press.

Gesell, A. 1947. *The child from five to ten.* New York: Harper and Bros.

Greenacre, P. 1971. *Emotional growth.* Vol. 1. New York: International Universities Press.

Greenson, R. R. 1978. On transitional objects and transference. In *Between fantasy and reality: The transitional object,* ed. S. A. Grolnick and L. Barkin, 205–09. New York: Aronson.

Grinstein, A. 1968. *On Sigmund Freud's dreams.* Detroit: Wayne State University Press.

Grolnick, S. A. 1978. Dreams and dreaming as transitional phenomena. In *Between fantasy and reality: The transitional object,* ed. S. A. Grolnick and L. Barkin, 213–31. New York: Aronson.

Guntrip, H. 1969. *Schizoid phenomena, object relations and the self.* New York: International Universities Press.

————. 1971. *Psychoanalytic theory, therapy and the self.* New York: Basic.

Harrison, I. B. 1966. A reconsideration of Freud's "A disturbance of memory on the Acropolis" in relation to identity disturbance. *Journal of the American Psychoanalytic Association* 14:518–27.

Hartmann, E. 1966. The psychophysiology of free will: An example of vertical research. In *Psychoanalysis—A general psychology,* ed. R. M. Loewenstein, L. M. Newman, M. Schur, and A. J. Solnit, 521–36. New York: International Universities Press.

Hartmann, H. [1939] 1958. *Ego psychology and the problem of adaptation.* Reprint. New York: International Universities Press.

————. [1955] 1964. Notes on the theory of sublimation. Reprinted in H. Hartmann, *Essays on ego psychology,* 215–40. New York: International Universities Press.

————. 1960. *Psychoanalysis and moral values.* New York: International Universities Press.

Holt, R. R. 1965. A review of some of Freud's biological assumptions and their influence on his theories. In *Psychoanalysis and current biological thought,* ed. N. S. Greenfield and W. C. Lewis, 93–124. Madison: University of Wisconsin Press.

————. 1972. Freud's mechanistic and humanistic images of man. In *Psychoanalysis and contemporary science,* ed. R. R. Holt and E. Peterfreund, 1:3–24. New York: Macmillan.

Home, H. J. 1966. The concept of mind. *International Journal of Psycho-Analysis* 47:42–49.

Hougaard, E. 1981. Some reflections on the relationship between Freudian psychoanalysis and Husserlian phenomenology. *Journal of Phenomenological Psychology* 9:1–90.

Irwin, J. E. G. 1973a. Oskar Pfister and the Taggert Report: The "first pastoral counselor" and today's role problems. *Journal of Pastoral Care* 27:189–95.

————. 1973b. Pfister and Freud: The rediscovery of a dialogue. *Journal of Religion and Health* 12:315–27.

Jacobsen, T. 1963. Ancient Mesopotamian religion: The central concerns. *Proceedings of the American Philosophical Society* 107:473–84.

James, W. [1902] 1961. *The varieties of religious experience.* New York: Collier.

Jones, E. 1953. *The life and work of Sigmund Freud.* Vol. 1. New York: Basic.

————. 1955. *The life and work of Sigmund Freud.* Vol. 2. New York: Basic.

————. 1957. *The life and work of Sigmund Freud.* Vol. 3. New York: Basic.

Jung, C. G. 1963. *Memories, dreams, reflections.* New York: Pantheon.

Kanzer, M. 1969. Sigmund and Alexander Freud on the Acropolis. *American Imago* 26:324–54. Reprinted in Kanzer and Glenn (1979), 259–84.

————. 1976. Freud and his literary doubles. *American Imago* 33:231–43. Reprinted in Kanzer and Glenn (1979), 285–96.

Kanzer, M., and J. Glenn, eds. 1979. *Freud and his self-analysis.* New York: Aronson.

Kernberg, O. F. 1977. Boundaries and structure in love relations. *Journal of the American Psychoanalytic Association* 25:81–114.

Klein, G. 1976. *Psychoanalytic theory: An exploration of essentials.* New York: International Universities Press.

Knight, R. P. 1946. Determinism, "freedom" and psychotherapy. In *Psychoanalytic Psychiatry and Psychology,* ed. R. P. Knight, 365–81. New York: International Universities Press.

Kohut, H. 1966. Forms and transformations of narcissism. *Journal of the American Psychoanalytic Association* 14:243–72.

————. 1971. *The analysis of the self.* New York: International Universities Press.

Lehman, H. 1978. A dream of Freud in the year 1910. *International Journal of Psycho-Analysis* 59:181–87.

Lewy, E. 1961. Responsibility, free will and ego psychology. *International Journal of Psycho-Analysis* 42:260–70.

Loewenberg, P. 1971. A hidden Zionist theme in Freud's "my son, the myops . . . dream." *Journal of the History of Ideas* 31:129–31.

McGuire, W., ed. 1974. *The Freud/Jung letters.* Princeton: Princeton University Press.

Mahler, M. S. 1968. *On human symbiosis and the vicissitudes of individuation.* New York: International Universities Press.

Mahler, M. S., F. Pine, and A. Bergman. 1975. *The psychological birth of the human infant.* New York: Basic.

Masson, J. M. and T. C. Masson. 1978. Buried memories on the Acropolis: Freud's response to mysticism and anti-semitism. *International Journal of Psycho-Analysis* 59:199–208.

Meissner, W. W., S.J. 1964. Prolegomena to a psychology of grace. *Journal of Religion and Health* 3:209–40.

————. 1966a. *Foundations for a psychology of grace.* New York: Paulist Press.

————. 1966b. The operational principle and meaning in psychoanalysis. *Psychoanalytic Quarterly* 35:233–55.

————. 1969. Notes on the psychology of faith. *Journal of Religion and Health* 8:47–75.

————. 1971. Notes on identification, part 2: Clarification of related concepts. *Psychoanalytic Quarterly* 40:227–302.

————. 1976. New horizons in metapsychology: View and review. *Journal of the American Psychoanalytic Association* 24:161–80.

————. 1977. The psychology of religious experience. *Communio* 4:36–59.

————. 1978a. *The paranoid process.* New York: Aronson.

————. 1978b. Psychoanalytic aspects of religious experience. *Annual of Psychoanalysis* 6:103–41.

————. 1979a. Methodological critique of the action language in psychoanalysis. *Journal of the American Psychoanalytic Association* 27:79–105.

————. 1979b. Critique of concepts and therapy in the action language approach to psychoanalysis. *International Journal of Psycho-Analysis* 60:291–310.

————. 1981. *Internalization in psychoanalysis.* Psychological Issues Monograph Series, no. 50. New York: International Universities Press.

————. 1983. Notes on the potential differentiation of borderline conditions. *International Journal of Psychoanalytic Psychotherapy* 9:3–49.

————. N.d. Values in the psychoanalytic situation. *Psychoanalytic Inquiry*, forthcoming.

Mendel, W. M. 1968. Responsibility in health, illness, and treatment. *Archives of General Psychiatry* 18:697–705.

Meng, H., and E. L. Freud, eds. 1963. *Psychoanalysis and faith: The letters of Sigmund Freud and Oskar Pfister.* New York: Basic.

Modell, A. H. 1968. *Object love and reality.* New York: International Universities Press.

Nuttin, J. 1956. Human motivation and Freud's theory of energy discharge. *Canadian Journal of Psychology* 10:167.

Pfister, O. 1928. "Die Illusion einer Zukunft" (The illusion of the future). *Imago* 14:149–84.

————. 1948. *Christianity and fear.* London: Allen and Unwin.

Rahner, K. 1961. Concerning the relationship between nature and grace. In *Theological investigations,* vol. 1. Baltimore: Helicon.

Rapaport, D. [1957] 1967. The theory of ego autonomy. Reprinted in *The collected papers of David Rapaport,* ed. M. Gill, 722–44. New York: Basic.

Ricoeur, P. 1970. *Freud and philosophy: An essay on interpretation.* New Haven: Yale University Press.

Rizzuto, A. M. 1979. *The birth of the living God.* Chicago: University of Chicago Press.

Rochlin, G. 1965. *Griefs and discontents: The forces of change.* Boston: Little, Brown.

Rose, G. J. 1978. The creativity of everyday life. In *Between fantasy and reality: The transitional object,* ed. S. A. Grolnick and L. Barkin, 345–62. New York: Aronson.

Ryle, G. [1949] 1965. *Concept of mind.* Reprint. New York: Barnes and Noble.

Schafer, R. 1973. Action: Its place in psychoanalytic interpretation and theory. *Annual of Psychoanalysis* 1:159–96.

————. 1976. *A new language for psychoanalysis.* New Haven: Yale University Press.

Schorske, C. 1973. Politics and parricide in Freud's *Interpretation of dreams. American Historical Review* 78:328–47.

Schur, M. 1966. Some additional "day residues" of "the specimen dream of psychoanalysis." In *Psychoanalysis—A general psychology,* ed. R. M. Loewenstein, L. M. Newman, M. Schur, and A. J. Solnit, 45–85. New York: International Universities Press. Also in Kanzer and Glenn (1979), 87–116.

————. 1969. The background of Freud's "disturbance" on the Acropolis. *American Imago* 26:303–23. Reprinted in Kanzer and Glenn (1979), 117–34.

————. 1972. *Freud: Living and dying.* New York: International Universities Press.

Shengold, L. 1966. The metaphor of the journey in *The interpretation of dreams. American Imago* 23:316–31. Reprinted in Kanzer and Glenn (1979), 51–65.

————. 1972. A parapraxis of Freud's in relation to Karl Abraham. *American Imago* 29:123–59. Reprinted in Kanzer and Glenn (1979), 213–44.

————. 1979. The Freud/Jung letters. In Kanzer and Glenn (1979), 187–201.

Stamm, J. 1969. The problems of depersonalization in Freud's "Disturbance of memory on the Acropolis." *American Imago* 26:364–72. Reprinted in Kanzer and Glenn (1979), 135–42.

Teilhard de Chardin, P. 1959. *The phenomenon of man.* New York: Harper and Bros.

Tustin, F. 1980. Autistic objects. *International Review of Psycho-Analysis* 7:27–39.

Vergote, A. 1969. *The religious man.* Dayton, Ohio: Pflaum.

Waelder, R. 1936. The problem of freedom in psychoanalysis and the problem of reality-testing. *International Journal of Psycho-Analysis* 17:89–108.

Waelhens, A. de. 1959a. Réflexions sur les rapports de la phénoménologie et de la psychoanalyse. In *Existence et signification,* 191–211. Paris: Beatrice-Nauwelaerts.

————. 1959b. Réflexions sur une problématique husserlienne. In *Edmund Husserl, 1859–1959.* The Hague: Nijhoff.

Wallace, E. R. 1978. Freud's mysticism and its psychodynamic determinants. *Bulletin of the Menninger Clinic* 42:203–22.

Wallerstein, R. S. 1973. Psychoanalytic perspectives on the problem of reality. *Journal of the American Psychoanalytic Association* 21:5–33.

Weisman, A. D. 1965. *The existential core of psychoanalysis.* Boston: Little, Brown.

White, R. W. 1959. Motivation reconsidered: The concept of competence. *Psychological Review* 66:297–333.

————. 1963. *Ego and reality in psychoanalytic theory.* New York: International Universities Press.

Winnicott, D. W. 1965. *The maturation process and the facilitating environment.* New York: International Universities Press.

————. 1971. *Playing and reality.* New York: Basic.

Wittels, F. 1931. *Freud and his time.* New York: Liveright.

Zetzel, E. R., and W. W. Meissner, S.J. 1973. *Basic concepts in psychoanalytic psychiatry.* New York: Basic.

Zilboorg, G. 1958. *Freud and religion.* Westminster, Md.: Neuman Press.

INDEX